PENGU

PIERS THE PLOUGHMAN

ADVISORY EDITOR: BETTY RADICE

Nothing is known for certain about the life of WILLIAM LANGLAND, an obscure fourteenth-century cleric, but a tentative outline can be made from supposedly autobiographical elements in the manuscripts of his poem. Born in about 1332 at Cleobury Mortimer in Shropshire, the son of a small Oxfordshire landholder, he was probably educated at the monastery of Great Malvern; he trained to be a priest but due to the death of his patrons he only took Minor Orders and was unable to advance in the Church. He wandered a good deal in England and was clearly familiar with London; he also lived for some while in a cottage on Cornhill with his wife Kit and his daughter Colette, making a meagre living by singing the Office of the Dead for wealthy patrons. Langland lived an unconventional life, constantly writing verse, and was thought by some to be crazed. Tall and thin, he was nicknamed 'Long Will'. He died at the end of the century.

•

FRANK GOODRIDGE was Senior Lecturer in English at the University of Lancaster from 1965 until his death in 1984. Born in 1927, he graduated from Magdalen College, Oxford, and after teaching English for four years he was Senior Lecturer at St Mary's College of Education, Twickenham, until 1965. He published poems, criticism and educational articles in various journals and was the author of a critical study of Emily Brontë's *Wuthering Heights*.

PIERS
THE PLOUGHMAN

*

William Langland

**TRANSLATED
INTO MODERN ENGLISH
WITH AN INTRODUCTION BY**
J. F. Goodridge

PENGUIN BOOKS

PENGUIN BOOKS

Published by the Penguin Group
Penguin Books Ltd, 27 Wrights Lane, London W8 5TZ, England
Penguin Putnam Inc., 375 Hudson Street, New York, New York 10014, USA
Penguin Books Australia Ltd, Ringwood, Victoria, Australia
Penguin Books Canada Ltd, 10 Alcorn Avenue, Toronto, Ontario, Canada M4V 3B2
Penguin Books (NZ) Ltd, 182–190 Wairau Road, Auckland 10, New Zealand

Penguin Books Ltd, Registered Offices: Harmondsworth, Middlesex, England

This translation first published 1959
Revised edition 1966
20

Copyright © J. F. Goodridge, 1959, 1966
All rights reserved

Printed in England by Clays Ltd, St Ives plc
Set in Monotype Garamond

For Alan Morrison

CONTENTS

CONTENTS

INTRODUCTION

WILLIAM LANGLAND was an obscure fourteenth-century cleric, of whom no contemporary record exists and of whose life nothing is known for certain. The only reliable external evidence we have for the authorship of *Piers Plowman*[1] is an ascription on the reverse side of the last leaf of one of the manuscripts,[2] which gives his name and parentage. Apart from this, we have to rely solely on the clues given in the successive versions of the poem, where the dreamer of the visions is gradually identified with a self who is also their author. Here we are on uncertain ground, since the poem cannot be read as spiritual autobiography. The dreamer is primarily a dramatic *persona* whose function, as in other medieval dream-poems, is to provide a link between the reader and the visions. Yet he reveals his baptismal name as William; in one place (XV, 145) he appears to surrender his full name by means of a cryptogram (a common method of signature in medieval poems); and in the later versions of the poem he takes on a waking existence that is convincingly life-like.* There is no reason to doubt that there are here elements of genuine autobiography. On this basis we may work out a tentative outline of the poet's life.

He was born about the year 1332 at Cleobury Mortimer in Shropshire and lived till the end of the century. He was the son (possibly illegitimate) of Stacy (Eustace) de Rokayle, who held land under the Despensers at Shipton-under-Wychwood in Oxfordshire. He was probably educated at the monastery of Great Malvern, where he passed through the usual theological training of a priest. But owing to the death of his patrons he only took Minor Orders and was unable to advance in the church. Mr W. A. Pantin[3] describes the class of unbeneficed clergy to which Langland belonged as a clerical proletariat: 'Socially and economically, this class must have been poles apart from the "sublime and literate persons", though the case of Langland shows us that a more or less submerged cleric might be the intellectual equal of anybody.'

Langland seems to have wandered a good deal from place to place and mixed with all kinds of people. He knew London well

*See Appendix A.

and worked on his poem there. He tells us that he lived with his wife Kit and his daughter Colette in a cottage on Cornhill, and made a meagre living by singing the Office of the Dead for wealthy patrons. He certainly knew poverty at close quarters.* We also hear his nickname, Long Will, and he frequently refers to his own tallness and leanness. He sometimes lived an unconventional life, dressed like a beggar; he was inclined to treat self-important people with little respect; he was constantly preoccupied with writing verses and some people thought him mad.

Langland must have spent a large part of his life revising and adding to his poem, for the surviving manuscripts belong to three distinct types representing three different stages in the poet's conception. These are known as the A, B and C texts. The B text is the best known, and has therefore been chosen for the present translation.

The A text consists of a Prologue and eight books of the *Vision of Piers Plowman* followed by four books of the *Life of Do-well* – so that it ends inconclusively with the dreamer's rejection by Learning and Scripture. The B text has a Prologue and twenty books and the C text, a revised and expanded version of this, a Prologue and twenty-three books. Langland calls his Books *Passūs*, which suggests the idea of steps in a developing argument.

Professor J. A. W. Bennett has brought forward convincing evidence[4] to show that the A text was composed about the year 1370, and the B text recension between 1377 and 1379. The C text must have been composed some time after 1390. The controversial theory of multiple authorship has now been disposed of[5] and students of the poem may safely regard the three versions as the work of one author.

To judge from the large number of manuscripts that still survive, *Piers Plowman* was very much a 'living' text in its day, being widely read throughout the fifteenth century and well into the sixteenth.[6] But in the latter part of the sixteenth century its West Midland dialect began to present serious difficulties. Langland's terms seemed (as Puttenham put it[7]) 'hard and obscure', and he came to be regarded chiefly as 'a malcontent of his time' – a precursor of the Reformation, admired for the bitterness of his invective against the Roman church. Between 1561 and 1813 no edition of *Piers* was printed and its reputation remained more or less unchanged. Whenever it was mentioned it was described as a satire, and Dr T. D. Whitaker, Langland's first modern editor,

*See Appendix B.

referred to Langland as 'the first English satirist', praising him chiefly for his rich Hogarthian scenes of medieval life. The more allegorical parts were considered 'insipid'.

The rediscovery of Langland's full range as a great English poet – representative of his age as Spenser, Milton, Wordsworth or Yeats were of theirs – has been a slow process. There have been genuine difficulties, as well as prejudices, to overcome. In the nineteenth century many readers were still dominated by the image of Langland as a dour Wycliffite preacher, and tended to regard his allegorizing as a mode of abstraction. Even in this century progress has frequently been held up – by controversy over side-issues, by misleading ideas about the limitations of allegory and also by the largely groundless assumption that Langland wrote carelessly and was no artist. As recently as the fifties, when the present translator was working on this version, there was surprisingly little help to be gleaned from the mass of scholarly material available, and no up-to-date editions of the texts. I was consequently obliged to do a good deal of pioneer work in interpreting the more neglected parts of the poem, and some of this was embodied in a lengthy Introduction and Appendices, large parts of which have been dispensed with in the present edition, since adequate criticism is now available elsewhere. For textual criticism, students should go to George Kane's edition of the A text and his discussion of the evidence for authorship; for closer critical study, to works like those of Elizabeth Salter and John Lawlor.[8]

*

In common with Dante's *Divine Comedy* and Milton's *Paradise Lost*, *Piers Plowman* deals with the largest of all themes: the meaning of man's life on earth in relation to his ultimate destiny. Like Milton, Langland seeks to 'justify the ways of God to men'. But his perspective is different from either Dante's or Milton's. He does not take us on a journey through worlds other than this, or ask us to look back on life from the point of view of hell, purgatory or heaven. Nor does he remove us, as Milton does, to a distant vantage-point in time from which to survey human history. His poem is no epic in the ordinary sense of that word. Langland's cycle of visions begins and ends with fourteenth-century England. His pilgrimage, like Bunyan's, is that of man's individual life and his life in society, as it has to be lived on this middle-earth between the 'Tower of Truth' and the 'Dungeon of Falsehood'. Langland was concerned, as Blake was, both with the condition of society and with the history of the human soul struggling to 'cleanse the doors of perception' and come to terms with ultimate truth. But for Langland, this meant translating his visions, at every point, into an art that had an immediate application to practical life. Though epic in scope and constantly rising to a prophetic point of view, *Piers Plowman* is cast in the didactic form of medieval moral allegory – a spiritual journey which, though it takes place in a series of dreams dreamt by an imaginary dreamer, is constantly related to life as it has to be lived. The form allows various different time-scales, and with them different levels of meaning, to operate side by side, or be superimposed on one another. First there is the 'literal' life-span of the dreamer or poet. He is represented at the beginning as a lazy vagabond or ordinary human wayfarer whose interest in Truth amounts to little more than idle curiosity. But through his dreams he sees the world with fresh eyes, is bewitched into thinking seriously and is sent forth by Holy Church on a pilgrimage in search of Truth, which he can only find through learning the law of Love. So he must progressively meet and assimilate every aspect of reality, and rise from his preoccupation with physical, economic, social and political facts to the level of moral and spiritual vision.

Though the story of Will's growth in knowledge and understanding provides the poem's one consistent thread of narrative, it is no regular step-by-step progress. It is as irregular and unpredictable as life itself – there are moments that are crowded with vivid impressions, or flooded in solitude with the wonder of new realization, followed by long barren years of intellectual debate, uncertainty or, perhaps, complete unawareness. In Book XI the poet ironically allows forty-five years of the dreamer's life to drop out as if they had never existed, so that he passes in a moment from the struggles of early manhood to those of old age. Erratic, obstinate and often misguided, he constantly has to double back on his tracks to rediscover what he had half known before.

Unlike Milton or Blake, Langland was a master of comic effects. He could survey the world with humour, sometimes mocking or playful, more often wry and sardonic. So the pilgrimage is partly burlesque – the dreamer's over-eager curiosity and general lack of solemnity lead to many setbacks on his quest. Both he and the *personae* of his dreams bear witness, dramatically, to the absurdity of the human situation in the face of eternity's uncompromising demands. For Langland seems to combine opposite qualities – on the one hand, an almost exasperating sense of the absolute, that insists on following up every hint and will never leave a subject till

the truth of it has been pursued to its final conclusions ('I shal
tellen for treuth sake, take hede who so lyketh!'); on the other
hand a sense of man's almost incurable folly and waywardness, and
an awareness of the plain ungarnished facts of life as it has to be
lived from moment to moment. He likes to show common sense
confounding theory, but likes even better to show idealism con-
founding worldly common sense – as Conscience confounds Lady
Fee, or Patience subdues the worldly Haukyn by showing him
poverty. So the poem sometimes swings back and forth between
extremes: harsh prophecy or solemn warning, and Rabelaisian
satire that is not afraid to expose contradictions in terms of farce.
These opposites are most effectively combined in the swift, sure
satire of the final Book – and it is hard to see how such a resilient
response to experience can ever have given rise to the idea of Lang-
land as a grim pessimist. There is very little in his poem of the
'Nordic strain'.

One of the effects of Langland's self-mockery is to associate the
dreamer, and ourselves, with the action, so that we are directly
involved, and made to feel the difference between knowledge and
full participation, which is one of the poem's main themes. But the
dreamer seldom occupies the centre of the picture. The visions
themselves, with their 'higher' time-scales, dominate his life, and
the prime mover is an unseen providence that is always a little
beyond the horizon of vision. So we gain from the poem a sense of
reality as something objective and ineluctable, penetrating and
overshadowing life as we know it in the world.

Superimposed on the time-scale of a single fourteenth century
life-span, with its direct references to current political events, are
the further time-scales apprehended in higher moments of vision.
The painstaking allegorical expositions that describe the long way
of the commandments are broken by sudden moments of illumina-
tion – hard surfaces of doctrine and argument dissolve into kaleide-
scopic pictures, each revealing more than the last. One important
scale that holds these dramatic variations together, especially in the
last five Books, is that of the liturgical year, and we can observe in
Langland the process of ritual being turned into drama. Beginning
with the Nativity in the middle of Book XVI, the dreamer passes
on rapidly through Epiphany and Lent to the climax of Passiontide
and Easter (Book XVIII), then returns by way of Pentecost, in
Book XIX, to Advent in the final Book. Coupled with this liturgi-
cal cycle run the main themes of sacred history – the story of the
patriarchs and prophets followed by that of Christ and his church,

which leads on inevitably to the *terminus a quo* of the present.

But in Langland the contemporary scene is itself shifting and multi-dimensional. Here, as in the realm of spiritual experience, his clairvoyance can penetrate beyond appearances and show us what lies behind the façade of church and state. He is one of the few writers in whose work it is difficult to distinguish between prophetic insight – that sometimes works on a historical or eschatological level – and plain truthfulness, especially (as John Lawlor has put it) his 'unerring eye for woes that are actual'. He did not sympathize with the poor at a safe distance; he felt need and hunger as immediate sensations and could express them in sharply physical and kinaesthetic terms. His denunciation of hypocrisy therefore carries conviction. We do not dismiss his prophetic role as a preacher's mannerism. At almost any stage in his narrative, he can rise easily to a point of view from which he can relate present facts to first causes and final ends. The present fulfils past warnings and shows portents of what is still to come. Christ and Antichrist are here and now. This gift of prophetic vision lends to the poem a time-scale vaster than that of any epic, and fills it with glimpses of a divine economy that may ultimately lead to the salvation of all mankind. Behind Langland's 'animated foreground', there is always 'the long vista of eternity'.[9]

All these perspectives are present *within* the poem – in its flexible language and varied dramatic sequences: we need not look outside it to find the 'meaning'. Other medieval allegories are more formal and diagrammatic, but *Piers Plowman* does not depend on a fixed scheme of symbolic reference. There is little need, for example, to explain what 'Meed' (which I have translated 'Fee') is or was – her words and actions provide as full a context by which to judge her as any that Dickens could give. Allegory was for Langland a dynamic way of thinking or 'making out' the truth in pictorial and dramatic form, by intuition as well as by observation and logical argument. To do this, he freely used all the resources of the vernacular language, and the potentialities of the dream form. He moved easily from brisk reportage to grotesque nightmare, or from angry theological disputation to the dream-within-a-dream that is close to mystical vision. There is no infallible key to such dramatic poetry – we must be constantly alert to changes in tone and direction that would be impossible in the stately verse of a poem like *Paradise Lost*. We are required, in Book III, for instance, to move rapidly from a world that exhibits the perverse power of money, and jingles with thousands of florins, to a moving statement of the divine law of reward and restitution. This in turn is later associated with one Robert the Robber, who can never hope to repay his debts, and so is compared with the penitent thief on Calvary. The essence of Langland's dream technique is its capacity for what Elizabeth Salter has called 'rapid contraction and expansion of reference' – where vivid realism can play its part within a progressively widening field of religious vision.

Langland's imagination was essentially visual and dramatic, and there are parts of his poem that might make good material for a film. We are struck at once by the fullness and variety of his picture of the Plain of the world, with its crowded panoramas and ugly close-ups, its noisy comings and goings and its intimate details. In the early books we witness a constant clash of opposing forces, and the truth about human society is revealed in the guise of a powerful and absorbing drama. Familiar vices and virtues no longer appear commonplace, but grotesque or disturbing. The 'real' characters – pardoners, lawyers, friars or thieves – are so placed alongside allegorical ones that the latter assume the semblance of life. Guile, Fee, Civil-Law, Conscience and Reason become the dynamic forces that move the world, and all the others fall under their direction.

A character like Sloth or Fraud is the personification of a propensity found in many men; and by embodying it in a single person, the poet shows us what shapes it assumes in human society. He reveals to us our moral qualities, stripped of all the conventions by which we seek to hide them. A schoolboy who uses a nickname, or the dramatist who gives one of his characters a name like Sir Francis Wronghead, is usually pointing to some social foible which characterizes a particular type. Langland employs a similar idiom, but places his types in surprising contexts that shock us out of our stock associations, so that we cannot mistake the enormity of the evils they represent and the perversions of truth that they bring about. By this method of contrast and opposition, familiar virtues also take on a dramatic interest which they rarely have in naturalistic drama or fiction.

Each of the Deadly Sins carries a load of sins greater than any man could possibly carry: the dominant vice is displayed in all its grossest forms. Sloth is not merely a lazy priest who goes hunting when he should be saying his Office; he is all kinds of sloth, lay and clerical, rolled into one. The world is foreshortened, and the gluttony of Glutton is reflected in a crowd of others whom he meets in the tavern. In the description of the soiled coat of Haukyn the Active Man, all the sins of the Plain are run together, flourishing under the cloak of self-important worldliness – and it is he whom Langland chooses to test the power of the Christian absolutes, Patience and Poverty. After the dreamer's frustrating struggles with a succession of intellectual faculties and pursuits (Thought, Study, Intelligence, Imagination, etc.), he meets a being, Anima, in whom all the powers of the human soul are combined; and when he has afterwards encountered the separate god-given virtues in incarnate form, he falls in with the Samaritan who unites all these graces in the one attribute of Love. The Samaritan in turn dissolves into the person of Piers-Christ; and it is important to bear in mind that Christ himself in this poem is also an 'allegorical' person, representing a god-like potentiality in the soul – for Langland shared something of the view of Meister Eckhart that 'a good man is the only-begotten Son of God'.

So the *dramatis personae* of *Piers Plowman* are not static abstract categories. Each is a mirror that reflects those aspects of life that stand out at a particular stage of mental or spiritual development, defining its categories of thought or modes of perception. They are the means by which the relevance of those categories and concepts to everyday life can be put to the proof. Langland does not offer us the 'plane mirror reflection' of the comedy of manners, but rather a comedy of humours, where single properties assume a life more powerful than that of ordinary individuals and gather into themselves a large number of observations and experiences. The great strength of such a method lies in its power to cut across habitual expectations – our conceptions, for example, of classes of people or individual 'character' types, or our common notions of what we ourselves are or may become. Langland's form of allegory reorganizes human experience according to new patterns. The cells of the dreamer's thoughts and perceptions keep dividing and coming together again around fresh nuclei. The simplicity of Holy Church's teaching gives way to the multiplicity of Falsehood's following; that of Piers into the contradictions of the mental faculties encountered in the search for Do-well, which is a kind of psychological drama: the dreamer's attention is turned inwards as he seeks the truth among the conflicting powers of the mind. Here the dramatic effect lies in the individual confrontation between the dreamer and his various *alter egos* ('single figures or incidents etched in sharp relief'[10]) and in the vigorous to and fro of intellectual debate and homily. What Learning, Study, Intelligence and the rest have to say to him is seldom more than he is capable of seeing for himself at the time. They all reflect his limitations. But as he increases in self-knowledge, the selves whom he at first had failed to recognize slowly coalesce, and their powers are gathered round new centres, the heavenly graces or virtues. The dramatic technique again changes, leaving the dreamer a passive spectator: in place of personal encounters we have dramatized narrative or parable, culminating in the ritualized drama of religious contemplation. The various narrative modes of picture and dialogue, action and comment are now combined, since all the faculties and virtues are concentrated on the person of Piers or Christ. But though the texture is here multi-layered and demands the reader's full attention on various levels, the poem never loses its dramatic and pictorial impact. At the climax of the Harrowing of Hell Langland's style still has much in common with that of the Miracle Plays that were performed in the streets.

Langland was never wilfully an obscure poet: he sought strenuously to make all his meanings clear, weaving all the glosses and explanations into the body of his narrative. He preferred simple similes to complex symbols and metaphors; he transposed abstruse doctrines into everyday terms or embodied them in dramatic dialogue so as to render them immediately applicable to practical life; he carefully spelt out each step in an argument and exhibited the truth from many different sides. If the resulting structure is still in places confusing and complex, this is only because, to him, the application of simple truth to actual experience was no simple matter.

Langland's willingness to follow, at times, wherever the spirit leads – a characteristic of most medieval devotional writing – occasions many digressions, stoppings-short and unexpected transitions. The pattern is incomplete in parts, yet unified on a higher level as the dreamer becomes caught up in the mystery of Christ and his spokesman, Piers. Piers represents the human ideal which is the ultimate object of the search. In Books VI and VII he is the good ploughman who alone knows how to obey the natural law. During the debates of Do-well he disappears, for the dreamer has lost sight of his ideal and only hears of him in hints and riddles. When he reappears, he has undergone a change corresponding to the change in the dreamer's understanding of what Truth is and where it is to be found. He is the perfect Christian and the representative of Christ mirrored in the soul of everyman. Having failed to discover him in the priesthood of his day, the dreamer must look for his image reflected in the powers of his own soul.

Allegory, as Langland employs it, is a way of testing and proving experience. It allows him almost unlimited scope to vary his modes of thought and feeling as the subject-matter demands. He can mix realism and fantasy in whatever proportion he chooses, and rein-terpret for himself – in the concrete language of everyday life – traditional doctrines, symbols, legends and sacred histories. Since he did not write, like the 'court' poets, for a select audience of listeners, but rather for a wider literate public who were to read his poem in manuscript, he was able to employ every variety of speech, ranging from that of the theological lecture to the coarse vernacular of the street or tavern. There could be any number of *personae* – new ones might suddenly appear, while others merged together or disappeared. Through their mouths he could say what-ever he wished, twisting the narrative this way and that as his mental and spiritual horizon expanded or contracted. The secret of the poem's appeal to a modern reader may lie partly in this irregu-larity of construction, for instead of giving us a finished picture of the Christian view of life, it registers all our 'uncertainties, mys-teries, doubts' and shows a continuing process of thought: Truth is something to be appropriated to oneself, not merely understood by the mind.

Langland was not faced with the problem of finding a voice through which to project his response to the problems of his time. He had not to struggle for a style amid conflicting standards of poetic decorum. The alliterative verse that he used provided a comparatively easy, natural mode of utterance; its flexibility was perfectly adapted to the play and dramatic movement of the dream-allegory. In his day this form of verse seems to have been popular in the west and north of England – and though a court poet like Chaucer may have regarded it as provincial and old-fashioned, it is worth remembering that Langland was an educated cleric and also a Londoner, able to widen its range and assimilate into it many different traditions of speech. His was an age of oral learning and theological disputation, when the style of the homilist provided a matrix out of which writers could draw what they chose – even the Canterbury pilgrims tend to lecture one another. As Mr Owst has shown[11], the medieval sermon was a repository of vernacular speech, where graphic similes and proverbial phrases jostled with learned terms. In Langland's day, the English language was not stratified according to class, function or level of literacy so much as it has been since. The reservoir on which he was able to draw contained no less than the whole spoken and written speech of his time. Glutton with his Great Oaths, Sloth with his ballads of Robin Hood, the lazy workmen singing a snatch from a bawdy French song did not seem out of keeping in a poem that drew much of its finest language from the Vulgate, the Fathers and the mystics. Religious discourse was not a solemn and mannered performance, remote from the common vernacular, and Langland's medley of tongues is the characteristic voice of fourteenth-century England. His art consists largely in deploying all its arresting combinations and contrasts. One of his favourite devices is to allow the hieratic and the demotic, the learned riddle and the popular joke, to fall out in quick succession or change places. At its simplest, this is the means by which a particular speaker turns the tables on his opponent, unexpectedly adopting his mode of talk. So Langland's two-edged irony repeatedly plays on the contrasts between Latin and English, clerical and lay, elaborate commentary and simple text, learned word-spinning and proverbial wisdom – seeking thereby to distinguish what is genuinely profound from specious sophistry.

The weaving of heterogeneous dialects (typified by the voices of Piers and the priest flinging abuse and Scriptural texts at one another 'till their noise awoke me') provides a basis for all those bold contrasts and connexions on which Langland's purpose depends – to reconcile irreconcilables and break down men's defences against the divine command to seek perfection.

Such a design required a form of verse that could enlist without strain all the dramatic and rhetorical devices of prose. Langland had fortunately inherited a form of alliterative verse, ultimately derived from Old English, which had broken free from the strict 'classical' rules and reappeared as a fluent, 'free' verse that did not depend on poetic diction. Other poets of the 'Alliterative Revival' – the courtly poets of the north and north-west – developed for their special audiences a new and sometimes elaborate poetic diction, loading their lines with colourful words and strong alliteration. But in that part of the West Country from which Langland derived his basic style, the verse was comparatively unadorned and the alliteration was unobtrusive. This made possible a stark simplicity of statement and a sensitive use of natural speech responsive to the pressure of immediate feeling.

Middle English alliterative verse has no regular metre, but each line is divided by a natural speech-pause into two halves that are linked by three or four stressed syllables beginning with the same sound. In *Piers Plowman* there are usually two alliterative syllables in the first half-line echoed by one in the second – as in this passage from Book XX:

Somme lyked nouȝte þis leche   and lettres þei sent,
ȝif any surgien were in þe sege   þat softer couthe plastre.
Sire lief-to-lyve-in-leccherye   lay þere and groned;
For fasting of a fryday   he ferde as he wolde deye.

It will be noticed that the language and rhythm are colloquial, the length of line varies considerably and there can be any number of 'slack' syllables.

In verse that is based on metrical feet, the way we read each word and phrase depends on its placing in relation to a regular pattern of stresses. In alliterative verse the basic unit is simply the half-line, which is an ordinary phrase or speech-unit, to be read just as it would normally be spoken. Its poetic effect depends on the way it completes or contrasts with the other half-line, and on its rhythmic and dramatic relation to the sequence of phrases to which it belongs. The poet did not think so much in grammatical sentences, as in balanced, antithetical or accumulative sequences of phrases, each a separate unit that chimed or clashed with others. Sometimes they interact sharply as in the alternations of dialogue. At other times they grow from one another like the momentary inspirations of an eloquent speaker augmenting and amplifying his theme, and playing on his hearers by constant variations of pace. The effects nearly always appear spontaneous, even in the more laboured passages. Though he obeyed no formal pattern, Langland could build up his contrasted patterns of sound with the skill of a great dramatist. Sometimes the spate of his eloquence appears to flow on unchecked, running over from line to line and eddying hither and thither; but there comes a point of climax where the whole force of a speech is gathered together in a single transparent image, or breaks against an unexpected obstacle that gives an entirely new direction to the argument.

Langland's art is strictly functional: his language is always shaped for a specific didactic or religious purpose – to bring home some spiritual truth, either to himself or his contemporaries. But even from a prose translation the reader should gain some appreciation of the varied resources of poetic speech by which he sought to turn moral and spiritual truths into imaginable realities. I hope to have caught something of his sharp feeling for physical things, whether loathsome or lovely; of the limpid simplicity of single lines and arresting images; of the broad comedy and the bold dramatic turns and contrasts; of the ironic juggling with words and meanings, and the elaborate rhetorical climaxes built up by insistent repetition and parallelism, that suddenly turn inward on the reader; and occasionally, the magnificent cadences that remind us of the language of the King James Bible.

To discover all these riches, and many more, the reader must turn to the original text, for which a translation is no substitute. My chief aim here has been to render the full sense of the poem in a form that will be easily accessible to the general reader. I have put sense first, because Langland, more than any other poet, subordinated style to subject-matter – and because I think it essential for a person approaching the poem for the first time to gain some impression of his complete scope and design.

I have striven especially hard to do justice to those long homiletic and theological passages which are sometimes omitted, and to bring out their full depth and power. A comparison of the three texts shows Langland more scrupulous even than Wordsworth in his concern for detail, striving for clarity and precision in word and phrase and anxious that his intentions should not be mistaken. A prose translation that strives for the same clarity in a modern idiom may help to clear away the impression of looseness and archaism which some verse translations convey. My anxiety has been to present the poem in a form that will make a direct impact on a modern mind.

I experimented with alliterative verse for some time before deciding to write in prose. Verse certainly proved the easier, and I found in writing alliterative verse a facile tendency to blur the sense in order to retain an equivalence of sound alone. A hybrid language of Middle and Modern English appears to relieve the translator of the necessity to find a correct modern equivalent.

I think, too, that a great deal of Langland's strength and suppleness has survived among preachers and pamphleteers, and that the style of radical social commentary and journalism at its best, where abstract statements are lit up by vivid pictures and vernacular expressions, is derived from the preaching and satire of the Middle Ages. These, together with the prose of the medieval mystics and the translators of the Bible, may provide models for rendering Langland that are as good, at least, as the work of any modern poet.

The chief temptation in writing prose, which I have been careful to avoid, is to produce a tightened summary version, jettisoning part of Langland's cargo of phrases in order to improve the grammatical structure. I have also tried to avoid ironing out Langland's idiosyncrasies – asides, repetitions, parentheses and play on words – and have retained a good deal of the alliteration. The prose has this at least in common with Langland's verse, that it is meant to be read with the ear rather than the eye.

For Langland's texts I have substituted the Authorized Version or, in the case of the Psalms, that of the Book of Common Prayer. All the scriptural and other references are given in the Notes. I have also placed in the Notes a brief Book-by-Book commentary on the allegory, which the reader would do best to ignore until he has read the poem.

I wish to thank those friends who have helped me with particular passages, and I am especially grateful to my wife for extensive revisions. I owe my first interest in *Piers Plowman* to Professor J. A. W. Bennett, who has kindly discussed with me several difficulties in the text and corrected some errors. Naturally, he is not responsible for those that remain, and there may be readings here with which he disagrees.

Finally, I am grateful to Dr E. V. Rieu and Mrs Betty Radice for continued kindness and patience while the original work, and its recent revision, were in progress.

Lancaster, 1966   J. F. G.

PIERS THE PLOUGHMAN

PART ONE

*William's Vision of Piers
the Ploughman*

Prologue

THE PLAIN FULL OF PEOPLE

THE STORY. *The poet takes to the roads, and sets out to roam the world in search of marvels. One day he falls asleep, and dreams of the plain of this world, set between the Tower of Truth and the Dungeon of Falsehood. On this plain he sees a motley crowd of people, most of them seeking worldly gain, among whom the greedy, unscrupulous churchmen are the most conspicuous. He also sees a king set up to maintain law, and, in the fable of the rats and mice who tried to bell the cat, witnesses the failure of the Commons to hold their lawless master in check. Then once more he surveys the throng of people, moving about in a great hubbub of noise.*

ONE summer season, when the sun was warm, I rigged myself out in shaggy woollen clothes, as if I were a shepherd; and in the garb of an easy-living hermit[1] I set out to roam far and wide through the world, hoping to hear of marvels. But on a morning in May, among the Malvern Hills, a strange thing happened to me, as though by magic. For I was tired out by my wanderings, and as I lay down to rest under a broad bank by the side of a stream, and leaned over gazing into the water, it sounded so pleasant that I fell asleep.

And I dreamt a marvellous dream: I was in a wilderness, I could not tell where, and looking Eastwards[2] I saw a tower high up against the sun, and splendidly built on top of a hill; and far beneath it was a great gulf, with a dungeon in it, surrounded by deep, dark pits, dreadful to see. But between the tower and the gulf I saw a smooth plain, thronged with all kinds of people, high and low together, moving busily about their worldly affairs.

Some laboured at ploughing and sowing, with no time for pleasure, sweating to produce food for the gluttons to waste. Others spent their lives in vanity, parading themselves in a show of fine clothes. But many, out of love for our Lord and in the hope of Heaven, led strict lives devoted to prayer and penance – for such are the hermits and anchorites who stay in their cells, and are not forever hankering to roam about, and pamper their bodies with sensual pleasures.

Others chose to live by trade, and were much better off – for in our worldly eyes such men seem to thrive. Then there were the professional entertainers, some of whom, I think, are harmless minstrels, making an honest living by their music; but others, babblers and vulgar jesters,[3] are true Judas' children! They invent fantastic tales about themselves, and pose as half-wits, yet they show wits enough whenever it suits them, and could easily work for a living if they had to! I will not say all that St Paul says about them; it is enough to quote, 'He who talks filth is a servant of the Devil.'[4]

And there were tramps and beggars hastening on their rounds, with their bellies and their packs crammed full of bread. They lived by their wits, and fought over their ale – for God knows, they go to bed glutted with food and drink, these brigands, and get up with foul language and filthy talk; and all day long, Sleep and shabby Sloth are at their heels.

And I saw pilgrims and palmers[5] banding together to visit the shrines at Rome and Compostella.[6] They went on their way full of clever talk, and took leave to tell fibs about it for the rest of their lives. And some I heard spinning such yarns of the shrines they had visited, you could tell by the way they talked that their tongues were more tuned to lying than telling the truth, no matter what tale they told.

Troops of hermits with their hooked staves were on their way to Walsingham, with their wenches following after. These great, long lubbers, who hated work, were got up in clerical gowns to distinguish them from laymen, and paraded as hermits for the sake of an easy life.

I saw the Friars there too – all four Orders of them[7] – preaching to the people for what they could get. In their greed for fine clothes, they interpreted the Scriptures to suit themselves and their patrons. Many of these Doctors of Divinity can dress as handsomely as they please, for as their trade advances, so their profits increase. And now that Charity has

gone into business, and become confessor-in-chief to wealthy
lords, many strange things have happened in the last few years;
unless the Friars and Holy Church mend their quarrel, the
worst evil in the world[8] will soon be upon us.

There was also a Pardoner, preaching like a priest. He
produced a document covered with Bishops' seals, and claimed
to have power to absolve all the people from broken fasts and
vows of every kind. The ignorant folk believed him and were
delighted. They came up and knelt to kiss his documents,
while he, blinding them with letters of indulgence thrust in
their faces, raked in their rings and jewellery with his roll of
parchment! – So the people give their gold to support these
gluttons, and put their trust in dirty-minded scoundrels. If
the Bishop were worthy of the name, if he kept his ears open
to what went on around him, his seal would not be sent out
like this to deceive the people. But it is not by the Bishop's
leave that this rogue preaches; for the parish priest is in league
with the Pardoner, and they divide the proceeds between
them – money which, but for them, would go to the poor of
the parish.

Then I heard parish priests complaining to the Bishop that
since the Plague[9] their parishes were too poor to live in; so
they asked permission to live in London, where they could
traffic in Masses,[10] and chime their voices to the sweet jingling
of silver. Bishops and novices, Doctors of Divinity and other
great divines – to whom Christ has given the charge of men's
souls, and whose heads are tonsured to show that they must
absolve, teach, and pray for their parishioners, and feed the
poor – I saw them all living in London, even in Lent. Some
took posts at Court counting the king's money, or in the Courts
of Exchequer and Chancery, where they claimed his dues
from the wards of the City and his right to unclaimed pro-
perty. Others went into the service of lords and ladies, sitting
like stewards managing household affairs – and gabbled their
daily Mass and Office without devotion. Indeed, I fear that
there are many whom Christ, in His great Consistory Court,[11]
will curse for ever.

Then I understood something of that power which was

entrusted to Peter, to 'bind and unbind'[12] as the Scripture
puts it. Peter, by our Lord's command, left it in the hands of
Love, sharing it out among the four greatest virtues,[13] which
are called Cardinal. For these are the hinges on which swing
the gates of Christ's kingdom, closing against some, and
opening on the bliss of Heaven to others. But as to those other
Cardinals at Rome who have assumed the same name, taking
upon themselves the appointment of a Pope to possess the
power of St Peter, I will not call them in question. The election
of a Pope requires both love and learning. There is much more
I could say about the Papal Court, but it is not for me to say it.

*

Then there came into the field[14] a king, guided by the knights.
The powers of the Commons gave him his throne, and Com-
mon Sense provided men of learning to counsel him and to
protect the people.

The king, with his nobles and counsellors, decided that
the common people should provide them with resources; so
the people devised different trades, and engaged ploughmen
to labour and till the soil for the good of the whole community,
as honest ploughmen should. Then the king and the people,
helped by Common Sense, established law and order, so that
every man might know his rights and duties.

Whereupon a long, lean, crazy fellow[15] knelt before the
king and said gravely: 'God save you, your majesty, and pro-
tect your kingdom. May He grant you grace to be so just a
ruler, that you may win the love of your loyal subjects, and the
reward of Heaven hereafter.'

And then from the air on high an angel of Heaven[16] stooped
down and spoke something in Latin – for the ignorant folk
could not speak for themselves, they could only suffer and
serve; so the angel said:

'Sum rex, sum Princeps, – neutrum fortasse deinceps; –
O qui iura regis Christi specialia regis,
Hoc quod agas melius iustus es, esto pius!
Nudum ius a te vestiri vult pietate;

Qualia vis metere talia grana sere.
Si ius nudatur de iure metatur;
Si seritur pietas de pietate metas!'

A garrulous fellow, with his head full of quotations, took offence at these words, and retorted to the angel:

'*Dum rex a regere dicatur nomen habere,*
Nomen habet sine re nisi studet iura tenere.'†

Whereupon all the common people, wishing to add their own piece of advice to the king, shouted out a line of Latin – let him make what he could of it –

'*Precepta regis sunt nobis vincula legis.'‡*

Then all at once there ran out a horde of rats, and with them more than a thousand little mice,[17] all coming to hold a Council to discuss their common safety. For a cat[18] from a certain court used to come when he chose, to pounce on them and paw them, toss them about and play with them in the most alarming manner. 'We're surrounded with so many dangers,' they said, 'that we scarcely dare to move. And if we complain of his games, he'll plague us all the more and never let us alone – he'll scratch and claw us and trap us between his paws, till our lives are not worth living! If we could only think of some scheme to stop him, we could be lords in our own domain and live at ease.'

Then a certain rat, well known as an eloquent speaker, put forward an excellent plan of his own invention: 'I have noticed,' he said, 'certain liveried men in the City, who wear bright gold chains around their necks, and fancy collars. They behave like dogs off the leash, straying about wherever they

---

*"You say, "I am a king; I am a prince," – but in time you may be neither. It is your duty to administer the laws of Christ the King; the better to do this, be as mild as you are just. You should clothe naked justice with mercy, and sow those crops which you hope to reap. Strip justice of mercy, and you shall be judged by justice alone: sow mercy, and you shall reap mercy.'

†'Since a king is entitled to be a king only by the act of ruling, he is a king only in name if he does not maintain the laws.'

‡'The king's decrees are as binding to us as the Law.'

like over warrens and commons; and I'm told that they some-
times go wandering off and cause trouble elsewhere. Now it
has often occurred to me, that if they had bells attached to
their collars, people could hear them coming and run away!

'So,' continued the rat, 'I have thought of a good scheme
like that for us. We must buy a bell of brass or shining silver,
attach it to a collar and hang it round the cat's neck! Then we
shall be able to hear what he's up to – whether he's stirring
abroad or having a rest or running out to play; and if he's in a
pleasant, frisky mood, we can peep out of our holes and just
put in an appearance, but if he's in a bad temper, we can take
care and keep out of his way.'

The whole rat-assembly applauded this scheme. But when
the bell was bought and attached to the collar, there was not
a rat in the whole company who dared to fix it round the cat's
neck – not for the whole realm of England! So they were dis-
gusted with themselves and ashamed of their feeble plan, and
felt that all their long labour and planning had been wasted.

Then a mouse who looked very shrewd[19] pushed himself
boldly forward, and, standing before them all, spoke like this:
'Even if we killed the cat, another like him would come to
scratch us – and it would be no use our creeping under the
benches! So I advise all commoners to leave him alone: and
let's not be so rash as even to show him the bell.

'I heard my father say,[20] several years ago, that when the
cat is a kitten the court is a sorry place. And so it says in Holy
Scripture: "Woe to that land whose king is a child."[21] For
then no one can rest for the rats at night. In any case, the cat
is not after our blood while he's off catching rabbits;[22] let
us give him his due – he's content with his "venison". So
surely a little trouble now is better than long years of misery
and confusion. True, we should be rid of a tyrant, but what
would happen? – We mice would be eating up men's malt,
and you rats would tear their clothes to shreds. So thank God
the cat can outrun you! For if you had your own way, you
could never govern yourselves.

'Therefore my counsel is, don't offend the cat or the kitten
in any way; for I can foresee all the trouble it would lead to.

And let us have no more talk of this collar. – Not that I ever gave any money for it myself – though if I had, I must say I should have kept quiet about it. So let them both go, cat and kitten, leashed or unleashed, and catch what they can. Be sensible and mark my words – and let us keep out of what doesn't concern us!'

Now what this dream means you folk must guess for yourselves, for I haven't the courage to tell you – and that's God's truth!

*

Besides all this, a hundred men in silk gowns stood swaying from side to side and making speeches. These were the lawyers who served at the bar, pleading their cases for as much money as they could get. Never once did they open their mouths out of love for our Lord; indeed you could sooner measure the mist on the Malvern Hills, than get a sound out of them without first producing some cash!

I saw many more in this great concourse of people, as you shall hear presently: barons, burgesses, and peasants; bakers, brewers, and butchers; linen-weavers and tailors, tinkers and toll-collectors, masons and miners and many other tradesfolk. And all kinds of labourers suddenly appeared – shoddy workmen, who would while away their hours with bawdy songs – like 'Dieu vous save, Dame Emme!' – while cooks with their boys cried, 'Hot pies! Hot pies! Fat pigs and geese! Come and eat!' and inn-keepers were bawling, 'White wine! Red wine! Gascon and Spanish! Wash down your meat with the finest Rhenish!'

All this I saw in my dream, and a great deal more besides.

Book I

THE TEACHING OF HOLY CHURCH

THE STORY. *Langland dreams that the Lady Holy Church comes to explain his vision. Truth, who dwells in the Tower, she says, is God, who gave us worldly goods only as a means of life; but the Devil, who dwells in the Dungeon, uses them to deceive us. On finding out who she is, the dreamer asks her how he may save his soul. 'By seeking Truth,' she replies, and then describes how the Father of Lies fell from Heaven. Being questioned further, she explains that Truth is the same as Love, dwelling in the heart. Without it, faith and moral virtue are cold and useless.*

Now I will show you the meaning of the mountain, the dark valley, and the plain full of people.

A fair lady, clothed in linen, came down from a castle and called me gently, saying, 'My son, are you asleep? Do you see these people, moving about in such a turmoil of activity? Most people who pass through this world wish for nothing better than worldly success: the only heaven they think about is on earth.'

Lovely as she was, something in her face made me uneasy, and I said, 'Forgive me, Lady, but what does it all mean?'

'The tower on the hill,' she replied, 'is the home of Truth, and He would have you learn to obey His word. For He is the Father of Faith, who created you all, giving you a body and five senses with which to worship Him while you dwell below. And therefore He commanded the earth to provide wool and linen and food, enough for everyone to live in comfort and moderation.

'And of His goodness He ordained three things in common,[1] which are all that your body requires: clothing to protect you from cold, food to keep you from want, and drink when you are thirsty.

'But do not drink too much, so that you're the worse for it

32

when you ought to be at work. Remember the story of Lot,[2] whose fondness for drink drove him to consort with his daughters, to the Devil's great delight – how he revelled in strong drink, and this suited the Devil's purpose, and being consumed with lust, he slept with both his daughters. "Come," they said, "let us make our father drink wine, and we will lie with him, that we may preserve seed of our father." So Lot was overwhelmed by wine and women, and there, in his gluttony, he begat evil sons. So be guided by me, and avoid strong drinks. Moderation is always wholesome, though you may crave for more. Not all that the belly desires is good for the soul; nor is all that the soul loves, food for the body. Put no trust in your body, for its promptings come from the World, and the World is a liar out to betray you. And the Flesh and the Devil are in league to pursue your soul, and speak evil things to your heart. I give you this good counsel that you may be watchful.'

'Pardon me, Lady,' I said, 'I find your teaching good. But tell me, the money of this world, which men cling to so eagerly – whom does it all belong to?'

'Read the Gospel,'[3] she answered, 'and see what Christ said when the people brought Him a penny in the Temple, and asked Him whether or not they should honour Caesar. "Whose is the image and inscription?" He asked. "Caesar's," they answered, "We can all recognize him!" "Then render to Caesar," He said, "the things that are Caesar's, and to God the things that are God's; otherwise you wrong Him."

'For Right Reason should rule you in this matter, and Common Sense[4] look after your money for you, giving you some as you need it; for Thrift and these two go hand in hand.'

Then I begged her in God's name to tell me the meaning of the fearful dungeon in the dark abyss.

'That is the Castle of Sorrow,' she said, 'Whoever enters there may well curse the day he was born. In it there lives a creature called Wrong, who begat Falsehood, and first founded the dungeon. It was he who persuaded Adam and Eve to sin, who tempted Cain to murder his brother, and enticed Judas with the Jews' silver and then hanged him on an elder-tree.[5] He thwarts love and deceives everyone: those who trust in his riches are the first to be betrayed.'

Then I wondered what woman this could be to quote such wise words of Holy Scripture; and I implored her, in the name of God, before she left me, to tell me who she was that taught me so kindly.

'I am Holy Church,' she replied, 'You should recognize me, for I received you when you were a child, and first taught you the Faith. You came to me with godparents, who pledged you to love and obey me all your life.'

Then I fell on my knees and besought her mercy, begging her to take pity on me and pray for my sins; and I asked her to teach me plainly how to believe in Christ and do the will of Him who created me. – 'Teach me no more about earthly treasure, O Lady whom men call Holy, but tell me one thing: *How May I Save My Soul*?'

'When all treasures are tested,' she said, 'Truth is the best. And to prove it and test what is true, I appeal to the text "God is love".[6] For Truth is as precious a jewel as our dear Lord himself.

'For he who speaks nothing but the truth, and acts by it, wishing no man ill, is like Christ, a god on earth and in Heaven – those are St Luke's words.[7] Men of learning who know this teaching should proclaim it everywhere; for Christians and heathens alike are crying out for it.

'And kings and nobles should be Truth's champions: they should ride to war and put down criminals throughout their realms, and bind them fast till Truth has reached a final verdict on them. That is clearly the proper profession of a knight – not merely to fast one Friday in a hundred years, but to stand by every man and woman who seeks plain truth, and never desert them for love or money.

'King David in his time[8] dubbed knights, making them swear on their swords to serve Truth for ever. And if anyone broke that vow, he was an apostate to the Order.

'And Christ himself, the king of kings, knighted ten Orders

34

of angels:[9] Cherubim and Seraphim and seven like them – and one other, the Order of Lucifer. And God, in His majesty, made them His Archangels, the rulers over His whole household, and they rejoiced in the power which He gave them. And He taught them to understand Truth by the Holy Trinity,[10] and required nothing of them but to obey Him.

'But Lucifer, though he too, with others of his Order, had received this teaching in Heaven, broke the vow of obedience, lost his happiness, and, in the likeness of a fiend, fell from the angelic company into a deep, dark hell where he must abide for ever. And innumerable legions sprang out after him in loathsome shapes, for they believed his lying words – "I will exalt my throne above the stars of God: I will sit in the sides of the North . . . I will be like to the most High."[11] And all those who put their hope in these words, Heaven could hold no longer. And they fell in the form of devils, for nine days together, till God in His mercy stopped their fall, causing the spaces of Chaos to close and cohere, and bringing them to rest.

'They fell in so strange a way[12] that some remained in the air, some on earth, and some in the depths of hell. But Lucifer, on account of his pride, lies the lowest of all, and his pain will never cease. And all those who do wrong must go after death to dwell with him in the pit; but the righteous who die still honouring Truth may be sure their souls will go to Heaven, where Truth himself, dwelling in the Holy Trinity, will enthrone them.

'So I say again, that when all treasures are tested, Truth is the best; my two texts[13] prove it. Teach this to the ignorant, for the learned know it already: Truth is the most perfect treasure on earth.'

'But,' I said, 'I have no natural gift for grasping Truth. You must teach me better. How does truth grow in me? Is there some special faculty somewhere in my body?'

'You stupid fellow!' she said, 'Why are you so dull-witted? You can't have learnt much Latin at school – *Heu mihi, quod sterilem duxi vitam iuvenilem!**

*Alas! for my barren and misspent youth!

'There is a natural knowledge in your heart,[14] which prompts you to love your Lord better than yourself and to die rather than commit mortal sin. That, surely, is Truth. If anyone else can teach you better, listen, and learn accordingly.

'For this is the testimony of God's word, the word by which you must live: that Love is Heaven's sovereign remedy, and he who takes it has no trace of sin left. By Love, God chose to fashion[15] all His works. He taught Moses[16] that it was the dearest of all things, the virtue closest to Heaven, the plant of Peace [17] whose leaves are most precious for healing.

'Heaven could not hold Love, it was so heavy in itself. But when it had eaten its fill of earth, and taken flesh and blood,[18] then it was lighter than a leaf on a linden-tree, more subtle and piercing then the point of a needle. The strongest armour was not proof against it, the tallest ramparts could not keep it out.

'Therefore Love is first among the company of the Lord of Heaven; He is a mediator between God and man, as a Mayor is between king and people: He alone delivers judgement on man for his misdeeds, and assesses the penalties.

'And so that one can recognize love by natural instinct, it begins by some power whose source and centre is in the heart of man. For every virtue springs from a natural knowledge in the heart, implanted there by the Father who created us – He who looked upon us with love and let His Son die for our sins, wishing no evil to those who tortured Him and put Him to death, but praying for their forgiveness.

'From this you may see an example in His own person, that He was mighty yet gentle, and granted mercy to those that hanged Him on the Cross and pierced His heart.

'So I advise you who are rich to have pity on the poor; and though you have power to summon them before the courts, be merciful in what you do. For "with what measure ye mete"[19] – whether well or ill – you shall be measured with that when you leave this world.

'For though you speak the truth and are honest in your dealings, and as chaste as an innocent child that weeps at its baptism, unless you love men truly, and give to the poor, generously sharing the goods God has given you, you shall have no more merit from your Masses and Hours than old Molly from her maidenhead, that no man wants.

'For the great Apostle James laid down in his Epistle that faith without deeds[20] is worthless – dead as a door-nail. So Chastity without Charity shall lie bound in hell; it is no more use than a lamp without a light.

'Many chaplains are chaste, but lack all charity. There are no men more greedy, once they get preferment. Ungrateful to their own relations and to all their fellow-Christians, they swallow up everything they are given, and cry out for more. Such a loveless virtue as this shall be fettered in hell.

'And there are parish priests galore who keep their bodies pure, yet are so burdened with avarice that they cannot wrench it off; it is hinged on them like a lid. This is not the truth of the Trinity, but the treachery of hell, and it teaches the layfolk to give less readily of their goods.

'Therefore our Lord says, "Give and it shall be given to you,[21] since I gave you all that you have. This is the key which unlocks love, and sets free my grace to comfort the sorrowful, heavy-laden with sin."

'Love is the physician of life, the power nearest to our Lord himself, and the direct way to Heaven. Therefore I repeat from these texts, that when all treasures are tested, Truth is the best. Now I have told you what Truth is, and shown you that no treasure is better, and I can stay with you no longer. May our Lord protect you.'

Book II

THE MARRIAGE OF LADY FEE[1]

THE STORY. *The dreamer asks Holy Church how he may recognize Falsehood, and she shows him a vision of Lady Fee, Falsehood's daughter, at whose illicit wedding to Fraud, the poet sees all Falsehood's followers. The proceedings are stopped by Theology, and Fee, with her whole train, sets out for Westminster to put the case before the royal judges. But being forewarned of the king's intention to arrest them, they scatter, and Fee alone is taken by his officers.*

BUT again I fell on my knees and besought her help, saying, 'Forgive me, Lady, for the love of Mary Queen of Heaven, who bore the blessed child who died for us – but show me some way by which I can recognize Falsehood.'

'Look to your left and see,' the Lady said. 'There he stands, Falsehood himself, with Flattery[2] and all their companions.'

I looked to the left[3] as the Lady told me, and saw a woman, richly dressed, whose robe was trimmed with the finest fur in the land. She was crowned with a coronet like a queen's, and her fingers were prettily adorned[4] with gold filigree rings, set with rubies that glowed like red-hot coals, with priceless diamonds and sapphires, both deep-blue and azure, with amethysts and with beryls to protect her from poisons.[5] Her dress was gorgeously coloured with rich scarlet dye, set off with bands of bright gold lace studded with gems. I was dazzled by her magnificence, for I had never seen such riches before; and I wondered who she was, and whose wife she could possibly be.

'Who is this woman,' I asked, 'that wears such splendid garments?'

'That is Fee the Maiden,' said the Lady. 'Many is the time she has injured me, slandering my dear friend Honesty, and denouncing her before the magistrates. She comes and goes in the Pope's palace as familiarly as I do, though Truth objects to this, because she is illegitimate. For her father was Falsehood, who has a deceitful tongue, and has never told the truth since he came into this world. And Fee has inherited his character, according to the law of nature, for it is written: "Like father, like son: Every good tree bringeth forth good fruit."[6] So I ought to take precedence over her, for I came of better stock.

'My father is the great God, the source of all graces – the one God who had no beginning; and I am his good daughter, to whom he has given Mercy as a marriage portion; so that any man who is merciful, and who truly loves me, shall be my lord, and I his lover, in Heaven.[7]

'And I swear by my life, the man who takes Fee to wife will lose for her love all his portion of mercy. What does David say in the Psalter about those who take fees, and about the way of salvation for men in authority? –

> "Lord, who shall dwell in thy tabernacle:
> or who shall rest upon thy holy hill? . . .
> He who taketh no bribes against the innocent."[8]

'And now this Fee is to be married to one Fraud Serpent's-tongue,[9] a cursed creature begotten by a devil. Flattery first paved the way for her, enchanting all the folk with his charming speech, but it was Liar who made the match.

'Tomorrow is the Maiden's wedding-feast, where you will be able to meet all their retinue, and learn what sort of people they are. Get to know them all if you can, but hold your tongue and say nothing against them; let them be, till Honesty comes as a Judge with power to punish them; then you may speak out.

'Now I commend you to Christ,' she said, 'and His spotless Mother. And never let your conscience be burdened through coveting fees.'

*

Thus the Lady left me lying asleep; and dreaming still, I saw the marriage of Lady Fee. All the rich company who owe their places to Falsehood were invited to the wedding, both by bride and bridegroom. In this vast assembly were men of every status, high and low: knights and clerics, jurors and summoners,[10] sheriffs with their clerks, beadles and bailiffs, business brokers and purveyors, victuallers[11] and advocates – I cannot number the throng that ran at Fee's heels.

Those who seemed most familiar with her face were Father Simony and Lord Civil-Law,[12] with his host of jurymen. But Flattery led the way to her chamber to fetch her out, for he was the agent commissioned to hand her over. And Simony and Civil-Law, when they realized what the couple wanted, had agreed for a certain sum to say whatever they were asked. Then Liar pushed himself forward, saying, 'See! Here's a deed of conveyance, that Guile, with his great oaths, has given them both'; and he begged Lord Civil-Law to look it over, and Father Simony to read it. Whereupon Simony and Civil, standing up before the guests, unfolded this solemn deed drawn up by Falsehood, and began singing it out at the tops of their voices:

'*Sciant presentes et futuri*[13] . . . Be it known and witnessed by all the world, that the Lady Fee is married, not for her virtue, beauty, or kindness, but solely for her property. Fraud is glad to have her, because he knows her wealth. And, by this charter, Sir Flattery-of-the-Double-tongue invests them with the following assets: to live as princes, to be proud and despise poverty, to backbite, boast, and bear false witness, to mock, scorn, and slander, and to break the commandments boldly without restraint.

'And he bestows upon them the Earldom of Wrath and Envy, together with the Castles of Strife and Senseless-Chattering; also the County of Covetousness and all the adjacent lands, including the twin towns of Usury and Avarice, both of which I grant them, with all their hagglings and traffickings besides, and furthermore the Borough of Theft. And, moreover, I grant them the whole lordship of Lechery from end to end, with all its appurtenances of clothes, words, and deeds, of wishing, and eager watching with the eyes, and of idle thoughts that persist when the powers of performance fail.'

Besides all this, he gave them the apanage of Gluttony, with its many privileges, viz. to swear great oaths and drink all day in diverse taverns, and gossip and joke there, and judge one's fellow-Christians; to eat before the proper time on fast-days, and then sit gorging till overpowered by sleep; to breed like town-pigs, and wallow luxuriously in bed till their sides were fattened with sloth and sleep; and finally to awake in despair, with no will to amend, and in their last agonies, to believe themselves lost.

'And to have and to hold, and all their heirs, a dwelling with the Devil, and be damned for ever; therewith all the dependencies of Purgatory extending into the pains of Hell; giving in return, at the end of one year, their souls to the Devil, to dwell with him and suffer torment as long as God is in Heaven.'

And these were the witnesses: first, Wrong himself; then Piers the Pardoner, of the Pauline Order;[14] Bett, the beadle of Buckinghamshire; Randolph, the reeve of Rutland; Mund the Miller, and many others.[15] It was signed and sealed, in the year of the Devil, in the presence of Simony, by authority of Civil-Law.

Theology, when he heard this recital, could contain himself no longer. 'The Devil take you and your weddings!' he said to Sir Civil-Law, 'contriving such mockeries in defiance of Truth! I hope you'll be sorry for this affair before it is finished!

'For Fee is an honest woman,[16] and the daughter of Restitution. God intended her for Honest Work, and you have given her to a rogue – God confound your impudence! Is that how you understand the text "The labourer is worthy of his hire"?[17] – A plague on your Law! You earn your living by lying and pimping, you and all your notaries and your fine friend Simony – you ravage Holy Church and rob the people. By God, you shall pay for it dearly! Fraud, as you well know, you hypocrites, is a faithless, treacherous bastard descended from Beelzebub; and Fee is a well-born lady, who might kiss the king himself as a true cousin, if she chose.

'So use your intelligence, and take her to London to put the case before the Law, and see if any law will allow such a shocking match. And if by any chance the judges do permit it, yet mind what you're up to, for Truth is no fool, and Sir Conscience, who knows you both, is one of His council. If He finds you guilty of helping Fraud, it will go hard with your souls on the Day of Judgement.'

Sir Civil agreed to go to London, but neither Simony nor the notaries would assent until they had silver for their services. So Flattery produced a great supply of florins, and bade Guile hand out gold to all and sundry, especially to the notaries, 'that none of them fail us'; and he retained False-Witness by means of a large sum, 'for he knows how to manage Fee and put her at my disposal.'

Everyone thanked Fraud and Flattery profusely for their golden gifts, and came along to reassure Fraud, saying, 'Never fear, dear sir, we shall not cease from our efforts until, by our combined influence, Fee is your wedded wife. Already, with a little gentle encouragement, we have persuaded the Lady to come to London and hear what the Law will say; and we feel sure that before long you will both be united for ever.'

Then Fraud and Flattery were pleased, and they summoned all the men in the neighbouring shires, beggars included, to be ready to accompany them to Westminster[18] and act as witnesses.

Then they wanted some horses to take them there, so Flattery procured a supply: he set Fee on a newly-shod Sheriff, Fraud on a gently-trotting Juryman, and himself on a finely-harnessed Sycophant.

But the notaries were annoyed because they had no horses, and Civil-Law and Simony were left to go on foot. So Civil and Simony swore they would saddle the Summoners, and have those petty inquisitors harnessed as palfreys. 'Father Simony shall bestride them himself,' said Sir Civil. 'Bring together all the deans, sub-deans,[19] archdeacons, Bishops' Officers, and registrars, and have them saddled with silver bribes, so they'll condone our sins – adultery, divorce, and private usury – and let them carry the bishops about on their visitations. The Paulines will help as well; they know everyone's secrets, and will draw up law-suits for me in the Consistory Courts. And put a bridle on the Commissary[20] too – he shall draw our waggon, and will get us provisions with fines from fornicators.

'And as for all the others still on foot, the friars and rogues and the rest, yoke Liar to a big cart and make him draw them all.'

So Fraud and Flattery set out together with Fee between them, and all these men behind. I haven't the time to describe all the rag-tag that followed them – men of every sort on earth. But Guile was at their head directing them all.

However, Honesty saw him, and although he said nothing, he spurred his palfrey and passed them all by; and coming to the king's court, he told the news to Sir Conscience; and Sir Conscience informed the king.

'By God!' said the king, 'if I could catch Fraud or Flattery or any of their crew, I'd teach those wretches to stir up trouble! I shall have them hanged by the neck, and their accomplices along with them! No one shall go bail for them; they shall feel the full force of the Law.' And he commanded an Officer, who came forthwith, to arrest them at all costs, and put Fraud in fetters, regardless of bribes. 'And strike off Guile's head before he goes a step further. And if you take Liar, hold him fast till you have put him in the pillory, and don't listen to his pleadings. And then bring Fee here to me.'

Dread stood at the door and overheard this decree; so he went quickly and warned Fraud and his followers to scatter.

Then Fraud fled in fear to the Friars. And Guile, in terror of death, was searching round for a way of escape, when some merchants met him and took him in with them, shutting him up in their shop as a salesman; and they rigged him up as an apprentice to serve the customers.

Then Liar nimbly bounded away, to skulk in the alley-ways, and be lugged about by all and sundry. He was nowhere welcome, in spite of his many tales; everywhere he was jeered at and sent packing. But at last the Pardoners took pity on him.

and pulled him indoors. They washed and wiped him and wrapped him in rags, and sent him on Sundays to the churches with seals, selling pounds-worths of Pardons. Then the doctors were annoyed, and sent him an urgent letter asking him to join them, and help them analyse urine. And the grocers also sought his help for hunting out their wares, for he knew something of their trade, and had all the drugs and spices at his command. But then he fell in with some minstrels and messengers, and they kept him with them for six months and eleven days.[21] And finally the Friars lured him away and disguised him in their own habit so that visitors should not recognize him; but he has leave to come and go at his pleasure, living with them on and off whenever it suits him.

Thus they all fled in terror and went into hiding, except for Fee the Maiden, who alone made no attempt to escape. And even she trembled with fear when she was arrested, weeping and wringing her hands.

Book III

LADY FEE AT WESTMINSTER

THE STORY. *Lady Fee is well received at Court, and the Judges and Counsellors seek her favour with promises of help. The king decides to pardon her, provided she will marry his knight Conscience, and to this she consents. But Conscience himself will not hear of it, and violently denounces her before the king. He defeats Fee's arguments and prophesies the coming of a Messianic kingdom of truth and peace, where Fee shall be no more.*

LADY FEE, deserted by all her companions, was brought before the king by the beadles and bailiffs. And the king, calling one of his counsellors (I need not mention his name), told him to take her and see that she was properly looked after. 'I shall examine her myself,' the king said, 'and ask her outright which man she would really prefer. If she proves amenable and is willing to do as I tell her, I intend, God willing, to pardon her for this offence.'

Then, as the king commanded, this counsellor politely put his arm round Fee and guided her to her chamber, where music and other entertainments were provided for her amusement.

All those who resided at Westminster treated Fee with the greatest respect. Some of the judges, with the Clergy's permission, hastened along full of gallantry and good humour, to console her as she sat in her boudoir. 'Do not lose heart, Lady Fee,' they said. 'You have no cause for distress. We will speak to the king and smooth the way for you. And we can promise you that you will be able to marry whom you wish, in spite of Conscience and all his tricks!'

Fee thanked them graciously for their great kindness, giving everyone presents of gold and silver vessels, with rings, rubies, and valuables of all kinds, not forgetting a gold piece even for the lowest of their retainers. Then the judges took their leave of her.

Whereupon the Clergy and Counsellors came to comfort her in the same way, saying, 'Take heart, Lady, for we will always be at your disposal, for as long as there's life left in you; don't hesitate to make full use of us.' Fee politely returned the compliment, and said that for her part she would always be faithful to them, get them titles, and obtain seats for them[1] in the Bishop's Court, 'You needn't worry about your education,' she said, 'as long as you're friends of mine; I'm well known in places where learning gets you nowhere.'

Her next visitor was a Friar, come to hear her confession. Speaking in the dulcet undertones of the confession-box,[2] he said to Fee, 'Don't worry how many men you have had to do with, clerics or laymen, or if Falsehood has hung at your heels for half a century, I will still give you absolution – for a small fee, of course – shall we say one horse-load of wheat? For that I will undertake to be your own beadsman,[3] and spread your influence among the gentry and clergy, undermining Conscience wherever I go.'

So Fee knelt before him and made her confession, shamelessly; and when she had told him a suitable tale or two, she gave him a coin accepting him as her beadsman and personal agent. Then, after gabbling through the form of absolution, he added, 'We are having a stained-glass window made for us, and it's proving rather expensive. If you would care to pay for the glazing yourself, and have your name engraved in the window,[4] you may have no doubts of your eternal salvation.'

'Ah! If I can be sure of that,' the woman said, 'I will do anything for you, Father. You can count me your unfailing friend – but never be hard on those lords and ladies who give way to their lusts. Do not blame them for it, for lechery is a frailty of the flesh, a natural instinct, Father – that's what all the books say. We all began that way, so there can't be much harm in it, as long as one avoids a scandal. And it's quite the easiest to forgive of all the Seven Deadlies. So you be kind to them, and then I will roof your church, build you a cloister, whitewash your walls, glaze your windows, have paintings and images made, and pay for everything. People will all be saying I am a lay-sister of your Order.'[5]

*

But God forbids us to blazon our good deeds on walls and windows, lest they become mere monuments of pride and worldly pomp. For all your motives and purposes lie open to God; He sees your natural greed, and knows where the money really belongs.

Therefore I advise you, lords and ladies, have done with such inscriptions, and do not cry for the notice of men of God[6] when you want to give alms, lest you have your reward on earth,[7] and your Heaven too. And 'Let not thy left hand know what thy right hand doeth,'[8] for so the Gospel bids men do good deeds.

And you Mayors and Officers who uphold the Law, and are the chief link between king and people, be sure that you punish all fraudulent tradesmen, the brewers, the bakers, the butchers, and the cooks, in your pillories and ducking-stools. For these are the men who do most harm to the poor, poisoning them with adulterated food, at extortionate prices. They grow rich by selling at retail prices, and invest in properties by robbing the bellies of the poor. For how could they build themselves such tall houses, and buy up lands and tenements, if they were honest dealers? But Fee has begged the Mayor to accept money from them – or if not money, plate, and gold rings and other valuables – to let them stay in business undisturbed. 'For my sake,' she says, 'leave them all alone, and let them overcharge just a wee bit.'

Now hear what Solomon said for the benefit of such Mayors and officials: 'Fire shall consume the tabernacles of those who freely take bribes'[9] – that is, all who expect gratuities or New Year boxes because they hold office will have their houses and homes burned to ashes.

*

The king, coming from his Council, sent for Fee at once, and a band of his officers, in great high spirits, escorted her to his private chamber.

Then the king spoke graciously to her and said, 'This is not the first time, Lady, that you have acted unwisely, but you never did worse than when you accepted Fraud! However, I will forgive you this time – but never do such a thing again, as long as you live.

'Now I have a knight called Conscience, who has recently come from overseas. If he is willing to make you his wife, will you have him?'

'Certainly, my liege,' answered the Lady. 'God forbid that I should refuse! Hang me if I'm not completely in your hands.'

So Sir Conscience was summoned to appear before the king and Council. He made a low obeisance to the king, and knelt to hear his wishes.

'Are you willing to marry this woman, if I give my consent?' said the king. 'She would gladly accept you as a husband.'

'God forbid!' said Conscience, 'I'd rather be damned than marry such a wife! She is fickle and faithless, and has led count-less men into sin. Thousands already have been betrayed by trusting in her riches. She makes wantons of wives and wid-ows, using presents as baits to lure them into sin. She has poisoned Popes[10] and corrupted Holy Church, and your own father[11] she ruined by her false promises. I swear to God you won't find a greater bawd between Heaven and hell, though you search the whole earth! She's as lecherous as a monkey – a tale-bearer too! – and as common as a cart-track to every way-faring wretch – monks and minstrels and the lepers that lie under the hedges. The only men who treat her with respect are jurors and summoners and suchlike, and County Sheriffs who would be ruined without her; for by bribing them she causes men to lose their lands and their lives. She gives gold to the gaolers to let prisoners loose, and lets criminals wander at large, while honest men, who have done no harm, are seized, cast into irons, and hanged, to satisfy her spite.

'What does she care about threats of excommunication? She keeps the Bishop's men in clothes, and can get absolution whenever she likes. Her purse can do more in a single month than the king's privy seal[12] can do in six. Even the Pope con-fides in her – as is well known to those who buy livings in

Rome; for it is she and Simony who seal her Papal mandates.

'She makes bishops of men who can scarcely read. She provides livings for parsons and for lawless priests to spend their lives with mistresses and concubines, and rear families. Heaven help that land where she wins the king's favour! For she will always smile on falsehood and trample on the truth.

'Christ! How her jewels mow down the magistrates! How she perjures herself in the law-courts, and chokes up the course of justice! Her florins fly so thick, that truth is smothered with them. She bends the Law as she likes, chooses her own days for settling disputes, and makes men lose for her sake what the Law might have won them. A poor man is bewildered and confused: he may plead in the courts for ever, but the Law will not move an inch; it hates to reach a verdict, and without bribes or presents Fee will satisfy no one.

'So she brings disaster upon barons and burgesses, and all commoners who try to lead honest lives. This, my liege, is her way of life – and may God confound her and all her supporters! For she has coupled Education with Avarice, and she holds such sway over men of property that, no matter how the poor are wronged, there is nothing they can do about it.'

Then Fee looked aggrieved, and whined to the king for a chance to speak and defend herself; and the king willingly allowed her. 'Excuse yourself if you can, by all means,' he said, 'for with all these accusations of Conscience, you are like to be packed off for good.'

'Ah, my good lord,' said the Lady, 'when you know the truth of the matter you will credit him less. In times of trouble, Fee is very useful. – And you know well enough, Conscience, that I did not come here in pride, to quarrel, or slander you. You know too, you liar, unless you try to gloss it over, that you have come crawling to me many times in the past, and laid your hands on my gold and doled it out as you liked. So why you should be so angry with me now, I can't imagine. For I can still honour you with my favours, if I choose, and bolster up your courage in ways that you never dreamt of.

'But you have foully slandered me before the king here. For

I never killed, or planned the death of a king, nor did any of
the things that you say – I swear by the king! And in the
French Wars,[13] I did him no wrong at all – unlike you, who
shamed him again and again, creeping into hovels[14] to keep
your fingers warm, fearing the winter would last for ever,
frightened to death of a few storm-clouds – and then rushing
home because your belly was empty!

   'And you robbed the poor men without pity, you thief, and
carried their money away on your back, to sell at Calais. And
meanwhile, I stayed behind with my lord, to protect his life. I
cheered his men up and made them forget their miseries, and
slapped them on the back to liven up their spirits, till they
fairly danced for joy, hoping to have me all to themselves. By
God, if I had been Commander of his men, I wager my life I'd
have made him master of that whole land, from end to end –
and king, too, and what an honour that would have been for
his family – the smallest brat among them would now be as
good as a baron!

   'But then you, Conscience, stepped in with your coward's
advice – to give it all up,[15] the richest realm under the sun, for
a handful of silver!

   'Why, a king, as guardian of the realm, is bound to fee those
who serve him, and show courtesy to all men, especially to
foreigners, with handsome gifts. It is for fees that people love
and respect him. And without me, how could the nobles, or
even emperors, retain young men to ride about for them?
Even the Pope and the prelates accept offerings, and pay fees to
those who uphold their laws. Servants all get fixed wages for
services rendered; beggars demand fees for their begging, and
minstrels fees for entertaining. The king receives fees from his
men, to keep peace in the land.[16] Schoolmasters get fees for
their pupils; skilled workmen take fees for their apprentices;
and even priests expect a fee, in food or Mass-offerings, for
teaching people virtue; and surely merchants must make a
profit, to carry on their trade. There's not a man on earth that
can live without fees!'

   'By Heaven!' said the king to Conscience, 'Fee has cer-
tainly won her point, it seems to me.'

'No,' said Conscience, and he knelt down on the ground. 'By your leave, my lord, there are two different kinds of payment. The one is the gift of Heaven which God, of His grace, gives to those who do their work well on earth. The Psalmist speaks of this: "Lord, who shall dwell in thy tabernacle, with thy saints? Who shall dwell in thy holy hill?"[17] And King David answers the question too: "He that walketh uprightly, and worketh righteousness" – that is, he who is unspotted from the world, and single-minded, who has acted with reason and justice, and sought after truth; who has taught the poor, and has not lived by usury – "Who putteth not out his money to usury, nor taketh rewards against the innocent." So all who help the innocent and side with the righteous, doing good to them without fees and maintaining truth, shall have this payment from God in time of greatest need, when they leave this world.

'But there is another kind of payment, a lucre without measure, which men in authority grasp at – the bribes they get for supporting evil-doers. And of them the Psalter also speaks:

"In whose hands is wickedness:
    and their right hand is full of gifts."[18]

And even the man who receives money from them shall pay a bitter price for it, unless the Scripture lies![19] And priests who seek their own pleasure, exacting money for the Masses they sing, gain all their reward on earth, as we read in St Matthew: "Verily I say unto you, they have their reward."[20]

'The money, my liege, which labourers receive from their master, is not a fee at all, but a fair wage. Nor are there any fees for trading with goods: it is simply an exchange, one pennyworth for another.

'Tell me, you shameless Fee, did you never read the Book of Samuel,[21] nor notice why vengeance fell on Saul and his children? For God sent a message to Saul, by his prophet Samuel, that Agag, king of the Amalekites, and all his people, must die for a deed done by their ancestors. "Therefore," said Samuel to Saul, "God himself commands you to obey Him and do His will, to go with thy host to the land of the Amalekites, and slay all that you find there – men and beasts alike, burn them to death; wives, widows, and children, all their estates and belongings, and everything you find, burn it, and carry nothing away, no matter how valuable. Take no booty; destroy it all; spare nothing, and it will be better for you."

'And because Saul coveted the booty, and spared the life of the king and of his beasts, against the prophet's warning, God told Samuel that Saul and all his seed should die, and come to a shameful end. This was what your fees did for Saul – such harm that God hated him for evermore, and all his heirs after him. But I had better draw no conclusions from this, lest anyone should be offended. For this world is so changed now, that the man who tells the truth to those in power is condemned first.

'Yet I am certain of one thing, for Common Sense has taught me to believe it: that Reason shall reign supreme and rule over the nations. And there are many who shall share the fate of Agag;[22] for once more Samuel shall slay him, and Saul shall be condemned, and David shall be crowned king[23] and subdue all kingdoms. Then one Christian king shall rule over the whole world.

'And no more shall Fee prevail, as she does now; but Love and Meekness and Honesty shall be the rulers of the earth, and the guardians of truth.

'And if any man commits a sin against truth, or takes a bribe to permit a falsehood, he shall have but one judge, and that is Honesty. Lawyers shall no longer plead at the bar with their hoods of silk and cloaks of ermine. For as it is now, Fee is a law unto herself: she makes lords of criminals, and rules kingdoms over the heads of judges.

'But Natural Love and Conscience shall come together, and turn Law into an honest workman. – Such love shall arise,[24] and such peace and perfect truth among the people, that the Jews, amazed that men should be so truthful, will be filled with joy, thinking that Moses or the Messiah has come to earth.

'And any man who carries a sword,[25] a lance, an axe, a dagger, or any kind of weapon, shall be put to death, unless he sends it to the smithy to be turned into a scythe, a sickle, or a ploughshare. – "They shall beat their swords into plough-shares, and their spears into pruning hooks."[26] And men will pass their time in digging or ploughing, spinning yarn or spreading dung, or else there will be nothing for them to do.

'And the only kind of hunting left to priests will be for the souls of the dead;[27] and they will hammer at their Psalms from morn till night. For if any of them hunt with hawks and hounds, they shall lose their boasted livings.

'No king or knight or officer or Mayor shall tyrannize over the people, or summon them to serve on juries and compel them to take oaths. But each criminal will be punished accord-ing to his crime, heavily or lightly as Truth shall decide. And the King's Court, the Common Court, the Church Court, and the Chapter shall all be one Court, with a single judge, one True-tongue, an honest man who never opposed me. There shall be no more battles, and any blacksmith who forges a weapon shall perish by it.

– "Nation shall not lift up sword against nation,
    neither shall they learn war any more."[28]

'But before this comes to pass, men shall see the worst; and the sign of its coming will be six suns in the sky,[29] with a ship and half a sheaf of arrows. And then an Easter full moon shall convert the Jews; and when they see these things, the Saracens shall sing the *Gloria in Excelsis*. But to you, Fee, and to Maho-met, will come disaster; for it is written,

"A good name is rather to be chosen than great riches,
    and loving favour rather than silver or gold." '[30]

Then Fee suddenly grew as furious as the wind, 'I don't know any Latin,' she said, – 'I leave that to the scholars. But you should read what Solomon says in the Book of Proverbs: "He that giveth gifts winneth the victory, and hath much honour withal." '[31]

'Your quotation is quite correct, Madam,' said Conscience. 'But you are like a certain lady reading the Scripture, who, when she came to the words "Prove all things",[32] was highly delighted. However, the text broke off at the end of a page, and if she had turned over, she would have found the rest of it – "Hold fast to that which is good."

'You, my lady, have done the same as she did. You've discovered half the text, but you could never find the rest, not if you pored over Proverbs all day long: you need a scholar to turn the pages for you! Your vision would suit the lords of this world very well, but the sequel is bitter medicine for those who take bribes. For this is the text complete –

> "He that giveth gifts winneth the victory, and hath much honour withal, *but he taketh away the soul of him that receiveth them.*" '33

Book IV

THE DOWNFALL OF LADY FEE

THE STORY. *As Conscience still refuses to be reconciled with Fee, the king resolves henceforth to act on Reason's advice, and sends Conscience to fetch him. On their return to Court, there arises a test case; for Crime, a purveyor, is accused of oppressing the people, and Worldly Wisdom and Fee are intriguing for his release. But Reason pleads eloquently against them, and finally gains the support of the king and the majority of the Court. So Fee and her lawyers are defeated, and the king vows to follow Reason and Conscience in everything.*

'STOP!' said the king, 'I will not allow this any longer. You must be reconciled and obey me, both of you. Conscience, I command you to kiss her and make it up.'

'Good God, no!' said Conscience. 'Banish me for ever first! I'd rather die than kiss her unless Reason says so.'

'Then I command you to ride quickly and fetch Reason at once. Tell him to come quickly, as I have some news for him. From now onwards, he alone shall direct my kingdom and be my Chief Counsellor. And he shall discuss with you, Conscience, how you teach the people, clerics, lay folk and all.'

'I am very glad of this,' said Conscience. And he rode directly to Reason, whispered the king's command in his ear, then took his leave.

'Stay and rest for a bit,' said Reason, 'while I go and get ready.' And he called for his servants, Cato[1] Fairspeech and Tom True-tongue-tell-me-no-idle-tales-for-I-don't-find-them funny, and said, 'Set my saddle on Wait-till-I-get-a-chance, gird him with a belly-band of Good Advice, and put on the heavy bridle to hold his head down, for he's sure to start neighing before we get there.'

Then Conscience and Reason rode as fast as they could,

conferring privately about Fee and the subtle hold she had on mankind.

But before long, they were pursued by two men, Worldly Wisdom and his friend Cunning, who had certain matters to clear up in the Courts of Exchequer and Chancery, and were galloping hard to catch up with Reason. For they hoped, for a small fee, to get his advice; he might save them a great deal of trouble and embarrassment.

But they were both covetous men, and Conscience, who knew them well, told Reason to ride faster, and take no notice of them. 'Their talk is deceptive,' he said. 'The truth is that they spend their time with Fee, and make their money out of strife and quarrels; Love and Honesty they avoid like the plague.

> "Destruction and unhappiness is in their ways
>   and the way of peace they have not known."[2]

They don't give a straw for God – "There is no fear of God before their eyes." These men, I tell you, would do more for a horse-load of oats or a dozen chickens, than for all the love of our Lord and His blessed Saints. So let them ride by themselves, Reason, and keep their money-bags. Conscience does not acknowledge them, nor I think does Christ.'

So, with Conscience to guide him, Reason galloped full tilt along the highway, till he came to Court.

The king courteously came to meet him, and offered him a seat on the dais between himself and his son. And they spoke together very seriously for a long time.

*

Then a man named Peace came to Parliament bringing in a petition[3] against one Crime. 'He has run away with my wife,' he said, 'and assaulted Rosy, Reg's girl, and had his way with Margaret too, for all her struggling. And besides that, his ruffians have seized my pigs and geese, and I'm too scared of him to argue or put up a fight. He has borrowed my horse and never brought it back, and refused to pay a farthing for it though I begged him for the money. He stands by and eggs his men on to murder my servants, and forestalls my goods[4] and starts a brawl over them at the market. He breaks down my barn doors and carries off my corn, and all I get is a tally-stick for two hundredweight or more of oats. And on top of all this, he beats me up and goes to bed with my daughter, and I live in such terror of him, I daren't lift a finger.'

The king was aware that Peace was telling the truth; he knew already from Conscience of the misery that this ruffian caused among his subjects. So Crime began to feel alarmed, and applied to Worldly Wisdom to smooth things over with money. 'If only I could get in the king's good books,' he said, offering Wisdom a large bag of silver, 'Peace and all his gang could howl on for ever and it wouldn't worry me!'

But in view of the terrible sins Crime had committed, Wisdom and Cunning decided to read him a lecture before helping him: 'People who act on impulse,' they said, 'will always be running their heads into trouble. Such is the case with you, my good man, and you'll soon discover how right we are. It looks as though you're in a bad way, unless Fee can fix things up for you, for the king holds your life and lands at his mercy.'[5]

Then Crime began imploring Worldly Wisdom to settle the matter for him – a few coins in his palm and a little juggling, and all would be well! So Wisdom and Cunning, taking Fee with them, went off together to get Crime a pardon.

Then Peace held forward his blood-stained head to show them, saying, 'God knows, I've done nothing to deserve a blow like this. Conscience and all the people will vouch for that.' But Wisdom and Cunning set to work quickly, and tried to bowl the king over with solid cash.

The king, however, stood his ground, and swore by God and his crown that Crime should suffer for his offences; and he commanded an officer to cast him in irons at once – 'And make sure he never sees his feet for years,' he added.

'Good heavens above!' said Worldly Wisdom, 'that is surely very ill-advised. If the man is willing to pay compensation, why not let him have bail? And then his surety can pay a ransom for him,[6] and the whole affair will be straightened out. That will be much better for all concerned.'

Cunning agreed with him and urged the same course. 'There's no sense in making matters worse,' he said. 'Two wrongs don't make a right.'[7]

Then Fee thought it was her turn, and, begging the king to show mercy, she offered Peace a gift of pure gold. 'Accept this from me, my good fellow,' she said, 'as a little something to make up for your injury. I'll promise you Crime will never do it again.'

So now Peace himself, with tears in his eyes, begged the king to have mercy on the man who had done him so many wrongs – 'for he has given me good security, as Sir Wisdom advised, and with your consent, I am quite willing to forgive him. For my part, it seems the best way out; Lady Fee has paid me the damages, and what more could I ask?'

'No!' said the king. 'Crime shall not be allowed to escape; I will learn more of this matter first. If he gets off lightly, he will treat the whole affair as a joke, and beat up my servants more boldly than ever. Unless Reason takes pity on him or he is ransomed by Humbleness, he shall sit in my stocks till his dying day!'

Then some of the court pleaded with Reason to take pity on the poor wretch, and persuade the king and Conscience to let Fee ransom him.

'It's no use asking me to have mercy,' answered Reason, 'till lords and ladies learn to love the truth, and turn away from filth and ribaldry; and Lady Peacock casts her finery off, and locks her furs away in her clothes-chest; and parents spoil their children only with rods, and jesters become famous for their holy living; till the clergy are greedy to clothe and feed the poor, and men of Religion who wander off to Rome sing Mass in their cloisters instead, as Benedict, Bernard, and Francis ruled that they should; till preachers prove what they preach by their own practice, and the king's Council serves the public good; and bishops sell their horses to buy shelter for beggars, and their hawks and hounds to help poor monks and friars; till St James is sought[8] in a place of my own choosing, and no one goes to Galicia except to stay there; till no more money bearing the king's image, stamped or unstamped, gold or silver, is carried abroad to fill the pockets of Papal robbers;[9] and till all who go running off to Rome or Avignon[10] are searched for money at Dover[11] – except, of course, for all the merchants[12] and their men, the messengers with their letters, the priests, the penitent pilgrims, and those seeking livings from Rome!

'Yet I shall still have no pity,' continued Reason, 'while Fee has any hold on this Court. I have seen so much of the havoc she creates, and could give you proof if you wished. If I, for my part, were a king, with a realm to protect, I should leave no wrong unpunished, on peril of my soul. Nor, God willing, would anyone win my favour with gifts, or gain my mercy through Fee; only their Meekness would influence me.

'For a man named *Nullum Malum* met with one called *Impunitum*, and bade *Nullum Bonum* be *irremuneratum*.[13] Let your confessor, my lord, interpret this riddle for you, without glossing over it. And if you carry it out, I swear that the Law shall turn labourer and drive a muck-cart, and Love shall rule over your land as you have always wished.'

Then the king's confessors put their heads together, to see if they could interpret this sentence in the king's interests – though not for the good of his soul or his people's benefit. For I noticed how Fee, as she sat in the Council-Chamber, made signs to the lawyers, and how they, chuckling to themselves, left Reason's side and skipped across to her. And Worldly Wisdom winked at her and said, 'I'm the very man for you, Madam. For however well I may argue when pleading a case, I haven't a word to say once I light on some money!'

But all the just men among them, including most of the Court and many great nobles, declared in favour of Reason; and even Cunning agreed, and praised Reason's speech. And they thought Meekness a true scholar, and Fee no better than a common slut. Love himself turned against her, and Honesty despised her, and voiced his opinion so loudly that the whole Court heard him. 'If anyone marries her for her money,' he said, 'he'll soon be a fine cuckold!'

But Fee sat there sullen and crestfallen, branded as a whore by the greater part of the Court. Yet one of the jurors and a summoner still went after her eagerly; and a sheriff's clerk swore at the whole assembly, saying, 'Many's the time I've assisted you at the bar, and none of you ever gave me a brass farthing!'

Then the king, calling Reason and Conscience to his side, gave his verdict in favour of Reason. He frowned threateningly on Fee, and turned angrily to Law – the Law that Fee had almost overthrown – saying, 'I have you to thank, no doubt, for the loss of half my estates.[14] This Fee of yours has choked up the truth and trampled on your justice. But Reason will settle with you before I have reigned much longer, and judge you as you deserve, make no mistake. Nor shall Fee stand bail for you either! From now on I will have honest lawyers, and there's an end of the matter! As for Crime, the majority of this Court have judged him guilty, and he shall be sentenced accordingly.'

Then Conscience said to the king, 'Unless you win the support of the common people, you will find it very hard to bring this about, and govern your subjects strictly according to justice.'

'I'd rather be drawn alive,' exclaimed Reason, 'than rule your kingdom in any other way. And you must give me the power to command obedience.'

'I swear by our blessed Lady,' answered the king, 'I will support you in this, once I have called together my Council, the nobles and clerics. I gladly accept you, Reason, and while I live you shall never leave my side.'

'And for my part, I am ready to stay with you for ever,' said Reason, 'but you must let Conscience remain here as our adviser; that is all I ask.'

'I grant it,' answered the king. 'God forbid we should fail! Let us live together for the rest of our lives.'

Book V

THE CONFESSION OF THE SEVEN DEADLY SINS AND THE SEARCH FOR TRUTH

THE STORY. *The dreamer awakes, only to fall asleep again almost at once. Then he dreams of Reason preaching in the Plain to the whole realm and rousing all the people to confess their sins. Each of the Seven Deadly Sins makes a confession to Repentance, who then prays to Christ to forgive them all. The people afterwards set out as pilgrims in search of Truth, but they are still ignorant and soon lose their way. Then Piers the Ploughman suddenly speaks up from among the crowd, and claims that he is the servant of Truth and can direct them to His mansion. They listen patiently to his directions, but when they learn how difficult the way is, some desert him and return home.*

THE king and his nobles went to church to hear Mass and Matins for the day. And then I awoke from sleep, disappointed that I had not slept more soundly and seen more. But scarcely had I gone two hundred yards, when I felt so faint and sleepy that I could walk no further. So I sat down quietly and said my Creed, and dropped asleep muttering my Rosary.

Then I saw much more than before. For again I beheld the field full of people, and now Reason, standing before the king with a Cross in his hand, and preparing to preach to the whole kingdom.

He made it plain to them that their sin alone had caused the Plagues, and that the great gale[1] which came from the South-west on Saturday evening was clearly the judgement of God on their excessive pride. 'Your pears and plum-trees toppled before the blast,' he said, 'as a parable to warn you to do better. And beeches and mighty oaks were dashed to the ground, with their roots twisted high in the air, as a terrible sign of the

61

destruction that deadly sin will bring upon you all, on the Day of Doom.'

I could preach a long sermon on this myself, but I will speak only of what I saw – how clearly Reason preached before the people.

He told Waster to go and work, at whatever trade he could do best, and so win back the money that he had squandered. He begged Lady Peacock to leave off wearing her furs, and put them by in a chest against time of need. He directed Tom Stowe to take a couple of cudgels, and rescue his wife Felicity from the ducking-stool.[2] He warned Walter that his wife was much to be blamed for wearing a headdress worth five guineas, while his ragged old hood would hardly fetch threepence. And he bade Mr Bett cut himself some birch-rods, and beat his daughter Betty till she was willing to work.

Then he told the merchants to discipline their children. 'If you make a lot of money, don't pamper them with it,' he said, 'and even if the Plague carries off half the neighbourhood, still you must never spoil them unreasonably. My mother and father used to say to me, "The more you love the child, the more you must correct him."[3] And Solomon, the author of Wisdom, said the same – "He that spareth his rod hateth his son." [4]

And then he admonished the priests and Bishops, saying, 'Prove by your own lives what you preach to others. This will bring blessing to yourselves, and encourage us to have better faith in your teaching.'

Next, he exhorted the monks and friars to keep to their Rule – 'lest the king and his Council cut down your supplies, and decide to manage your property for you until you are better governed.'

Then he counselled the king to love his people – 'for they are your greatest treasure in times of peace, and in times of trouble your chief support.' And he begged the Pope to have pity on Holy Church, and govern himself before distributing grace to others.

'And as for you men who maintain the laws,' he said, 'you must covet Truth, and not gold or gifts if you would please

God. For the Gospel tells us that neither God nor His saints in Heaven will acknowledge any man who opposes the truth – "Verily I say unto you, I know you not."[5]

'And you folk who go on pilgrimages and visit the shrines of St James and the saints in Rome, must seek instead for the blessed Saint Truth,[6] for He alone can save you, who with the Father and the Son liveth and reigneth for ever and ever. And may He bless and save all who follow my teachings.'

So ended Reason, and Repentance ran to take up his theme, till William wept bitterly to hear him.

Pride[7]

The Lady Peacock Proud-heart threw herself flat on the ground and lay there for a long time. Then she raised her head, crying 'Lord, have mercy,' and vowed to God that she would slit her smock and fasten a hair-shirt on the inside, to tame the fierce lusts of her flesh. 'Here's an end to all my swaggering airs,' she said. 'For now I intend to take a humble place and endure insults gladly – that will be something new for me! And I will be meek and beseech God for mercy, for this is the thing my heart has always loathed.'

Lechery[8]

Then Lecher cried 'Alas!' and besought Our Lady to intercede for his soul, and pray God to have mercy on his sins; and for this he made her a vow, that every Saturday for many years to come, he would drink nothing but water and be content with only one meal.

Envy

Then with a heavy heart Envy asked for penance, and sorrowfully began to say the *Confiteor*. He was as pale as ashes, and shook like a man with the palsy. His clothes were so coarse and shabby, I can scarcely describe them – a rough tunic with a kirtle below, a knife by his side, and foresleeves cut from a Friar's habit. With his shrivelled cheeks, and scowling horribly, he looked like a leek that has been lying too long in the

sun. His body was all blistered with wrath, and he went about
biting his lips and twisting his fingers, always scheming some
vengeance by word or deed, and looking for a chance to carry it
out. His tongue was like an adder's: every word he spoke was
backbiting and detraction. He made his living by slander and
bearing false witness; and in whatever company he showed his
face, he displayed his manners by flinging dirt at everyone.

'I would be shriven, if only I dared,' said this creature, 'but
I am far too ashamed. For I swear I would far rather see Bert,
my neighbour, get into trouble, than win half a ton of Essex
Cheese tomorrow.

'There's one near neighbour of mine whom I've almost
ruined. I've so slandered him to the gentry that he's lost all his
money, and my lies have turned even his friends against him.
It makes my blood boil to see him in luck, or getting credit for
anything.

'I cause such strife among folk with my evil talk, that it
sometimes ends in loss of life or limb. Yet when I meet the man
I detest most, in the market place, I greet him politely, as if I
were his best friend. For I daren't offend him – he's far stronger
than I am. But if once I got him in my power, God knows
what I'd do to him!

'And when I go to church, and the priest tells us to kneel
before the Rood and pray for pilgrims and all the people, then
on my knees I call down curses from Heaven on the thieves
who've run off with the bowl I use for rubbish, and my
tattered sheet! And then I turn my eyes away from the altar,
and seeing that Ellen has a new coat, I wish to God it were
mine, together with all the cloth from which it was cut.

'I gloat over other men's losses, and bewail their gains. I
condemn their actions, while my own are much worse. And if
anyone tells me off, I hate him for ever. I could only be happy
if everyone were my slave, for it drives me mad to think that
anyone else should have more than I have.

'And so I live, without love, like a mangy cur, my whole
body swollen with bitter gall. Why, for many years I could
scarcely eat, Envy and Ill-will are so hard to digest. Haven't
you got some sweet syrup that can soothe my swellings, some

gentle linctus of shame or penance, to drive it out of my heart?
– or will you have to scour my stomach?'

'Yes, indeed I have,' said Repentance, and he advised him
what was best – 'Sorrow for sin always save a man's soul.'

'But I *am* sorry,' said the man, 'I am seldom otherwise.
That is why I'm so thin – because I can never get my revenge!
When I was living in London, among the rich merchants, I
would use Backbite as my private agent, to run down other
men's wares! And when mine wouldn't sell, and theirs would,
then you should see how I scowled and slandered them and
their goods! Still, if I can, through the grace of Almighty God,
I intend to make amends for all these things.'

Anger[9]

Then Anger, with staring eyes, was roused to repentance, and
hanging his head came forward snivelling. 'I am Anger,' he
said. 'I used to be a friar, and worked at the Friary as a gar-
dener, grafting shoots. So I grafted on to those beggars such
lies and tales that they bore great branches of flattering words
to please the gentry, and blossomed out into ladies' bowers to
hear confessions. And now this tree of mine has borne strange
fruit: for the people would rather go to the friars for Con-
fession, than to their parish priests. And the salaried priests,
finding they have to share their profits with the friars, de-
nounce them from the pulpits. Then the friars retaliate in kind,
and wherever they go on their rounds preaching, I, Anger,
walk with them, and teach them from my holy books.

'Both parties will boast of their own spiritual power, and
despise each other, till either they all become beggars and live
by *my* spiritual power, or else grow rich, and ride about on
horseback![10] So I never rest from pursuing these wicked folk,
for I reckon that's my vocation.

'I have an aunt who's a nun – an Abbess in fact. She would
rather drop down dead than suffer a moment's pain! For many
months I served as a cook in her convent kitchen, and in the
monastery too. My chief job was concocting soups for the
Prioress, and the other poor ladies. So I brewed them broths

of every conceivable slander – that Mother Joanna was an illegitimate child, that Sister Clarice might be a knight's daughter, but her mother was no better than she should be, and that Sister Peacock had an affair with a priest – "She'll never be Prioress," they said, "She had a baby last year in cherry-time;[11] it's the talk of the Convent!"

'And I fed them with such a hash of spiteful gossip, that two of them would sometimes burst out "Liar!" together, and slap each other across the face. Christ! If they'd both had knives, they'd have slaughtered each other!

'St Gregory was a good Pope, with great foresight, for it was he who laid down that no Prioress could hear confessions.[12] Otherwise they would all have been disgraced on the very first day, for women can never keep anything secret.

'I might, of course, live with the monks, but I mostly avoid them. They have too many fierce fellows watching out for men like me, Priors and Sub-Priors and Father Abbots. If I tell any tales there, they hold a special meeting, and make me fast every Friday on bread and water. Then they give me a telling-off in the Chapter-house, as though I were a child, and have me whacked with my trousers down. I am not very fond of living with fellows like that. There's nothing to eat there but stinking fish and watery ale. So that if, once in a while, they get in some good wine and I manage to drink in the evening, it gives me a flux of foul talk for five days after. I repeat all the evil I know about any of our brethren, till the whole house has heard it.'

'You must repent,' said Repentance, 'and never again repeat anyone's secrets, no matter how you came by them. And do not take too much pleasure in drink or swallow too much, lest it weakens your will and you get another attack of malice. For the Scripture says, "Be ye sober." '[13] And then he gave Anger his absolution, bidding him try to be contrite and weep for his sins.

Avarice

And then came Covetousness; no words can describe him, he looked so hungry and hollow, such a crafty old codger! He had beetling brows and thick, puffy lips, and his eyes were as bleary

as a blind old hag's. His baggy cheeks sagged down below his
chin, flapping about like a leather wallet, and trembling with
old age. His beard was all bespattered with grease, like a serf's
with bacon fat. He wore a hood on his head with a lousy cap
on top, and a dirty-brown smock at least a dozen years old,
torn and filthy and crawling with lice. It was so threadbare that
even a louse would have preferred to hop elsewhere.

'I have been covetous,' said this old wretch, 'I confess it all
now. I began as an apprentice under Sim-at-the-Stile, and I had
to make his business pay. I learnt to lie in a small way to begin
with, and my first lesson was in giving false weights. Then my
master would send me to the fairs at Weyhill and Winchester,
with all kinds of wares; and God knows they would still be un-
sold to this day, but for the grace of Guile which crept amongst
them!

'Then I went to school with the drapers, and was shown
how to stretch the selvedge and make the cloth look longer.
My chief lesson was with the best, striped stuff – how to pierce
it with pack-needles and join the strips together and lay
them in a press, till ten or eleven yards were stretched into
thirteen.

'My wife was a weaver of woollen cloth. She employed
spinners to spin it out for her, and paid them by the pound.
But if truth be known, the pound weight she used weighed a
quarter more than my own steelyard.[14]

'Then I bought her some barley-malt, and she took to brew-
ing beer for retail. She would mix a little good ale with a lot of
small beer, and put this brew on one side for poor labourers
and common folk. But the best she always hid away in the
parlour or in my bedroom; and if anyone took a swig at that,
he paid for it through the nose – four bob a pint at least, and
that's God's truth. Even so, she would measure it out in cup-
fuls – she was a crafty old girl! They called her Rose the Racket-
eer, and she's been a regular huckster all her life.

'But now I swear to break myself of these sins – no more
selling short weight or swindling the customers. And I'll make
a pilgrimage to Walsingham, with my wife as well, and pray
to the Rood of Bromholm[15] to get me out of debt.'

'Have you ever repented,' said Repentance, 'or made any restitution?'

'Yes, indeed I have: I was staying at an inn once, with some merchants, and while they were asleep I got up and burgled their bags.'

'That wasn't restitution, that was robbery!' said Repentance. 'You ought to be hanged for that, more than for everything else you've told me.'

'I though restitution meant robbery,' he said, 'I never learned to read, and the only French I know comes from the wilds of Norfolk!'

'Have you ever in your life practised usury?'

'No, certainly not, except in my young days. I did pick up a thing or two then, I admit, chiefly from Jews and Lombards.[16] They showed me how to weigh coins with a balance, clip the heavier ones, and then lend them out, all for love of the cross[17] – the one on the back of the gold pieces! The borrower would give me a pledge he was almost certain to lose, and that was worth more to me than the clipped coins. And you should have seen the agreements I used to draw up in case my debtors didn't pay on the nail. I've acquired far more properties through arrears of debt, than I ever could have got by "showing kindness and lending".[18] Why, I have lent money and goods to lords and ladies[19] before now, and afterwards been their broker, and bought them out for nothing!

'I do a roaring trade in barter and money-lending; people lose the better part of every crown I lend them. And sometimes, when I've carried the Lombards' letters to Rome with their gold, I have taken the money by tally here in London, and counted it out as a good deal less when I got to the other end.'

'But did you ever pay noblemen money to connive at your crimes?'

'I have certainly paid out money to noblemen, but they didn't love me for it, I assure you! I've turned many a knight into a mercer or draper[20] – and they never paid me a thing for their apprenticeship, not so much as a pair of gloves!'

'Then are you merciful to poor men who are forced to borrow?'

'I pity them as much as a pedlar pities cats – he'd kill them for their skins if he could only catch them!'

'Well, are you kind at least to your neighbours? Do you invite them in for a meal?'

'My neighbours think I'm as kind as a dog in a kitchen,' he said.

'Then you had better repent soon,' said Repentance, 'or the only prayer I can say for you is this: that you may never live to make good use of your riches, that your children after you may never enjoy them, nor your executors put them to any good purpose; but that all you have wickedly gained may be spent by the wicked.

'For if I were a Friar, and belonged to an honest, charitable House, I should never consent to spend money of yours on vestments or church repairs. Nor would I accept an extra penny on my allowance, if I knew, or had any suspicion, that it came from a man like you – not if you were to give me the best manuscript in the Friary, with leaves of burnished gold! For it is written, "Thou art the slave of another, when thou seekest after dainty dishes; feed rather upon bread of thine own, and thou shalt be free."[21]

'You are a vile wretch, and I cannot give you absolution. You must first settle accounts with all the people you have robbed. I have no power to pardon you till all their losses are made good, and Reason has entered it in the register of Heaven. For it is written, "The sin is not remitted unless restitution be made."[22] And all who have received any part of your wealth are bound before God to help you pay it back. If you doubt it, read what is written in the Psalter Commentary, under the verse, "Behold, Thou desirest truth in the inward parts."[23] For no man who uses your ill-gotten gains can ever prosper.

–"With the merciful Thou wilt show thyself merciful:
    and with the froward Thou wilt show thyself froward." '[24]

Then this scoundrel fell into despair, and would have hanged himself, had not Repentance offered him comfort at once, saying, 'Think of God's mercy, and pray aloud for it. For it is written, "God's tender mercies are above all His works,"[25] and again, "Compared with the mercy of God, all the evil that man can do or think in this world, is as a spark quenched in the ocean."[26]

'So fill your heart with thoughts of mercy. And as for your business, give it up. You have no right to buy yourself so much as a roll of bread, unless you can earn the money with your own hands, or beg it. All your wealth sprang from deceit, so you cannot live by it; and if you do, you are not paying for what you buy, but living on credit. And in case you are not sure whom to repay, take your money to the Bishop, and ask him to dispose of it for you, in whatever way is best for your soul. He shall answer for you before the Judgement of God – for you, and many more besides. For believe me, every bishop will render an account to God,[27] both of what he taught you in Lent, and what he gave you from the riches of God's grace, to guard and keep you from sin.'

Gluttony

And then Gluttony set out to go to Confession. But as he sauntered along to the church, he was hailed by Betty, the ale-wife, who asked him where he was going.

'To Holy Church,' he replied, 'to hear Mass and go to Confession; then I shan't commit any more sins.'

'I've got some good ale here, Glutton,' she said. 'Why don't you come and try it, ducky?'

'Have you got hot spices in your bag?'

'Yes, I've got pepper, and peony-seeds, and a pound of garlic – or would you rather have a ha'porth of fennel-seed, as it's a fish-day?'[28]

So Glutton entered the pub, and Great Oaths followed him. He found Cissie the shoemaker sitting on the bench, and Wat the gamekeeper with his wife, and Tim the tinker with two of his apprentices, and Hick the hackneyman,[29] and Hugh the haberdasher, and Clarice, the whore of Cock Lane, with the parish clerk, and Davy the ditcher, and Father Peter of Prie-Dieu Abbey, with Peacock the Flemish wench,[30] and a dozen others, not to mention a fiddler, and a rat-catcher, and a Cheapside scavenger, a rope-maker and a trooper. Then there was Rose the pewterer, Godfrey of Garlick-hithe, Griffiths the Welshman, and a crew of auctioneers. Well, there they all were, early in the morning, ready to give Glutton a good welcome and start him off with a pint of the best.

Then Clement the cobbler pulled off his cloak and flung it down for a game of handicap.[31] So Hick the hackneyman threw down his hood and asked Bett the butcher to take his part, and they chose dealers to price the articles and decide on the odds.

Then the two dealers jumped up quickly, went off into a corner, and began in whispers to value these rubbishy garments. But as they had scruples about it and couldn't agree, they asked Robin the ropemaker to join them as an umpire, and so they settled the business between the three of them.

As it turned out, Hick the hostler got the cloak, while Clement had to fill the cup and content himself with Hick's hood. And the first man to go back on his word was to do the honours, and stand Glutton a gallon of ale.

Then there were scowls and roars of laughter and cries of 'Pass round the cup!' And so they sat shouting and singing till time for vespers. By that time, Glutton had put down more than a gallon of ale, and his guts were beginning to rumble like a couple of greedy sows. Then, before you had time to say the Our Father, he had pissed a couple of quarts, and blown such a blast on the round horn of his rump, that all who heard it had to hold their noses, and wished to God he would plug it with a bunch of gorse!

He could neither walk nor stand without his stick. And once he got going, he moved like a blind minstrel's bitch, or like a fowler laying his lines, sometimes sideways, sometimes backwards. And when he drew near to the door, his eyes grew glazed, and he stumbled on the threshold and fell flat on the ground. Then Clement the cobbler seized him round the middle to lift him up, and got him on to his knees. But Glutton was a big fellow, and he took some lifting; and to make matters worse, he was sick in Clement's lap, and his vomit smelt so foul that the hungriest hound in Herttordshire would never have lapped it up.

At last, with endless trouble, his wife and daughter managed to carry him home and get him into bed. And after all this dissipation, he fell into a stupor, and slept throughout Saturday and Sunday. Then at sunset on Sunday he woke up, and as he wiped his bleary eyes, the first words he uttered were, 'Who's had the tankard?'

Then his wife scolded him for his wicked life, and Repentance joined in, saying, 'You know that you have sinned in word and deed, so confess yourself, and show some shame and make an act of contrition.'

'I, Glutton, confess that I am guilty,' said the man, 'I have sinned by word of mouth more often than I can remember: I have sworn by "God's Soul" and said "God and the saints help me" hundreds of times when there was no need to.

'And I have let myself go at supper, and sometimes dinner too, so badly that I have thrown it all up again before I have gone a mile, and wasted food that might have been saved for the hungry. On fast-days I have eaten the tastiest foods I could get, and drunk the best wines, and sometimes sat so long at my meals that I've slept and eaten both at the same time. And to get more drink and hear some gossip, I've had my dinner at the pub on fast-days too, and rushed off to a meal before midday.'

'God will reward you for this good confession,' said Repentance.

Then Glutton began to weep and bewail his vicious life; and he made a vow of fasting, saying, 'Every Friday from now on, I shan't give my belly a morsel of anything, not even fish, no matter how hungry and thirsty I get – not till my Aunt Abstinence gives me permission – though up to now I have always loathed her!'

Sloth

Then came Sloth, all beslobbered, with his gummy eyes. 'I shall have to sit down,' he said, 'or I'll fall asleep. I cannot stand or prop myself up all the time, and you can't expect me to kneel without a hassock. If I had been put to bed now, you'd never get me up before dinner was ready, not for all your bell-ringing – not unless nature called.'

Then, with a loud belch, he started his 'Bless me, father,' and beat his breast, but as he stopped to stretch, he yawned, grunted, and finally started to snore.

'Hey! Wake up, man!' shouted Repentance. 'Get a move on, and make your confession.'

'If this were my dying day,' said Sloth, 'I still couldn't be bothered to keep awake. I don't even know the Paternoster perfectly, not as a priest should really sing it. I know plenty of ballads about Robin Hood and Randolph Earl of Chester,[32] but I don't know a verse about our Lord or our Lady.

'I have made hundreds of vows, and forgotten them the next morning. I have never yet managed to do the penance the priest has given me, or felt sorry for my sins. And when I'm saying my Rosary, my heart is miles away from the words, except when I say them in a fit of temper. I spend every day, holydays and all, gossiping idly at the pub – sometimes even in church – and I never give a thought to the Passion of Christ.

'Nor have I ever once visited the sick or the prisoners chained in the dungeons. For I enjoy a bawdy joke, or a riotous day at the village wake, or a juicy bit of scandal about some neighbour, more than all that Matthew, Mark, Luke, and John ever penned. I don't keep account of vigils or fast-days – they just seem to slip by. And in Lent, I am lying in bed with my mistress in my arms till long after Mass and Matins are over, then I go to the Friary for a late Mass. And once I get to the "Ite, Missa est", I've had enough! Why, unless illness drives me to it, I sometimes go a whole year without making a confession, and then I do it by guesswork.

'I have been a parish priest for more than thirty years, yet I can neither sing my notes right, nor read a Lesson. I can start a hare in a ploughed field better than I can construe a single verse in the Psalms, or expound it to the parish. I'm good at presiding at Settlement Days, and auditing Reeves' accounts,[33] but I can't read a line of Canon Law. And if I take anything on credit, it goes clean out of my mind unless it is marked on a

73

tally. The man can ask for it six or seven times over, but I'll swear blind I know nothing about it. That's the way I ill-use honest men, day in and day out.

'It is a grim day for all concerned when I have to read the accounts of my servants' wages, and find how far behind I am with them. So I pay them off – with arrears of spite and resentment.

'And if someone does me a good turn, or helps me in need, I pay him back with rudeness; for I can never understand courtesy. My manners have always been like those of a hawk: you can't lure me by love alone, you must always hold a tit-bit under your thumb. My fellow-Christians must have done me hundreds of favours in times past, but I have forgotten them all. And I have wasted good foodstuffs, deliberately or through carelessness – meat, fish, bread, butter, cheese, and ale – all gone to waste till they weren't fit to eat.

'When I was a boy I never got down to my studies, but I trotted about from place to place instead; and this vile sloth had made me a beggar ever since. – *"Heu mihi, quod sterilem duxi iuvenilem*!"'*

'Do you repent?' said Repentance – but at that moment Sloth dozed off again.

Then the Watcher, whose name is *Vigilate*,[34] threw some cold water over his face and dashed it into his eyes, shouting earnestly, 'Look out! For Despair is out to betray you! Say to yourself "I am sorry for my sins," and beat your breast and beseech God for grace. For His goodness is greater than all the guilt in the world.'

Then Sloth sat up, blessed himself hastily, and made a vow before God to fight against his foul sloth, saying, 'Not a single Sunday shall pass from now on – unless sickness prevent me – but I will go to holy church before dawn, and hear Mass and Matins like a monk. And I will never again sit over my ale after dinner, but go to church and hear Evensong instead. I make this vow before the Holy Rood. Moreover I intend, if I can find the means, to pay back all that I have wrongfully acquired since I was a boy. I will not stint anyone, even if I go

*Alas! for my barren and misspent youth!

without myself; every man shall have what is his, before I leave this world. And with whatever is left, I swear by the Rood of Chester,[35] I will turn pilgrim, and seek Truth first, even if I never see Rome!'

Then Robert the Robber began weeping bitterly, for he remembered the text, 'Render to all men their dues,'[36] and had no means of making restitution. And yet this wretched sinner was praying under his breath, 'O Jesus, who died on the Cross of Calvary, and took pity even on Dismas my brother,[37] because he said, "Remember me, Lord, when thou comest into thy kingdom",[38] have mercy now on this robber who has not wherewith to repay.[39] For I can never earn enough with my hands to repay all that I owe. Yet I beseech You, out of Your great mercy, to accept what little I can do. Do not condemn me at Doomsday for doing so ill.'

I cannot tell for sure what happened to this robber. But I know that he wept bitter tears, and acknowledged his guilt to Christ again and again. And he promised to polish afresh his pikestaff of penance, and tramp the world with it for the rest of his life – because he had slept with Latro,[40] Lucifer's Aunt.

Then Repentance had pity on all the penitents, and bidding them kneel, he said, 'And now I will beg our Saviour's grace for all sinners, that He may have mercy on us all and help us to do better –

'O God, who in Your goodness[41] created the world, and fashioned all things out of nothing, making man the closest to Your image – and yet allowed him to sin, and so bring a sickness upon us all – and all for the best, for so I believe, whatever the Scriptures say –

"O felix culpa, O necessarium peccatum Adae!"[42]

– for through that sin, Your Son was sent to this earth, and became a man, and was born of a Virgin to save mankind; and in the Person of Your Son, O God, You made yourself like us sinful men, for it is written, "Let us make man in our own image, after our likeness,"[43] and again, "He that dwelleth in love, dwelleth in God, and God in him" – [44]

'So You, O God, robed in our flesh with Your Son, died for our sake on that Good Friday, at high noon – though neither You nor Your Son felt any sorrow in death, for the anguish was felt only in our human flesh, and Your Son overcame it – "He led captivity captive"; yet on account of the weakness of the flesh, Your Son closed His eyes for a while, at about midday when the light is greatest which is the meal-time of Your saints;[45] and then You fed with Your fresh Blood our forefathers who dwelt in darkness –

> "The people that walked in darkness,
> have seen a great light"[46]

– and by the Light which leapt forth from you then, Lucifer was blinded, and with Your dying breath You swept all those blessed souls into the bliss of Paradise.

'And the third day after, You walked again in our flesh, and the first to see You was not Mary Your Mother, but a sinful Mary; and You allowed it to be so, in order to comfort the sinful, for it is written, "I came not to call the righteous, but sinners to repentance."[47]

'And since Your most mighty deeds, all that Matthew, Mark, Luke, and John recorded, were done in our human coat-armour (for "The Word was made flesh and dwelt among us"[48]), so I believe we may confidently pray and beseech You, who art our Father and our Brother, to have mercy on us, and, if it be Your will, to take pity on these wretched sinners here, who repent so sorely that they ever offended You, in thought, word, or deed.'

Then Hope seized a horn of *Yet-didst-thou-turn-and-refresh-me*,[49] and blew it to the tune of *Blessed-is-he-whose-sins-are-forgiven*,[50] till all the saints in Heaven took up the song –

'Thou, Lord, shalt save both man and beast; How excellent is thy mercy, O God:
and the children of men shall put their trust under the shadow of thy wings.'[51]

Then a thousand men thronged together, crying aloft to Christ and His Virgin Mother, that Grace might go with them in their search for Truth.

But not one of them had the wisdom to know the way. So they blundered on like beasts,[52] over humps and hills, till at last, late in the day and far from home, they met a man dressed like a strange Saracen,[53] as pilgrims are. He carried a staff, with a broad strip of cloth twisted round it like bindweed. By his side were slung a bag and begging-bowl,[54] and souvenirs[55] were pinned all round his hat – dozens of phials of holy oil, scallop-shells from Galicia, and emblems from Sinai.[56] His cloak was sewn all over with devices – Holy Land crosses, cross-keys from Rome, and a St Veronica handkerchief [57] across the front – to let everyone know how many shrines he had seen.

'Where have you come from?' the people asked.

'From Sinai,' he said, 'and from Our Lord's Sepulchre. I have also visited Bethlehem, Babylon,[58] Armenia, Alexandria and many more holy places. You can see by the signs in my hat how widely I've travelled – on foot and in all weathers, seeking out shrines of the saints for the good of my soul.'

'Do you know anything about a saint called Truth?' they said. 'Can you tell us where to find him?'

'Good Heavens, no!' said the man. 'I've met plenty of palmers with their staffs and scrips, but no one ever asked for a saint by that name.'

'By St Peter!'[59] said a ploughman, pushing his way through the crowd, 'I know Him, as well as a scholar knows his books. Conscience and Common Sense showed me the way to His place, and they made me swear to serve Him for ever, and do His sowing and planting for as long as I can work. I've been His man for the last fifty years; I've sown His seed and herded His beasts, and looked after all His affairs, indoors and out. I ditch and dig, sow and thresh, and do whatever Truth tells me – tailoring and tinkering, spinning and weaving – I put my hand to anything He bids me.

'And Truth is pleased with my work, though I say it myself. He pays me well, and sometimes gives me extra; for He's as ready with His wages as any poor man could wish, and never fails to pay His men each night. Besides, He's as mild as a lamb, and always speaks to you kindly. – So if you would like to know where He lives, I'll put you on the track in no time.'

'Thank you, Piers old fellow,' the pilgrims said; and they offered him money to guide them to Truth's castle.

'No, by my soul!' swore Piers, 'I wouldn't take a farthing, not for all the riches in St Thomas's shrine![60] Truth would find it hard to forgive me for that! But if you want to go the right way, listen now, while I set you on Truth's path.

'You must all set out through *Meekness*, men and women alike, and continue till you come to *Conscience*; for Christ may know by this that you love God above all things,[61] and your neighbour next, and treat others as you would like them to treat you.

'Then turn down by the stream *Be-gentle-in-speech*, till you come to a ford, *Honour-thy-father-and-mother*. There you must wade into the water and wash yourselves thoroughly, then you'll step more lightly for the rest of your life. Next, you will see a place called *Swear-not-without-necessity-and-above-all-take-not-the-name-of-the-Lord-thy-God-in-vain*.

'After that, you will pass by a farm where you must not trespass on any account, for its name is *Thou-shalt-not-covet-thy-neighbour's-cattle-nor-his-wives-nor-any-of-his-servants-lest-you-do-him-an-injury*. So take care not to break any branches there, unless they are your own property.

'You will also see there two pairs of stocks; but do not stop, for they are *Steal-not* and *Kill-not*. Go round and leave them on your left, and don't look back at them. And remember to observe Holy Days, and keep them holy from morning till nightfall.

'Then you will come to a hill, *Bear-no-false-witness*. Turn right away from it, for it is thickly wooded with bribes, and bristling with florins. At all costs gather no blossoms there, or you will lose your soul. And so you will arrive at a place called *Speak-the-truth-and-mean-it-and-never-swerve-from-the-truth-for-any-man*.

'From there you will see a mansion[62] as bright as the sun, surrounded by a moat of *Mercy*, with walls of *Wisdom*, to keep out passion. It has battlements of *Christendom* to save mankind, and is buttressed with *Believe-or-you-cannot-be-saved*.

'And all the buildings, halls, and chambers are roofed, not with lead, but with *Love*, and are covered with the *Lowly-speech-of-brothers*. The drawbridge is of *Ask-and-you-shall-receive*, and each pillar is built of penance and prayers to the saints, and all the gates are hung on hinges of almsdeeds.

'The doorkeeper's name is Grace, a good man, who has a servant, Amendment, well known among men. And this is the password you must give him so that Truth may know you are honest: "I have done the penance which the priest gave me; I am very sorry for my sins, I always shall be whenever I think of them, and still should be even if I were Pope!"

'Then you must ask Amendment to beg his Master to open the wicket-gate that Eve shut in the beginning, when she and Adam ate the sour apples. For "Through Eve the door was closed to all men, and through the Virgin Mary it was opened again."[63] So Mary always has the key, even when the King is sleeping.[64]

'And if Grace gives you leave to enter by this gate, you will find Truth dwelling in your heart, hung on a chain of charity. And you will submit to Him as a child to its father, never opposing His will.

'But then beware of the villain Wrath, who envies Him who dwells in your heart. For he will push Pride in your way and make you feel so pleased with yourself that you are blinded by the glory of your own good deeds. So you will be driven out "as the early dew",[65] the door will be locked and bolted against you, and it may be a hundred years before you enter again. Thus by thinking too much of yourself, you may lose God's love, and enter His courts no more, unless His grace intervenes.

'But there are also seven sisters,[66] the eternal servants of Truth, who keep the postern-gates of the castle. These are Abstinence and Humility, Chastity and Charity, His chief maidens, Patience and Peace, who help many people, and the Lady Bountiful, who opens the gates to still more, and has helped thousands out of the Devil's pound.

'Anyone related to these seven is wonderfully welcome there, and received with honour. But if you are kin to none of

79

them, it is very hard for you to get in at all, except by the special mercy of God.'

'Christ!' said a cutpurse, 'I've got no relatives there!'

'Nor me, as far as I know,' said a juggler with a monkey.

'Lord 'a mercy!' said a market woman, 'if it's as bad as that, I'm not going a step further – not for no Friar's preaching!'

'Yes, but listen,' said Piers, still trying to spur them on, 'Mercy[67] herself is a maiden there, with power over all the others. She and her Son are akin to all sinners. So if you will put your trust in them, you may still find grace – but you must go quickly.'

'By St Paul!' said a Pardoner. 'It maybe that they don't know me there. I'll go and fetch my box of indulgences and my Bishop's Letters.'

'By Jesus, I'll go with you!' said a prostitute. 'You can say I'm your sister.' – But what became of these two I cannot tell.

Book VI

PIERS SETS THE WORLD TO WORK[1]

THE STORY. *Piers offers to go with the pilgrims himself, on condition that they first help him to sow his field. They agree to do so, and after setting them all to work, Piers makes his will in preparation for the pilgrimage. The work in the field goes well until Piers finds some of the men shirking. He tries to make them work, but they defy him, and he is forced to call up Hunger to punish them. Hunger chastises them soundly, they all return to work eagerly, and at last produce enough food to put Hunger to sleep. Then the men relapse into idleness.*

THEN the people complained to Piers and said, 'This is a grim way you've described to us. We should need a guide for every step of the road.'

'Now look,' said Piers the Ploughman, 'I have half an acre[2] of land here by the highway. Once I can get it ploughed and sown, I will go with you and show you the way myself.'

'We should have a long time to wait,' said a veiled lady. 'What work could we women be doing to pass the time?'

'Why, some of you can sew up the sacks,' said Piers, 'to keep the seed from spilling. And you fair ladies with slender fingers – you have plenty of silks and fine stuffs to sew. Make some vestments for priests, while you've got the time, and lend a hand in beautifying the churches. And those of you who are married or widows can spin flax and make some cloth, and teach your daughters to do it too. For Truth commands us to take care of the needy and clothe the naked. I'll give them food myself, so long as the harvest doesn't fail. For I don't mind working all my life for the love of God, to provide meat and bread for rich and poor.

'So come along now, all you men who live by food and drink – lend a hand to the man who provides you with it, and we will finish the job quickly.'

'By Heavens!' said a knight,[3] 'this fellow knows what's good for us! But to tell the truth, I've never handled a team of oxen. Give me a lesson, Piers, and I'll do my best, by God!'

'That's a fair offer,' said Piers. 'And for my part, I'll sweat and toil for us both as long as I live, and gladly do any job you want. But you must promise in return to guard over Holy Church, and protect me from the thieves and wasters who ruin the world. And you'll have to hunt down all the hares and foxes and boars and badgers that break down my hedges, and tame falcons to kill the wild birds that crop my wheat.'

Then the knight answered courteously and said, 'I give you my word, Piers, as I am a true knight; and I'll keep this promise through thick and thin and protect you to the end of my days.'

'Ah, but there's one thing more I must ask you,' said Piers. 'Never ill-treat your tenants, and see that you punish them only when Truth compels you to – even then, let Mercy assess the fine, and be ruled by Meekness, and at all costs have no truck with Fee. And if poor men offer you gifts, don't ever accept them – it may be that you do not deserve them, and will have to pay them all back at the year's end, in a perilous place called Purgatory!

'And take care also that you never ill-use your serfs. It will be better for you in the long run, for though they are your underlings here on earth, they may be above you in Heaven, in greater happiness, unless you lead a better life than they do. For Our Lord said: "When thou art bidden, go and sit down in the lowest room; that when he that bade thee cometh, he may say unto thee, Friend, go up higher."[4] And it is very hard to tell a knight from a serf when he comes to lie in the church-vaults – so lay that to heart.

'And you must always speak the truth, and show contempt for all tales that are told you, except such as are wise, and apt for rebuking your workmen. Have nothing to do with jesters and don't listen to their tattle, least of all when you sit at meals in your hall. For believe me, they are the Devil's minstrels!'

'Now, by St James,' the knight answered, 'I'll abide by your words for ever.'

'Then I will dress as a pilgrim,' said Piers, 'and go with you till we find Truth. I will put on my working clothes, all darned and patched, my leggings, and my old gloves to keep my fingers warm; and I'll hang my hopper around my neck for a scrip, with a bushel of rye inside. And then, when I have sown my seed, I will turn palmer, and go on a pilgrimage to gain a pardon.

'And those who help me to plough and sow before I set out, shall have leave to glean here in harvest-time, and make merry with what they can get, no matter what people say. And I will provide food for men of all trades, so long as they are faithful and honest. – But there'll be none for Jack the juggler[5] or Janet from the stews, none for Daniel the dice-player or Doll the Whore, nor Friar Rogue nor any of his Order, nor Robin the ribald with his bawdy jokes. For Truth once told me to have no dealings with such men – "Let them be blotted out of the book of the living"[6] – and so He bade me tell others. Holy Church is forbidden so much as to take tithes from them, for the Scripture says: "Let them not be written with the righteous." And they get off lightly at that, God help them!'

Now Piers' wife was called Dame *Work-while-you've-got-a-chance*, his daughter was called *Do-as-you're-told-or-you'll-get-a-good-hiding*, and his son's name was *Always-give-way-to-your-elders-and-don't-contradict-or-maybe-you'll-wish-you-hadn't*.

Then Piers turned to his wife and children, saying, 'May God be with you all, as His word teaches. For now that I am old and grey, and have enough to live on, I am going away with these folk on a pilgrimage, to do penance. So before I go, I will have my will written: –

Piers' Will. 'In the name of God, Amen. I, Piers, make this will myself. My soul shall go to Him who has best deserved it, and He shall, I trust, defend it from the Devil till I come to the day of reckoning, as my Creed tells me. And then I shall have a release and a remission from all the rent I owe on it.

'The Church shall have my flesh and shall keep my bones. For the parish priest took his tithe of my corn and earnings, and for my soul's sake I always paid it promptly; so he is bound, I hope, to remember me in his Mass, when he prays for all Christians.

'My wife shall have what I've earned by honest toil alone; and she shall share it among my daughters and my dear children. For though I should die this very day, my debts are all paid, and I've always returned what I've borrowed, before going to bed.[7]

'And now I swear by the Holy Rood of Lucca[8] to devote all that is left to the worship of Truth, and to serve Him for the rest of my life. And I will be His pilgrim, following the plough for poor men's sake; and my plough-shoe shall be my pike-staff, to cleave through the roots, and help my coulter to cut and cleanse the furrows.'

And now Piers and his pilgrims have gone to the plough, and many folk are helping him to till his half acre. Ditchers and diggers are turning up the headlands, and others, to please Peter, are hoeing up the weeds, while he is delighted with their labours and quick to praise them. They are all eager to work, and every man finds something useful to do.

Then at nine o'clock in the morning Piers left his plough in order to see how things were going, and pick out the best workers to hire again at harvest-time. At this, some of them sat down to drink their ale and sing songs – thinking to plough his field with a '*Hey-nonny-nonny*'!

'By the Lord!' said Piers, bursting with rage, 'Get up and go back to your work at once – or you'll get no bread to sing about when famine comes. You can starve to death, and to hell with the lot of you!'

Then the shirkers were scared, and pretended to be blind, or twisted their legs askew, as these beggars can, moaning and whining to Piers to have pity on them. – 'We're sorry, master, but we've no limbs to work with. But we'll pray for you, Piers – God bless you, sir, and may God in His goodness multiply your grain, and reward you for the charity you give us here. For we're so racked with pain, we can't lift a finger.'

'I shall soon see if what you say is true,' said Piers. 'But I know quite well you are shirking – you can't get away from Truth. I'm an old servant of His, and I've promised to keep an eye open for folk in the world who wrong His workmen, and warn Him about them. You are the men who waste the food that others sweat for. Still, Truth will soon teach you to drive His oxen – or you'll be eating barley-bread and drinking from the stream!

'If anyone is really blind or crippled, or has his limbs bolted with irons, he shall eat wheaten bread and drink at my table, till God in His goodness sends him better days. But as for you, you could work for Truth well enough if you wanted: you could earn your food and wages by herding cattle or keeping the beasts from the corn, or ditch or dig or thresh away at the sheaves; or you could help mix mortar or cart muck to the field. The fact is you would rather have a life of lechery, lying, and sloth, and it is only through God's mercy that you go unpunished.

'No, I would rather give my earnings to hermits and anchorites, who eat nothing from one noon to the next; and those who have cloisters and churches to maintain – I'm quite willing to keep them in clothes. But Robert Runabout will get nothing from me, nor the wandering preachers,[9] unless they know how to preach, and have the Bishop's licence. And if that is so, they can make themselves at home, and I'll give them bread and soup – for even an Apostle can't live on air!'

Then one of the vagabonds lost his temper with Piers, flung out a challenge and squared up for a fight. And a blustering Frenchman shouted out, 'Go and stuff your plough, you stingy old scoundrel! We'll do as we please – you can take it or leave it. We shall fetch as much of your flour and meat as we want, and make a feast with it – so you go and hang yourself!'

Then Piers the Ploughman begged the knight to keep his promise, and protect him from these damned villains, the wolves who rob the world of its food. 'For while they devour it all,' he said, 'and produce nothing themselves, there will never be plenty for the people. And meanwhile my plough lies idle.'

So the knight, who was courteous by nature, spoke kindly

to Waster, and warned him to mend his ways – 'or, by my Order of Knighthood,' he said, 'I shall bring you to justice.'

'I have never worked yet,' said Waster, 'and I don't intend to start now' – and he began to jeer at the Law and rail at the knight, and told Piers to go and piddle with his plough, for he'd beat him up if ever they met again.

'By God!' said Piers, 'I'll teach you all a lesson!' And with that he holloed out for Hunger; and Hunger heard him at once and started up. 'Avenge me on these wretches who eat up the world,' cried Piers.

Then Hunger leapt at Waster and seized him by the belly, wringing his guts till the water ran from his eyes. And he gave the Frenchman such a drubbing that he looked as lean as a rake for the rest of his life. He pasted them so soundly that he almost broke their ribs; and if Piers hadn't offered Hunger a pease-loaf and besought him to leave off, by now they'd both be pushing up the daisies! 'Spare their lives,' said Piers, 'and let them eat with the hogs and have bean and bran swill, or milk and thin ale.'

Then these rogues fled in terror to the barns, and threshed away with their flails from morning till night; and Hunger did not dare to molest them, because Piers had made them a pot of pease-pudding. And a crowd of hermits, cutting their cloaks to make jerkins and seizing some tools, went to work with spades and shovels, and dug and ditched like mad to stave off Hunger. Then thousands of blind and bed-ridden folk suddenly recovered, and men who used to sit begging for silver were miraculously cured! And the starving people appeased their hunger with bran-mash, and beggars and poor men worked gladly with peas for wages, pouncing like sparrowhawks on any work that Piers gave them. And Piers was proud of his success, and he set them all to work, giving them a fair wage and as much food as he could spare.

Then Piers took pity on the people, and begged Hunger to go home and stay in his own country. 'For thanks to you,' he said, 'I am well avenged on these wastrels. – But before you go, there's one thing I would like to ask you. What is the best thing to do with beggars and loafers? Once you've gone, I know quite well they will start slacking again. It is only their misery that makes them so submissive, and famine which has put them in my power. Yet they are truly my blood-brothers,'[10] said Piers, 'for Christ redeemed us all, and Truth once taught me to love all men alike and give freely to everyone in need. So I should like you to tell me what would be best, and advise me as to how to control them and make them work.'

'Listen then,' said Hunger, 'and mark my words. The big tough beggars who are capable of hard work, you can keep alive with horse-bread and dog-biscuits, and bring their weight down with a diet of beans – that will flatten their bellies! And if they grumble, tell them to go and work, and they'll get tastier suppers when they've earned them.

'But if you find a man who has fallen on evil days or been ruined by swindlers, for the love of Christ do your best to relieve him. You must seek out such folk and give them alms, and love them, as the law of God teaches – "Bear ye one another's burdens, and so ye shall fulfil the law of Christ."[11] So give all you can spare to those who are penniless – show them charity and do not reproach them; leave God to punish them if they have done wrong – "Vengeance is mine; I will repay, said the Lord."[12] For if you wish to find favour with God, you must obey the Gospel, and make yourself beloved among humble folk – "Make to yourselves friends of the mammon of unrighteousness"[13] – and then God will reward you.'

'I would not offend God for all the world,' said Piers. 'Are you sure I can treat the shirkers as you say, without committing a sin?'

'Yes, I assure you,' said Hunger, 'or else the Bible is wrong. Ask the giant Genesis, the begetter of all men: "In the sweat of thy brow," he says, "shalt thou eat bread"[14] – that is God's command. It says the same in the Book of Proverbs –

"The sluggard will not plow by reason of the cold:
    therefore shall he beg in harvest, and have nothing."[15]

And St Matthew, whose sign has a man's face,[16] tells this parable:[17] – There was a worthless servant who had only one talent; and because he would not work and trade with it, he lost his master's favour for evermore. And his master took his talent away from him, and gave it to the one who had ten, saying: "He that hath shall receive, and find help when he needs it; but he that hath not shall receive nothing, and no one shall help him; and I shall take away from him even that which he thinks he hath."

'It is common sense that every man must work, either by ditching and digging, or by travailing in prayer – the active or the contemplative life – for such is God's will. And according to Psalm 128, a man who lives by his own honest labour is blessed in body and soul –

"For thou shalt eat the labours of thine hands:
    O well is thee, and happy shalt thou be." '[18]

'Thank you,' said Piers, 'and now, friend Hunger, if you have any knowledge of medicine, I pray you, teach me it, for the love of God. For I and a number of my servants have got such a belly-ache, that we've been off work now for a whole week.'

'Ah! I know what's wrong with you,' said Hunger; 'you've been eating too much – no wonder you are in such agonies. If you want to get better, follow these instructions: never drink on an empty stomach, and never eat till hunger pinches you and sends you some of his sharp sauce to whet your appetite. And don't sit too long over dinner and spoil your supper; always get up before you've eaten your fill. What is more, never allow Sir Surfeit at your table – don't trust him, he's a great gourmand and his guts are always crying out for more dishes.

'If you follow these instructions, I'll bet you the doctors will soon be selling their ermine hoods and their fine cloaks of Calabrian fur with gold tassels, to get themselves a square meal; and you'll see them gladly giving up their medicine for farmwork to avoid starvation. For these doctors are mostly murderers, God help them! – their medicines kill thousands before their time.'

'By heaven!' said Piers. 'This is the best advice I've heard. And now, Hunger, I know you must be anxious to go – so the best of luck, and God reward you for all you have done for me.'

'Good gracious!' said Hunger, 'I'm not going yet – not until I've had a square meal and something to drink.'

'I haven't a penny left,' said Piers, 'so I can't buy you pullets or geese or pigs. All I've got is a couple of fresh cheeses, a little curds and cream, an oat-cake, and two loaves of beans and bran which I baked for my children. Upon my soul, I haven't a scrap of bacon, and I haven't a cook to fry you steak and onions. But I've some parsley and shallots and plenty of cabbages, and a cow and a calf, and a mare to cart my dung, till the drought is over. And with these few things we must live till Lammas time, when I hope to reap a harvest in my fields. Then I can spread you a feast, as I'd really like to.'

Then all the poor folk came with peas-cods, and brought beans and baked apples by the lapful, and spring onions and chervils and hundreds of ripe cherries, and offered these gifts to Piers, to satisfy Hunger.

Hunger soon gobbled it all up and asked for more. So the poor folk were afraid, and quickly brought up supplies of green leeks and peas, and would gladly have poisoned him. But by that time the harvest was approaching, and new corn came to market. So the people took comfort, and fed Hunger royally – Glutton himself couldn't wish for better ale. And so they put him to sleep.

And then Waster would not work any more, but set out as a tramp. And the beggars refused the bread that had beans in it, demanding milk loaves and fine white wheaten bread. And they would not drink cheap beer at any price, but only the best brown ale that is sold in the towns.

And the day-labourers, who have no land to live on but their shovels, would not deign to eat yesterday's vegetables. And draught-ale was not good enough for them, nor a hunk of bacon, but they must have fresh meat or fish, fried or baked and *chaud* or *plus chaud* at that, lest they catch a chill on their stomachs!

And so it is nowadays – the labourer is angry unless he gets high wages,[19] and he curses the day that he was ever born a workman. And he won't listen to wise Cato's[20] advice – 'Bear the burden of poverty patiently.' But he blames God, and murmurs against Reason, and curses the king and his Council for making Statutes on purpose to plague the workmen! – Yet none of them ever complained while Hunger was their master, nor quarrelled with *his* Statutes, he had such a fierce look about him.

But I warn you labourers, work while you have the chance, for Hunger is coming fast, and shall awake with the floods to deal justice on wastrels. And before five years have passed, a famine shall arise, and floods and tempests shall destroy the fruits of the earth. For so Saturn had predicted,[21] and has sent you this warning: *When you see the sun awry[22] and two monks' heads in the Heavens – when a Maiden has magical power, then multiply by eight – the Black Death shall withdraw, and Famine shall judge the world, and Davy the ditcher shall die of hunger – unless God, in His mercy, grants us all a truce.*

Book VII

PIERS THE PLOUGHMAN'S PARDON

THE STORY. *Truth, who is likened here to a Pope granting men a Bull of Indulgence, sends Piers a Pardon for his sins. And all Piers' helpers, that is, those who work honestly in any calling, are to have a share in it. After explaining how much pardon various callings are to have, the poet tells of a priest who asks Piers to let him read it, and who finds that it is not a pardon at all, but only a clause from the Athanasian Creed stating that those who do well will go to Heaven, and those who do evil, to hell. Then Piers tears the Pardon up in anger, and vows to give up farming and begin a life of prayer and penance. There follows an argument between Piers and the priest, the noise of which awakes the dreamer. Since then, he says, he has often puzzled over the meaning of the dream, and has reached the conclusion that to do well is more important for salvation than to gain indulgences. So the Vision of Piers the Ploughman ends, and we are prepared for the search for Do-well.*

WHEN Truth heard of these things, He sent a message to Piers telling him to take his team of oxen and till the earth, and He granted him a Pardon from guilt and punishment,[1] both for himself and for his heirs for ever. And He said that Piers must stay at home[2] and plough the fields, and whoever helped him to plough or plant or sow, or did any useful work for him, would be included with him in the Pardon.

All kings and knights who defend Holy Church and rule their people justly, have a pardon to pass lightly through Purgatory, and enjoy the company of the patriarchs and prophets in Heaven.

And all truly consecrated Bishops who live up to their calling, so long as they are well versed in both the Laws[3] and preach them to the laity, and do all in their power to convert sinners, are equal with the Apostles (as Piers' Pardon shows), and will sit with them at the high table on Judgement Day.

In the margin of the Bull, the merchants too had many years' indulgence, but none from guilt as well as punishment – the Pope would never grant them that, for they will not keep Holy Days as the Church requires, and they swear 'By my soul!' and 'God help me!' against their conscience, in order to sell their wares.

But Truth sent the merchants a letter under His secret seal, telling them to buy up boldly all the best goods they could get, then sell them again, and use the profits to repair the hospitals and to help folk in trouble – to get the bad roads mended quickly and rebuild the broken bridges – to enable poor girls to marry or to enter nunneries – to feed the poor and the men in prisons – to send boys to school or apprentice them to a trade, and to assist Religious Orders and give them better endowments. – 'And if you will do these things,' said Truth, 'I myself will send you St Michael my Archangel when you die, so that no devil shall harm your souls or make you afraid; and he will ward off despair, and lead your souls in safety to meet my saints in Heaven.'

The merchants were pleased with this, and many of them wept for joy, praising Piers for gaining them such an indulgence.

But the men of Law who plead at the bar were to receive the least pardon of all. For the Psalm denies salvation to those who take bribes, especially from innocent folk who suspect no guile – 'He who taketh no bribes against the innocent.'[4] An advocate should do his utmost to help and to plead for such poor folk, and princes and prelates should pay him for it – 'Their wages shall be from kings and rulers.'[5] But I assure you, many of these Judges and jurymen would do more for their friend John than for the love of God himself. Yet if an advocate uses his eloquence on behalf of the poor, and pleads for the innocent and the needy, comforting them in their misfortunes without seeking gifts – if he explains the Law to them as he has learnt it, for the love of God, and does no man injury – he shall take no harm from the Devil when he dies, and his soul shall be safe. This is proved by the Psalm, 'Lord, who shall dwell in Thy tabernacle.'

For human intelligence[6] is like water, air, and fire – it cannot be bought or sold. These four things the Father of Heaven made to be shared on earth in common. They are Truth's treasures, free for the use of all honest men, and no one can add to them or diminish them without God's will. So when, at the approach of death, the men of Law seek for indulgences, there is very little pardon for them if they have ever taken money from the poor for their counsel. You lawyers and advocates can be sure of this – blame St Matthew if I lie, for he gave me this proverb for you: 'All things whatsoever ye would that men should do to you, do ye even so unto them.'[7]

But every labourer on earth who lives by his hands, who earns his own wages and gets them honestly, living in charity and obeying the Law, shall have for his humility the same absolution that was sent to Piers.

But beggars and tramps have no place in the Bull, unless they have an honest reason for begging. A man who begs without need is a swindler, and like the Devil, for he defrauds others who are really in need, and deceives men into giving against their will. For if the almsgiver knew the beggar was not in need, he would give his alms to someone who deserved it more, and help the most needy. Cato teaches this, and so does the author of the Scholastic Histories. 'Take care whom you give alms to' – so Cato[8] says. And this is Peter Comestor's[9] advice: 'Keep your alms in your hand until you have made sure whom you are giving them to.'

Yet Gregory the Great, who was a holy man, bade us give alms to all that ask, for the love of Him who gave us all things. 'Do not choose whom you pity,' he said, 'and be sure not to pass over by mistake one who deserves to receive your gifts; for you never know for whose sake you are more pleasing to God.'[10] Nor do you ever know who is really in need – only God can know that. If there is any treachery, it is on the beggar's side, not on the giver's. For the giver is repaying God's gifts,[11] and so preparing himself for death; but the beggar is borrowing, and running into debt, a debt which he can never repay, and for which Almighty God is his security; for only God can pay back the creditor, and pay him with interest. – 'Wherefore then gavest thou not my money into the bank, that at my coming I might have required mine own with usury.'[12]

So except in dire need, you tramps should avoid begging, for it is written that whoever has enough to buy bread, has all he needs, even if that is all he possesses. – 'He is rich enough who does not lack bread.'[13] Comfort yourselves, therefore, by reading the lives of the Saints, and profit by their example. The Scriptures strictly forbid begging, and condemn you in these words:

'I have been young, and now am old:
And yet saw I never the righteous forsaken, nor his seed
    begging bread.'[14]

For your lives are bereft of charity, and you keep no law. Many of you do not marry the women you consort with; you mount and set to work, braying like wild beasts,[15] and bring forth children who are branded bastards. Then you break their backs or their bones in childhood, and go begging with your offspring for ever after. There are more misshapen creatures among you beggars, than in all other professions put together! But be warned that on the day of your death, you will curse the time you were ever created men.

Not so the old men with white hair, who are weak and helpless, nor the women with child who cannot work, nor the blind and bedridden whose limbs are broken, nor the lepers, nor any such folk who bear their afflictions meekly: these shall have as full a pardon as the Ploughman himself. For out of love for their humility, our Lord has given them their purgatory and penance here on earth.

*

Then a priest spoke to Piers and said: 'Let me read your Pardon, Piers. I will construe each article for you and explain it to you in English.'

So Piers, at the priest's request, opened his Pardon, and I,

who was standing behind them both, could see the whole
Bull. It was contained entirely in two lines, and these were the
words, attested by Truth:

> '*And they that have done good shall go into life everlasting:*
> *And they that have done evil into everlasting fire.*'[16]

'By St Peter!' the priest said, 'I cannot find any Pardon here.
All it says is, "Do well and earn well, and God shall have your
soul: do ill and earn ill and the Devil will certainly have it after
you die." '

Then Piers, in sheer rage, tore the Pardon in two, and said:

> ' "Yea, though I walk through the valley of the shadow of
>   death, I will fear no evil:
> For Thou art with me."[17]

I shall give up my sowing, and cease from all this hard labour.
Why should I work so hard, merely to fill my stomach? From
now on, prayers and penance shall be my plough, and at night,
when I should be asleep, I shall weep instead for my sins. –
What does it matter if I have no wheaten bread! The prophet
ate his bread in penance and sorrow, and the Psalter tells of
many who did the same. If a man sincerely loves God, his
livelihood is easy enough to get, for it is written, "My tears
have been my meat day and night".[18] And St Luke teaches us
to live like the birds, and take no thought for the pleasures of
the world, "nor be solicitous, saying What shall we drink?"[19]
– showing us, by such examples, how to govern our lives.
Who is it that gives the birds in the fields their food in winter
time? They have no barns to go to, yet God provides for them
all.'

'What!' said the priest to Perkin, 'It sounds to me as if you
can read, Peter! Who taught you your letters?'

'Abstinence the Abbess,' answered Piers. 'She taught me
my ABC – then Conscience came and taught me a good deal
more.'

'Why, Piers, if only you were a priest, you would make a
real theologian, then you could preach on the text "The fool
hath spoken." '[20]

'You ignorant good-for-nothing!' said Piers. 'It is seldom you ever look at the Bible! When did you last read the Proverbs of Solomon? – "Cast out the scorner, and contention shall go out; yea, strife and reproach shall cease." '[21]

So the priest and Perkin argued, and their noise awoke me. And I looked about, and saw the sun to the southwards, and found myself on the Malvern Hills, starving and penniless. So I went on my way, puzzling over my dream.

Since then, I have thought many times about this dream, and wondered if what I saw in my sleep were really true. And I have often felt anxious for Piers, and asked myself what sort of pardon it was with which he consoled the people, and how it was that the priest gainsaid it with a few clever words. But I have no relish for interpreting dreams, I see how often it fails. Cato, and men skilled in Canon Law, advise us to put no faith in such divination – 'Pay no heed to dreams,'[22] says Cato.

Yet it is related in the Bible how Daniel expounded the dreams of a monarch whom the scholars call Nebuchadnezzar.[23] 'Your dream means, your Majesty,' he said, 'that strange warriors will come and divide your kingdom, and all your land will be parcelled out among petty princes.' And afterwards it fell out just as Daniel had foreseen. Nebuchadnezzar lost his kingdom, and it was seized by lesser lords.

Joseph also had a wonderful dream,[24] in which the sun and the moon and the eleven stars all made obeisance to him. And Jacob his father interpreted it, saying, 'This means, my son, that I and your eleven brothers will come and seek you and ask for your help in time of famine.' And it happened just as his father had said; for when Joseph was Lord Chief Justice of Egypt in Pharaoh's time, his father and brothers came to him for food.

All this makes me reflect on my dream – how the priest proved that no pardon could compare with Do-well, and thought Do-well surpassed indulgences, biennials, triennials,[25] and Bishops' Letters[26] – and how, on Judgement Day, Do-well will be received with honour, and exceed all the pardons of St Peter's Church.

Yet the Pope has the power to grant men pardon, so that they may pass into Heaven without doing any penance. This is our belief; the theologians teach it – 'And whatsoever thou shalt bind on earth shall be bound in Heaven: and whatsoever thou shalt loose on earth shall be loosed in Heaven.'[27] And so I firmly believe (God forbid otherwise!) – that pardons, penances, and prayers do save souls, even if they have committed deadly sin seven times over. But I certainly think that to put one's trust in these Masses is not so sure for the soul as is Do-well.

So I warn all you rich men who trust in your wealth to have triennials said for you after your death, not to be bolder therefore to break the Ten Commandments. And especially you men in authority, Mayors and Judges – no doubt you are thought wise, and possess enough of the world's wealth to buy yourselves pardons and papal Bulls – but on that dreadful day when the dead shall rise and all men shall come before Christ to render up their accounts, then the sentence shall state openly how you led your lives, how well you kept God's laws, and everything that you have practised day by day. Then, you may have pardons or provincials' letters[28] by the sackful, and belong to the Fraternity[29] of all the Four Orders, and possess double or treble indulgences, but unless Do-well helps you, I would not give a peascod for all your pardons and certificates!

So I advise all Christians to pray to God, and to His Mother Mary, our mediator, for grace to do such works in this life, that after our death and on the Day of Judgement, Do-well may declare that we did as he commanded.

HERE ENDS WILLIAM'S VISION OF
PIERS THE PLOUGHMAN

PIERS THE PLOUGHMAN

PART TWO

*William's Vision of Do-Well,
Do-Better, and Do-Best*

Book VIII

THE PROLOGUE: THOUGHT

THE STORY. *The poet wanders about in search of Do-well, and, after asking many people where Do-well lives, he questions two Friars, who answer that he lives with them. When Will disputes this, they reply with a parable intended to show that venial sin is unavoidable. So the poet leaves them to continue his search elsewhere, and, falling asleep in a wood, dreams that he meets one Thought, who is almost his own double. When the dreamer asks him about Do-well, he provides an answer that is correct in theory, but not enough to tell him what they are like in practice. So Thought advises him to ask Intelligence, and, after further wanderings, they meet and question him.*

So, in my rough woollen clothes, I wandered about all the summer, looking for Do-well. And many times I asked people I met if they knew where Do-well lived, and what kind of a man he was. But no one had any idea where his home was.

At last, one Friday, I happened to meet two Franciscan Friars,[1] Masters of Divinity, and men of great intelligence. I greeted them politely, as I had been taught to do, and begged them for the love of God to stop and tell me if they had ever found in all their travels a place where Do-well lived. For of all men on this earth who go on foot, the Friars travel most widely; they have been to many different courts and countries, and seen all kinds of places, from princes' palaces to poor men's cottages – so they surely know where Do-well and Do-evil live.

'He dwells among us,'[2] said one of the Friars Minor. 'He always has done, and I hope he always will.'

'I dispute that,' said I, in the fashion of the Schools, and began to dispute with him: 'For the Scripture says, "Even a righteous man falleth seven times a day."[3] Now whoever sins, it seems to me, does evil. But Do-well and Do-evil cannot live together, *ergo* Do-well cannot always be among you Friars. He must be elsewhere sometimes, or there would be no one to teach the people.'

'I will explain to you, my son,' said one of the Friars, 'how the upright man sins seven times a day. A parable[4] will make it clear. –

'Imagine a man in a boat on a wide stretch of water. What with the wind and the waves and the rocking of the boat, he is constantly falling and regaining his balance; for however firmly he stands, the least movement makes him stagger. Yet he is still safe and sound – and so he needs to be, for if he did not jump up quickly and reach for the tiller, the wind and water would capsize the boat, and his carelessness would cost him his life.

'It is like that,' said the Friar, 'with men here on earth. The water, which rises and falls, is like the world; the great waves are our worldly riches, that roll about as the winds and storms do; and the boat is our body, so frail by nature that even the upright man, buffeted by the fickle world and the flesh and the Devil, will sin seven times a day.

'But he commits no deadly sin, for he is protected by Do-well, that is, by Charity, who is our chief defender against sin. Charity gives you strength to stand,[5] and steers your soul, so that it is always safe, even if your body heels over like a boat in the water – unless, of course, you commit a mortal sin, and so drown your soul. If you choose to do that, God will not hinder you. For he has given you the means of taking care of yourself – free will and intelligence – gifts of which all his creatures, even the birds and beasts and fishes, have some share. But since man has the greatest share of them, he is the most to blame if he does not use them well, and obey Do-well's teaching.'

'I haven't the wits to grasp all this,' I said, 'but if I live long enough, I shall doubtless improve.'

'Then I commend you to Christ, who died on the Cross,' he said.

'May he keep you too,' I said, 'and give you long life, and the grace to be good men.'

*

So I wandered far and wide, and walked alone over a wild common and by a woodside, where I stayed listening to the singing of the birds. And as I lay down for a while in a glade under a lime-tree, listening to their sweet songs, their music lulled me to sleep. Then I dreamt the most marvellous dream, I think, that man has ever dreamt.

It seemed to me that a tall man, very like myself, came and called me by my own name. 'Who are you?' I said. 'And how do you know my name?'

'You know me well,' he said, 'no man better.'

'Are you sure I know you?'

'I am Thought,' he said. 'I have followed you for many years. Have you not seen me before?'

'Oh, so you are Thought?' I said. 'Then perhaps you can tell me how to find Do-well.'

'Do-well, Do-better, and Do-best,' he said, 'are not far to seek; for they are three fair virtues. Any man who is truthful in word and deed and earns his living by his own land or labour, who is honest in keeping accounts and takes no more than his due, and who is not scornful or given to drunkenness, is familiar with Do-well.

'Do-better does all these things, but much more besides. He is as meek as a lamb, charitable in speech, and willing to help all men according to their needs. For he has burst open all the money-bags that once belonged to Earl Avarice and his heirs, and plunged into the life of the cloister, and so made friends for himself with the money of Mammon.[6] And now he has entered an Order and translated the Bible, and he preaches to the people on the words of St Paul: *"Libenter suffertis insipientes, cum sitis ipsi sapientes"* – suffer the foolish to live with you, and do good to them gladly, for so God commands you.[7]

'Do-best is above both Do-well and Do-better. He bears the crozier of a Bishop, with a hook at one end[8] to drag men

out of hell, and a spike at the other to strike down the wicked
who lie in wait to injure Do-well.

'And Do-well and Do-better together have agreed to crown
a king to rule them, so that if either should wrong Do-best,[9]
the king will cast him in fetters, and never let him go unless
Do-best pleads for him. So all three have crowned one king
to protect them; and he must rule the country by their three
counsels, and never act without the consent of them all.'

Then I thanked Thought for his teaching; 'But still,' I said,
'this does not satisfy me. For I want to learn how Do-well,
Do-better, and Do-best work among the people.'

'Well,' said he, 'unless Intelligence can tell you, I don't know
any other living man who can.'

So for three days, Thought and I walked on together, dis-
cussing Do-well; and then, before we were aware of his
presence, we met Intelligence. He was so very tall and lean,
there is not another man like him, and in his dress there was no
sign of pride or of poverty. His looks were so grave and mild
that I dared not propose any subject to provoke him to argu-
ment. So I asked Thought to act as a go-between, and put for-
ward this topic to prove his intelligence: – what distinguished
Do-well from Do-better, and Do-best from both?

Then Thought said to Intelligence, 'This is Will, and he
would like to know where Do-well, Do-better, and Do-best
live, if Intelligence can direct him, and whether they are found
in human form. For he means to put their teaching into
practice.'

Book IX

INTELLIGENCE[1]

THE STORY. Intelligence explains to Will that Do-well is the guardian of a castle called the Flesh, which God, or Nature, has created, and in which He has placed the Soul under the rule of Good Sense. He then reproaches those who abuse this gift of Sense, adding that the Church should protect those people who lack it. After a digression about the duty of giving to the poor, he returns to the subject of the Flesh, and lectures the dreamer on the use and abuse of Marriage. He concludes by giving two definitions of Do-well, Do-better, and Do-best.

'SIR DO-WELL,' said Intelligence, 'lives less than a day's journey from here, in a castle made by Nature from four elements, a mixture of earth and air with wind and water.[2] And there also, subtly enclosed by him in the castle, dwells his mistress, one whom he loves as himself, and her name is Anima or the Soul. But Envy, a proud French knight known as the Prince of this World,[3] cannot abide her, and tries to entice her away from Nature by trickery.

'Nature, being well aware of this, keeps her guarded all the more carefully, having placed her under the charge of Sir Do-well, who is the Duke of these Marches. Sir Do-well's daughter, Do-better, is her maid-in-waiting, serving her faithfully at all hours; while above them both is Do-best, who is like a Bishop; for he rules over them all, his commands must be obeyed, and the Lady herself is guided by his instructions.

'The Warden of the castle and Commander of the Guard is a wise knight, Good Sense, who has five sons by his first wife – Sir See-well, Sir Say-well, and the gentle Sir Hear-well, Sir Work-well-with-your-hands (a very strong man), and Sir Godfrey Go-well – all of them mighty lords. They are employed to protect the Lady Anima until Nature sends for her, to keep her safe for ever.'

'What is Nature like?' I said. 'Can you describe him to me?'

'Nature,' said Intelligence, 'is a creator of all kinds of things; He is the Father and shaper of all that has ever been made. For he is the great God who had no beginning, the Lord of life and light, of pleasure and pain. Angels and all living creatures are subject to His will, but man is the most like Him of all in form and character.

'For it was through the word He spoke that the beasts came forth in the beginning – "He spoke," says the Scripture, "and they were created."[4] But when He created Adam, and Eve from Adam's rib, He formed them directly after His own image, using no intermediary.[5] For although He was One, God said "Let *us* make man,"[6] as if to say, "More is needed for this work than my word alone; my might, as well as my speech, must help in it."

'If a great prince wished to write a letter, but had no pen or parchment, the letter could never be written, for all his princely power and skill in writing. And it seems that God is the same, for the words "He spoke . . . etc." show that He must work through His Word, and thereby show forth His wisdom. So man was made through the power of Almighty God working with His Word and skill, and giving him everlasting life. For He gave to man the breath of His own Spirit from Heaven, and out of His great goodness bestowed on Adam and all his heirs the gift of eternal life and heavenly bliss.

'This, then, is the castle which Nature made: its name is Flesh, or man with a soul, created by the skill, the Word, and the sovereign power of God.

'For love of the Lady Anima, who is Life itself, Good Sense and all the other faculties are enclosed in this castle. And although she is free to wander through the whole of man's body, her chief resting-place and home is in the heart.[7] Good Sense, who watches over the heart, lives in the head, and Anima must obtain his consent in all that she seeks and avoids. For next to the Grace of God, Sense is the greatest among the guardians of the Soul.

'Great will be the misery of those that misuse their good

sense, especially those pampered gluttons "whose god is their belly"!⁸ As they serve the Devil, so he shall have their souls. All sinners have souls like Satan,⁹ and all who live good lives are like Almighty God, for "He that dwelleth in love dwelleth in God, and God in him."¹⁰

'Alas! that such a thing as drink should destroy those whom God redeemed so dearly, and make Him forsake the creatures He made in His own likeness! For it is written, "Verily I say unto you, I know you not,"¹¹ and again –

"So I gave them up unto their own hearts' lusts:
And let them follow their own imaginations."¹²

'But there are some who lack this good sense and cannot provide for themselves, and these, I maintain, should be supported by Holy Church – idiots and lunatics, for example, and also fatherless children, widows with no means of support, and helpless young women. All these lack the power to look after themselves and are in need of guidance. I could say much more about this, and quote many passages from the Four Doctors¹³ to bear me out; but if you do not believe me, you will find the same thing taught by St Luke.¹⁴

'And if any godfather or godmother sees his godchildren in pain or misfortune, he is bound to help them provided he has the means, or he will suffer for it in purgatory. For our duty to small children who do not yet know the Ten Commandments, does not consist merely in giving them names, for which they are none the wiser!

'If the prelates did their duty, no Christian man would ever stand at the gate crying for alms, or be without bread and soup. For never would a Jew see another Jew go begging, if he could help it, not for all the riches in the world! Alas! that one Christian should be unkind to another, when the Jews, whom we class with Judas, all help one another in need! Why cannot we Christians be as charitable with Christ's gifts as the Jews, who are truly our teachers, are with theirs? Shame on us all! I can see a time coming when the meanness of these prelates will be paid for by the whole community. Then the

Bishops will be justly blamed for all this beggary; for if a man gives silver to a jester and drives a beggar away because his clothes are ragged, he is worse than Judas – "The prelate who does not distribute Christ's patrimony is a traitor with Judas,"[15] and again – "He is a ruinous steward who wastes the rightful possessions of Christ's poor." Such a man does not do well, nor does he fear Almighty God; little does he care what wise Solomon said, that "The fear of the Lord is the beginning of wisdom."[16]

'The man who fears God DOES WELL; the man who fears Him out of love, and not in dread of punishment, DOES BETTER; but to DO-BEST is to abstain, by day and night, from wasting any words or time – "For whosoever shall keep the whole Law, and yet offend in one point, he is guilty of all."[17] Of all things on earth, God knows, nothing is more hated by those in Heaven than waste of time, and next to it waste of words. For speech is the first shoot of God's grace; it is the minstrel of God and one of the pleasures of paradise. It cannot please the faithful Father to hear his fiddle out of tune, and see his minstrel a vagabond hanging round the taverns.

'Our Lord loves all truthful, honest men who are willing to work, and gives them the grace to earn a living, come what may – "For there is no want to them that fear Him."[18]

'To live in true marriage is also Do-well; for married men must work and earn a living and keep the world going. All the Confessors of the Church, the kings and knights, the emperors and peasants, the virgins and martyrs, spring from marriage, and all arose out of one man. And woman was created as an agent, to assist in this work; and thus marriage was made – first by the consent of the father and the advice of friends, and then by the mutual agreement of the two partners. So marriage was established, and God himself made it; the heaven of wedlock is here on earth, and He himself was its witness.[19]

'But I believe that all traitors, thieves, liars, wasters, and other such idle wretches were conceived out of wedlock, or else in a forbidden time as Cain[20] was by Eve. For the Psalm says of such sinners –

"Behold, he travaileth with mischief:
He hath conceived sorrow, and brought forth ungod-
    liness."[21]

And all Cain's progeny came to an evil end. For God sent an
angel to Seth[22] saying, "I command that your issue be wedded
only with your issue, and never with Cain's." But some ig-
nored God's command and coupled Cain's children with
Seth's. Then God was angry with His creatures and said, "I
will destroy man whom I have created . . . for it repenteth me
that I have made them."[23] And He came to Noah and said,
"Go at once and build a ship of planks and timbers, and board
it quickly with your wives and three sons; and stay there till
forty days have passed, when the Flood will have washed
clean away all the cursed blood that Cain has engendered. The
beasts, too, shall curse the day that Cain was born, for they
shall all die for his misdeeds, on every hill and valley, and the
birds of the air besides – all but two of each kind, which shall
be saved in your wooden ark." Thus the children paid for their
forefather's guilt, and for him they had to suffer.

'Yet in one respect the Gospel contradicts this, for it is
written, "The son shall not bear the iniquity of the father,
neither shall the father bear the iniquity of the son."[24] But it
seems to me that if the father is a liar and a scoundrel, the son
will in part inherit his father's faults. Graft an apple on an
elder, and I doubt if your apple will be sweet; and it is even
less likely that the son of a villain should be without some
touch of his father. – "Do men gather grapes of thorns, or
figs of thistles?"[25]

'So, through this accursed Cain, misery first came into the
world – all because they contracted marriages against the will
of God. For all who marry off their children so, are bound to
suffer for it. And nowadays, to tell the truth, there are many
unnatural marriages, for many marry only for money, and
these marriages produce such wretched offspring as those
whom the Flood destroyed. Good men should marry good
women, even if they have no money. For Christ said, "I am
the Truth and the Life,[26] and can raise whom I will." I think

there is nothing more unseemly, than to give a young girl to a
doddering old man, or to marry for money some aged widow
who will bear no children, except in her arms! For since the
Plague hundreds of couples have married, yet the only fruit
they have brought forth are foul words; they live in jealousy,
without happiness, and lie in bed quarrelling, so that all the
children they get are strife and nagging! If they went to try
for the Dunmow flitch,[27] they wouldn't stand a chance with-
out the Devil's help; and unless they were both lying there'd
be no bacon for them.

'So I warn all Christians never to seek to marry for wealth
or rich relations. But bachelors should marry spinsters, and
widowers widows. And see that you marry for love, and not
for property, then you will gain God's grace and find money
enough to live on.

'Every layman who cannot keep himself chaste should be
wise enough to get married,[28] and so remain free from sin.
For the pleasure of lechery is a bait from hell. While you are
young and your weapon is virile, slake your lust in marriage
if you want an excuse for it. –

"While thou art strong, give not your strength to harlots,
  For it is written in the gates, a harlot is the entrance of
    death."[29]

And once married, be careful to observe the proper times –
not as Adam and Eve did when Cain was engendered. There
should be no love-making at forbidden times,[30] nor should you
ever come together unless both man and wife are clean in life
and soul, and in perfect charity. Then your marriage will be
pleasing to Almighty God; for He himself ordained marriage,
and said in the Scriptures: "To avoid fornication, it is good for
every man to have his own wife, and every woman her own
husband."[31]

'But those born out of marriage[32] are generally vagabonds –
swindlers, foundlings, imposters, and liars. Lacking the grace
to earn a living or gain people's affection, they turn beggars
and waste whatever they lay hands on. To spite Do-well, they

do evil and serve the Devil, with whom they will dwell when
they die, unless God gives them grace to amend their ways.

'So Do-well, my friend, is to do as the Law requires.
Do-better is to love both friend and foe. But to provide and
care for, heal and help young and old alike, that, believe me, is
Do-best of all.

'And Do-well is to fear God; Do-better is to suffer; and Do-
best springs from both the others. It subdues man's obstinate
nature, and destroys that wicked self-will which spoils so many
good works and driyes away Do-well through mortal sins.'

Book X

STUDY AND LEARNING

THE STORY. *Lady Study, the wife of Intelligence, reproaches her husband for condescending to teach the dreamer, whom she classes among those who do not care for intellectual pursuits, except to talk flippant theology over dinner. She inveighs against such men so strongly that the dreamer is compelled to beg her pardon on his knees. She is at once pacified, and directs him to the house of her cousins, Learning and Scripture.[1] He hurries there, is well received, and straight away is lectured by Learning about Do-well, etc. Learning then attacks the hypocrisy of the learned, especially those in Religious Orders, until the poet interrupts, and they discuss whether good works are necessary for salvation. Finally the dreamer delivers a long harangue to his teachers, in which he comes to the conclusion that learning is merely a hindrance to salvation, since men are predestined for Heaven or hell.*

Now Intelligence had a wife, sharp-featured and lean of figure, whose name was Lady Study. She was exceedingly angry with her husband for teaching me these things, and glaring at him she said furiously, 'How wise you are, to speak words of wisdom to flatterers and half-witted fools!' And so she blamed him and cursed him and would not let him speak. 'The folly,' she said, 'of trying to teach blockheads with such profundities![2] Do not cast your pearls before swine, man[3] – they have plenty of hips and haws! What can they do with pearls but slobber on them? Why, a bucket of hogwash gives them more pleasure than all the precious pearls that grow in paradise![4] And when I say swine, I mean men who show by their actions that they prefer worldly power, lands and riches and rents, with endless leisure, to all the wise maxims Solomon ever uttered.

'Wisdom and Intelligence are not worth a straw nowadays, unless they are carded over with covetousness, as clothiers comb their wool. A man only has to plot and scheme, contrive wrongs against others, and cover up the truth when he presides at Settlement-days, and his advice is sought by great men everywhere. Then he directs the policies of lords and twists the truth as he pleases.

'The world's wealth, says Job the prophet,[5] is in the hands of the wicked – of the men who live outside the Law, like barons, in every country. "Wherefore," he says, "doth the way of the wicked prosper? Wherefore are all they happy that deal very treacherously?"[6] And the Psalmist says the same – "Lo, these are the ungodly, these prosper in the world, and these have riches in possession"[7] – in other words, "Behold what mighty lords these wretches are!" Those to whom God gives most, give least to others, and the wealthiest are the most unkind to the common people. – "For lo, what Thou has perfected, they have destroyed; and what hath the righteous done?"[8] – Ribalds, clowns, buffoons, and ballad-mongers, these all get paid for their filth; but a man who has Holy Scripture always on his lips, who can tell the story of Tobit or of the Twelve Apostles, or preach on Christ's sufferings at the hands of Pilate and the Jews – a man who speaks of these things is little enough loved, God knows, and gets neither praise nor encouragement.

'As for those who set themselves up as fools and jesters, making a living under false pretences, which is forbidden by God's Law – who make up tales about themselves and spit and spew out their foul language, and drink and dribble and make men gape at them – who ridicule others and slander those who refuse to tip them – these men know about as much of music and minstrelsy as Munde the Miller knows of the Latin language! If it were not for their dirty jokes, Heaven knows, no one – king, knight, or canon of St Paul's – would give them so much as a farthing for the New Year! But nowadays entertainment and minstrelsy is nothing but lewdness, flattery, and filthy stories – Gluttony and Great-Oaths love such entertainment.

'But when these learned men and their ignorant jesters are sitting at table amidst their amusements, if the musicians are silent and the conversation turns to Christ, then they will crack a joke or two about the Trinity, and think up some crude argument, with St Bernard dragged in as their authority, and then prove their point by begging the whole question. They drivel at the high table as if they understood the Deity, and when their guts are full munch at God with their mouths.

'Meanwhile some poor wretch may cry at their gate, tormented by hunger and thirst and shivering with cold; yet no one asks him in or eases his suffering, except to shoo him off like a dog. Little can they love the Lord who gives them so much comfort, if this is how they share it with the poor! Why, if the poor had no more mercy than the rich, all the beggars would go to bed with empty bellies. For the gorges of these great theologians are often crammed with God's Name, but His mercy and His works are found among humble folk. That is the meaning of these words I have often noticed in the Psalter –

"... Until I found out a place for the temple of the Lord:

an habitation for the mighty God of Jacob.
Lo, we have *heard of* the same at Ephrata:
and *found* it in the wood."[9]

The clergy, and others like them, speak readily of God, and His name is often in their mouths; but lowly men have Him truly in their hearts.

'Since the Plague, Friars and other impostors have thought up theological questions just to please the proud. And they preach at St Paul's[10] out of sheer envy of the clergy, so that folk are no longer confirmed in the faith, or taught to be charitable with their goods and sorry for their sins. Not only in the Religious Orders, but among rich and poor throughout the whole realm, pride has spread so much that all our prayers are powerless to stop the pestilence. Yet not one of these worldly wretches takes warning from the fate of others; not even the fear of death will make them relinquish their pride or be generous to the poor, as charity plainly demands they should. But they gobble up all their wealth themselves in

merry-making and gluttony, and refuse to share a morsel with
a beggar, as Isaiah teaches[11] – " . . to deal thy bread to the
hungry, and bring the poor that are cast out to thy house."
For the greater the wealth and riches they amass, and the more
houses they have to let, the less are they willing to give away!
What Tobit[12] taught was very different; listen, all you rich folk,
to his words in the Bible – "If thou hast abundance, give alms
accordingly: if thou have but a little, be not afraid to give
according to that little." – In other words, give according to
your means. For we have no written contract to say how long
our lives will last. So you lords should be glad to hear such
warnings, and consider how you may provide most generously
for as large a household as possible – which is not the same as
following in search of feasts, like fiddlers or friars, and making
yourselves at home in other men's houses while despising
your own. For when the lord and lady eat elsewhere every day
of the week , their hall is a sorry, deserted place. And the rich
nowadays have a habit of eating by themselves in private
parlours – for the sake of the poor, I suppose – or in a special
chamber[13] with a fireplace of its own. So they abandon the
main hall, which was made for men to eat their meals in – and
all this in order to save money which a spendthrift heir will
afterwards squander.

'I have heard great men at their meals talking about Christ
and his divine powers as if they were clerics, finding fault with
the Father who created us all, and churlishly contradicting the
theologians. "Why," they say, "did our Saviour allow the
Serpent into the garden of Eden, to beguile first the woman
and then the man, and to lure them to hell? And why should
all their seed suffer the same death, for their sin alone?" And
then they begin to argue the point, saying, "Your own teach-
ing contradicts itself in this matter; for if we are to believe
what you priests tell us of Christ in the Gospel, He taught
that 'The son shall not bear the iniquity of the father.'[14] In
that case, why should we who are now living be corrupted
and destroyed for the deeds of Adam? There is no sense in it,
for as the Scripture says, 'Every man shall bear his own
burden.' "[15]

'This is the kind of argument which these lords stir up, so that men who take their words seriously are led into false beliefs. But Imagination will soon settle these problems for you.

'Augustine,[16] in answer to these rationalists, quotes this text, that we should "not be more wise than it behoveth to be wise". So never ask why God let Satan deceive his children, but believe steadfastly in the teaching of Holy Church, and pray God in His mercy to grant you His pardon and the gift of repentance, to purge yourself of sin while you are still on earth. And if you want to know why God allowed Satan to lead us astray or let Judas betray Christ, and if you insist on prying into the ways of Almighty God, you'd do better to keep your eyes in your backside! For everything in the world happened as God chose, and no matter how we argue, everything will continue as He chooses – and thank God for it! You deserve to go deaf for clouding men's minds with these fine distinctions between Do-well and Do-better! What use is it this fellow here asking about them, unless he lives the life that belongs to Do-well? I dare lay my life on it he'll never do better, though Do-best should drag him on by the scruff of his neck every day of his life!'

Now when it dawned on Intelligence what Lady Study was saying, he was so confused that he could not look her in the eyes, and became as silent as the grave, retreating into a corner. Then I begged him to speak and fell on my knees before him, but could not get another grain of wisdom out of him. His only answer was an embarrassed laugh, while he nodded and glanced furtively at Lady Study to hint that I should go and beg her pardon.

Once I grasped this meaning, I went and kneeled before his wife and said, 'Forgive me, madam, I beg you. I promise to be your slave and do your will diligently all my life, if only you will teach me what Do-well is.'

'Well, my man, since you are meek and have spoken so politely,' she said, 'I will direct you to my cousin, whose name is Learning. Within the last six months he has married a wife called Scripture, cousin to the Seven Arts.[17] The two of them

will gladly guide you to Do-well, I can vouch for that, for
they were both taught by me.'

Then I was as carefree as a bird on a sunny morning, and
happier than a minstrel with a gift of gold. So I asked her the
nearest way to Learning's home, saying, 'Please, Lady, give
me some token to prove I have come from you, for I must be
off at once.'

'Ask for the direct road,' she said, 'from here to Suffer-both-
weal-and-woe – if you are willing to learn that lesson. Then
ride on past Riches, and don't stop there, for if you become
attached to them you will never reach Learning. And avoid
the lecherous meadow that is called Lust; leave it a good mile
or more on your left, and continue till you come to a mansion
called Keep-your-tongue-from-lying-and-slander-and-your-
mouth-from-spicy-drinks. There you will meet Sobriety and
Simplicity-of-Speech, and while they are with you every man
will be glad to show you his wisdom. So you will come to
Learning, who knows most of the answers.

'To prove that you come from me, you had better say that I
am the one who put Learning to school, and that I send my
greetings to his wife. For I wrote her many books, and set her
to work on the Proverbs of Solomon and the Psalter Com-
mentary. And also I taught her Logic and many other prin-
ciples of philosophy, and explained to her all the different
measures of music.

'The philosophers Plato and Aristotle, and many more like
them, were first schooled by me. I was the first to have books
of Grammar written for children, and to cane them when they
would not learn. It was I that fashioned the tools for every
craft, for carpenters, sculptors, and masons; and though my
eyes may seem dim now, I taught them the use of the com-
passes and of the line and level.

'But Theology has always caused me a lot of trouble. The
more I ponder and delve into it, the darker and mistier it seems
to me to be. It is certainly no science for subtle invention, and
without love it would be no good at all. But I love it because
it values love above everything else; and grace is never lacking

where Love comes first. – If you wish to find Do-well you must love truly, for Do-better and Do-best are both akin to Love.

'In every science other than Theology, the rule, in Cato's words, is this: "If anyone tries to deceive you with words of flattery but is not a faithful friend to you in his heart, do the same to him, and answer guile with guile."[18] That is his advice to scholars. But Theology, you will notice, teaches the opposite. It commands us to live as brothers, to pray for our enemies, to love those who slander us and give to them in their need. And God himself bids us return good for evil – "As we have therefore opportunity, let us do good unto all men, especially unto them who are of the household of the Faith."[19] This is the teaching of St Paul, who loved perfection – to do good for the love of God and give to those that ask, and especially to the faithful. And Our Lord teaches us to love all who abuse or slander us, forbidding us to repay injury with injury – "Vengeance is mine; I will repay, saith the Lord."[20] So remember, all your life, to love others, for there is no knowledge on earth so healing to the soul.

'Astronomy is a difficult subject, and also very hard to learn. And Geometry and Geomancy[21] are sciences full of deceptive terms, and the way to success in them is long and hard, for they chiefly involve the study of Sorcery. And there is one other science that you must never touch if you intend to do-well, and that is Alchemy. For the occult experiments practised by alchemists are designed merely to take people in. All these sciences I invented myself, on purpose to delude men.

'These things which I have told you are the tokens which you must repeat to Learning and Scripture, and then they will gladly teach you how to understand Do-well.'

'Thank you very much, madam,' I said, and humbly took my leave of her. And without further hindrance I hurried on, and did not stop till I came into the presence of Learning.

Then I greeted the good man and his wife as Study had instructed me, and bowed to them both, repeating to them the tokens that I had been taught. And as soon as they knew that

I came from the house of Intelligence, they welcomed me with open arms and put me so much at my ease that I think no man on earth ever had a friendlier reception. So I told them truly why I had been sent there – to learn to understand Do-well, Do-better, and Do-best.

'Do-well,' said Learning, 'is a life among lay people, of believing in Holy Church and all the articles of faith which she requires us to know. That is to say, learned and unlearned alike must believe steadfastly in the great God who had no beginning, and His true Son who saved mankind from eternal death and from the power of the Devil, by the help of the Holy Ghost who proceeds from the Father and the Son. So there are three distinct Persons, though not making more than One, for all are but one God and each alone is God – God the Father, God the Son, and God the Holy Ghost, Creator of men and beasts.

'St Augustine wrote books on this doctrine, and was the first to formulate it, to establish us in our Faith. And on whose authority did he do this? – on that of all four Evangelists, for the Gospels bear witness that Christ spoke of himself as God: "I am in the Father, and the Father in me,"[22] and also, "He that hath seen me hath seen the Father." No Christian teacher could ever explain this doctrine fully; but the layfolk as well as the clergy must believe it if they wish to do-well. For if the Faith could be proved true, and there had never been men of subtle wit to dispute it, what merit would there be in believing? "Faith," St Gregory said, "has no merit where human reason supplies the proof."[23]

'Do-better is to suffer for your soul's health all that Scripture and Holy Church command, which is to strive with all your might, for mercy's sake, to practise what your words profess, and to be in fact what outwardly you seem. Let no man be deceived by your bearing, but be the same in soul as you appear to others.

'Do-best is to be bold in speaking out against the guilty, once you know that your own soul is innocent. But never blame others if you are guilty yourself – "For your teaching is contemptible if your conscience is troubled by faults of your own."[24] In the Gospel Christ sternly rebukes those who blame others while they have faults of their own – "And why beholdest thou the mote that is in thy brother's eye, but considerest not the beam that is in thine own eye? Thou hypocrite, first cast out the beam out of thine own eye"[25] – for it hinders your own sight.

'So, all you blind buzzards,[26] take my advice, and reform yourselves first. This text was meant for you Abbots and Priors, priests and curates, whose duty it is to teach and preach to all mankind and correct our faults with all your might. It was meant to warn you to practise what you preach, before you teach others the way to salvation. For even if you gave up preaching, the word of God would not be lost; it is always at work, and if it did no good to the people, it might still be of some use to yourselves!

'Yet from the world's point of view, it looks today as though God's word were not working at all, among clerics or laymen, except in the way which St Mark referred to in the Gospel – "the blind leading the blind, and both falling into the ditch."[27] No wonder the layfolk say of you that the beam lies in your own eyes, while the mote, through your fault, has fallen into the eyes of all other men – little wonder they blame you cursed priests for everything! The Bible tells what a bitter price all the Children of Israel had to pay for the guilt of two bad priests, Hophni and Phineas:[28] for it was their covetousness that caused the Ark of God to be lost, and Eli to break his neck.

'So for God's sake hold fast to what I say, you correctors of men, and correct yourselves first! Then you may safely say, as David said in the Psalter,

"Thou thoughtest that I was altogether such an one as thyself:
but I will reprove thee, and set before thee the things thou hast done."[29]

If you do that, then these lay-theologians will be ashamed to criticize or offend you, and will cease to talk as they talk now, calling you dumb hounds and saying, "His watchmen are blind: they are all ignorant, they are all dumb dogs, they cannot bark."[30] But instead, they will dread to say a word which might anger you or hinder you in your work, and they'll come quicker to your call than they would for a pound's worth of gold! And all because of your holy lives – so take my words to heart.

'Here is a rule which St Gregory, the great Pope and scholar, wrote in his *Moralia* for all Religious to carry out to the letter. He put it like this: "When the flood fails, and the fishes lack fresh water, they die gasping with drought on the dry land. Likewise a monk who takes delight in living outside the cloister or convent, and roves about stealing alms from noblemen, will at least go rotten and die." For surely, if Heaven is anywhere on earth and there is ease for any soul, it is in the cloister or the monastic school. I can think of many reasons for this: for no one enters the cloister to quarrel and fight: it is a life of complete obedience, among books and reading and learning; the only person to be despised there is the scholar who will not learn; otherwise there is nothing but love and sweetness.

'But today, Religion[31] is a rider of horses, a rover through the streets, an arbitrator at Days of Settlement, and a purchaser of land. He rides like a lord on his palfrey from manor to manor, with a pack of hounds at his heels; and if his lackey fails to kneel when he brings him his cup, he scowls and demands where he learnt his manners. The nobles should have more sense than to transfer property from their heirs to Religious Orders; for the monks are quite unmoved though the rain falls on their altars! Even where they have parishes to care for they live at ease, with no pity for the poor – such is their boasted charity! But their domains are so wide that they think of themselves only as landlords.

'Yet a king shall arise[32] who shall purge all you men of Religion, and scourge you for the breaking of your Rule as Christ scourged the money-changers out of the Temple. And he shall reform all you nuns and monks and canons, and put you to your penance, till you return at last to your original Rule. Then the Earls and Barons will thrash you till you are "like the chaff, which the wind scattereth away from the face of the

earth";[33] and even their children shall hoot and exult over you
crying –

"Some trust in chariots, and some in horses:
but we will remember the name of the Lord our God.
They are brought down and fallen:
but we are risen, and stand upright."[34]

'And then the Friars will cease begging, and find at last in
their ample refectories the key to Constantine's coffers,[35] the
ancient endowments of the Church; and they will use the
wealth which Gregory's children in God, the monks of Eng-
land, have so long put to misuse.

'At that time the Abbot of Abingdon,[36] and all his issue for
ever, shall get such a blow from this king that nothing will cure
it.

'For the proof of this prophecy, take a glance at the Bible,
you men who peruse it so often, and read: "How hath the
oppressor ceased! The exactress of gold ceased! The Lord hath
broken the staff of the wicked and the sceptre of rulers. He
who smote the people in wrath with a continual stroke, he that
ruled the nations in anger, is persecuted, and none hinder-
eth."[37]

'But before that king comes, Cain shall awake[38] from the
dead, and Do-well shall beat him down and destroy his power.'

'Then Do-well and Do-better,' I said, 'must be kingship
and knighthood.'

'No,' broke in Lady Scripture, 'I do not say this in scorn,
but unless scriveners have altered all the texts, there is nothing
to prove that kingship or knighthood ever got a man by a
hair's breadth nearer Heaven – and riches and power certainly
never did. St Paul shows[39] how impossible it is for rich men to
enter Heaven, and Solomon says "There is not a more wicked
thing than to love money."[40] And Cato teaches us not to covet
more of it than we need – "You should value the beauty of
money," he says, "but value it sparingly."[41] All the patriarchs,
prophets, and poets have written to warn us against it, and
have praised poverty borne with patience. And the Apostles

say[42] that the poor may claim their place in Heaven by right, while the rich can only gain it, if at all, by the grace and mercy of God.'

'I dispute that,' I said, 'and, by Christ, I can prove you wrong, from the words of St Peter and St Paul.[43] For every baptized person is saved, whether rich or poor.'

'That only applies,' she said, 'to men baptized on the point of death, such as Saracens and Jews. They can certainly be saved so – this is part of our Faith. Even if another heathen performs the baptism, such a man may attain Heaven like a Christian, for his true belief.

'But a Christian cannot reach Heaven by baptism alone, because Christ died for our sins, and in so doing He confirmed the Law. If we wish to rise with Christ ("If ye then be risen with Christ, etc."),[44] we must first have love and faith and fulfil the Law. And the Law is: "Thou shalt love the Lord thy God above all things,[45] and next to God all Christian men on earth." Without such love, it is little use our believing ourselves saved. If we fail to practise this charity, what use is all the silver we have hoarded, the clothes that we have left to get moth-eaten while beggars go naked, the pleasure we have taken in game and wine while others starve? – all these things will encumber us gravely on the Day of Judgement! And though our first duty is to show charity to each other, we must help the heathen as well, in the hope that they may be converted.

'For God's commandment is the same for high and low – never to injure any other man. "Unless I send thee some sign," He says, "slay not any creature made in my likeness," and again, "Do not kill, but suffer wrongs, and all will be for the best. Vengeance is mine, I will repay,[46] and unless my mercy restrain me, every man's misdeeds will be punished in purgatory, or in the pit of hell." '

'This is a long lesson,' I said, 'and I am not much the wiser for it. If this is meant to show me the way to Do-well, I must say your directions are very obscure. All you do is to lecture me on theology.

'But there is one thing that I do believe, on the authority of our Lord himself, which is better than any theological lecture: that I was made man, and that long before I existed my name was either entered in the Book of Life[47] or else on account of some wickedness was left unwritten. For the Scripture says, "No man hath ascended up to Heaven, but he that came down from Heaven."[48]

'Consider Solomon, the great sage and teacher of wisdom. God gave him the grace of wisdom and great riches, to govern his realm and make it prosperous. His judgements were good and wise[49] – the Scriptures vouch for that. And no one, unless it were Aristotle, ever taught men as well as he did. The theologians, when they preach to us of God's mercy, quote the words of Solomon and those of Aristotle as the wisest of their day – yet the whole Church considers them both damned![50]

'So if, to get to Heaven, I should imitate their deeds – the deeds of men who, for all their great words and wisdom, are now in hell – I should be acting very unwisely, no matter what you may preach!

'But truly, I am not surprised that so many men of intellect have such petty souls, incapable of pleasing God. For most men have set their hearts more on their goods rather than on God. No wonder if, at the point of death, when they need it most, they cannot find any grace. That was true of Solomon, and of many others like him. They may have shown themselves very intelligent, but their deeds, as Scripture says, were always foolish. They admit themselves, these philosophers and scholars, that they seldom act on their own wisdom. – "The scribes and Pharisees sit in Moses' seat: all therefore whatsoever they bid you observe, that observe and do; but do not ye after their works: for they say, and do not."[51]

'But I think that things are the same with many today as they were in Noah's time, when he built the Ark of planks and timbers: for none of the workmen and carpenters who fashioned it were saved, but only the birds and beasts and the blessed Noah with his wife and his sons, and their wives with them. – Not a single one of the craftsmen who built the ship

survived! Now God grant this may not happen to the men
who teach the Faith of Holy Church! For she is also the House
of God and a place of refuge, to save and shield us from shame
within her walls as Noah's Ark shielded the beasts – though all
the men who made her were drowned in the Flood. But the
men I mean here are the secular priests; they are the carpenters
who build Holy Church for Christ's own beasts – "O Lord,
thou preservest man and beast." [52] And on the Day of Doom
there shall be another Deluge, of death and fire at once. That
is why I say to you priests, the carpenters of God's Holy
Church, practise the things that you read in Holy Scripture –
lest perhaps when the Flood comes, you are not in the Ark.

'On Good Friday, a criminal who had lived all his life by
theft and lying was saved. Because he confessed on the cross
and Christ absolved him, he was saved before St John the
Baptist or Adam or Isaiah or any of the prophets who had lain
in hell for hundreds of years. And so a robber was ransomed
sooner than all the others, and was brought to perpetual bliss
without purgatory or penance.

'And what woman ever did worse than Mary Magdalen? Or
who worse than David when he plotted to do away with
Uriah? [53] – or than Paul the Apostle, who callously sentenced
many Christians to a cruel death? Yet these, whose works in
this life were more wicked than any in the world, are now like
kings among the saints in Heaven. While others, who spoke
with such wisdom and wrote books of philosophy and morals,
are dwelling with the damned in hell!

'So I think that what Solomon said [54] is true of us all –
"that the righteous, and the wise, and their works, are in the
hand of God: no man knoweth either love or hatred by all
that is before them." – Only God knows whether, on the Last
Day, a man will be praised for his love and loyal service, or be
judged for his ill will and envy of heart. For only by evil do
men know the good; how could we know white if all things
were black, or know a virtuous man unless there were also
some scoundrels? So let us live with the wicked as best we can,
for I believe there are few who are really good. "When neces-
sity is upon us, we must suffer." [55] And may He who can amend

all things, have mercy on us all! For the surest word that ever God spoke was "There is none that doeth good."[56]

'Our Lord never commended learning, for He said to St Peter and to those He loved: "When you stand before kings and rulers . . . take no thought beforehand what ye shall speak, neither do ye premeditate, etc."[57] – for He himself would speak through their lips and give to them all the wisdom they needed to refute those who opposed Christianity. And King David says[58] that when he spoke among kings, none could defeat him by skill in argument. For neither wisdom nor intelligence ever gave a man the upper hand in time of persecution, without some further grace from God.

'St Augustine, the mightiest of the Four Doctors and the greatest searcher into the Trinity, once said this in a sermon[59] – I came across it in my reading – "Lo, the ignorant arise and take Heaven by force, while we, with all our wisdom, are plunged into hell." In other words, none are more easily seduced from the right beliefs than clever scholars who study a lot of books; and none are sooner saved or are firmer in their faith, than simple ploughmen and shepherds and poor common labourers. For by pure faith, these cobblers, herdsmen, and peasants, who know so little and whose earthly lives are so imperfect, can pierce with a single Paternoster to the palace of Heaven; and when they die, pass through Purgatory unscathed into the bliss of Paradise. And so there are some scholars – you must have met them – who have cursed the day that ever they learnt more than the "I believe"; and many a priest has prized the "Our Father" higher than all his learning.

'I have often observed – and others must have noticed it too – how seldom the lower servants of noblemen fall into debt; whereas those who manage their property, the reeves and clerks, are frequently in arrears. And similarly the laymen and folk of little knowledge, seldom fall into sin so foully or so far, as the priests of Holy Church who are the wardens of Christ's treasure – the human souls they have to save, as God commanded them in the Gospel saying, "Go ye into my vineyard." '[60]

Book XI

FORTUNE, GOOD FAITH AND NATURE

THE STORY. *The dreamer, rebuked by Scripture for his presumption, falls into a deeper dream, in which he meets the goddess Fortune and follows her for forty-five years. Then he reaches Old Age, and Fortune and the Friars desert him. While he is reproaching the Friars about this, he suddenly sees Good Faith, and before long Scripture reappears as well. She preaches a sermon which makes the dreamer fear for his own salvation, but he is reassured by Trajan, the pagan Emperor who is said to have been released from hell. Then Good Faith teaches him the way of salvation, through the love and poverty of Christ. But the dreamer continues to argue till he meets Nature, and is shown all the wonders of creation; yet this only leads him to turn against Reason, at whose hands he suffers further reproach. So he wakes from his deeper sleep in shame and confusion, to find one called Imagination standing by him, whom he decides to follow.*

THEN Scripture condemned me and poured scorn on me, putting me to shame; and gave me her reason in this Latin saying '*Multi multa sciunt, et se ipsos nesciunt*[1] – There are many who know much, but themselves they do not know.' I wept with shame and resentment, and, in a drowsy ill-humour, fell asleep.

Then I dreamt a marvellous dream; suddenly, as I stood there, I was wafted away by the goddess Fortune, who brought me all aloue into the land of longing and made me look into a mirror – the Mirror of the World, – saying, 'Here you can see untold wonders – all the things you most long for – and reach them too, perhaps.'

In Fortune's train there were two handsome ladies, the elder called Lust-of-the-flesh, and the younger Lust-of-the-eyes. And after them came another, Pride-of-perfect-life,[2] who bade me forget about learning, and take more trouble over my looks. Then Lust-of-the-flesh threw her arms round my neck, and said: 'You are young and vigorous, and have many more years to live; are there not plenty of women to love? You see how many delights there are in this mirror; follow them, and they will give you a life-time of pleasure.'

The second lady said the same, and added: 'I will satisfy all your longings, and if it please Fortune, I'll stand by you till you get to be a lord with land of your own.'

'He will find a staunch friend in me,' said Fortune. 'No one who obeys my wishes ever fails to find perfect happiness.'

Then I saw one called Old-Age, very grave of aspect. 'By our Lady in Heaven,' he said, 'if I catch up with you, my man, you'll see how Fortune will desert you when you need her most – how Lust-of-the-flesh will clean forsake you. Then you will curse bitterly by day and night, and wish that you had never known Lust-of-the-eyes; it is then you will find what peril Pride-of-life has brought you to.'

'Pooh! Never you bother your head about that,' said Recklessness, appearing before me in rags and tatters; 'Go after Fortune! You've a long time yet before old age sets in. It's time enough to start stooping when your hair falls out! Now's the time to take it easy.

' "Man proposes, God disposes," '³ he continued – 'that's what Plato said – so let God do as He likes. Truth himself declares it's as well to follow Fortune,⁴ so neither Lust-of-the-flesh nor Lust-of-the-eyes can do you much harm – they'll not betray you unless you ask for it.'

'Hear! Hear! Cheerio, my old cock-sparrow!' said Childishness to Old-Age, and pulled me away. So it was not long before all my doings were governed by Lust-of-the-flesh.

'Alas!' said Old-Age and Holiness, 'that Intelligence should go to the dogs so that Will can follow his lusts!'⁵

But Lust-of-the-eyes at once consoled me. For forty-five winters she went with me, so that I no longer set any store by Do-well and Do-better; indeed, I had no wish to know anything of them. Amidst all my doings, Lust-of-the-eyes took first place in my mind – there was no room for Do-well and Do-better. And often she would comfort me, and say: 'Don't let your conscience fret over the way you made your money;

go and confess your sins openly to some friar. So long as
Fortune is your friend, the friars will always love you:[6] they
will make you one of their brotherhood, and beg their Prior
Provincial to get you a pardon, and say prayers and Masses
especially for you, as long as you are in the money.'

> '*Sed poena pecuniaria non sufficit pro spiritualibus delictis –*
> But a penance of money does not atone for spiritual
> offences.'[7]

So I followed up the woman's advice, for her words sounded
pleasant in my ear – till at last I left youth behind and ran into
old age. Then, in spite of all her fair promises, Fortune turned
against me, and poverty caught up with me and laid me low.
Then the Friars, ignoring our old connexion, began to avoid
me like the plague – all because I told them I would not be
buried in their graveyard, but at my parish church. For I had
heard Conscience say it was natural for a man to be buried
where he was christened, in his own parish. Yet when I re-
peated this to the Friars, they changed their opinion of me,
and seemed to think me a fool for uttering so simple a truth.
So I complained to my confessor, a man who prided himself
on his wisdom, saying, 'Why, Father, you are behaving like
those suitors who marry widows for money; for I'll swear by
the Rood, you've never cared where my body was to be buried
so long as you got my silver! And it strikes me as very strange
– and I'm not the only one – that your Community would
rather bury people[8] than baptize children who want to enter
the Church. It is true that both have to be done, but there's
surely more merit in baptizing than in burying. A man who is
baptized, so the theologians tell us, may go to Heaven, so long
as he is contrite – for "Only contrition can blot out sin."[9] But
a child without baptism cannot be saved – "Except a man be
born of water and of the spirit, he cannot enter the Kingdom
of Heaven."[10] Look it up, you scholars, and see if I am right.'

At that moment Good Faith[11] caught my eye, and I frowned.
'What are you frowning for?' he asked, staring hard at me.

'If only I dared tell this dream among the people!' I said.

'But of course you can, by St Peter and Paul,' he said, 'and you can quote both Apostles[12] to support you! For it is written, "Thou shalt not hate the *brothers* secretly in thy heart, but rebuke them publicly." '[13]

'But the Brother-Friars will quote a different text,' I said – ' "Judge not, that ye be not judged." '[14]

'What would be the use of a moral Law,' replied Good Faith, 'if no one stood out against fraud and falsehood? The Apostle said, "They that sin, rebuke before all,"[15] and listen to the words of the prophet David in the Psalter: "Thou thoughtest that I was altogether such an one as thyself, but I will reprove thee . . ."[16] So laymen are permitted to speak the truth if they choose – there is no law against it. The case is different with priests and prelates: they aren't allowed to tell tales about people's sins,[17] even if true. But when it concerns things already known to the whole world, why shouldn't you speak out openly in your writings? What is to prevent your denouncing deadly sins?

'But you should never be the first to expose a fault, and if you see something sinful, it is better to say nothing about it at first, but only be sorry that it is not put right. And you must never repeat anything that is secret, whether prompted by the desire to praise or belittle others. "Be sparing in praise, and yet more sparing in censure." '

'He is right,' said Scripture, and with that she leapt up into a pulpit and started to preach. Yet if laymen could have understood her, I doubt if they would have relished her sermon much. For this was her text[18] and theme – I took good note of it – '*Many* folk were called to a feast; and when they had all arrived, the porter unbarred the gate, quietly pulled in a *few*, and sent all the rest packing!'

I was so troubled by this text that my heart trembled within me, and I was filled with doubt and began to dispute with myself whether I was chosen or not. I thought of Holy Church, which had received me at the font as one of God's elect, and remembered how Christ called us all, even the Saracens, heretics, and Jews, to come to Him if we would – 'Ho, everyone that thirsteth, come ye to the waters'[19] – and how He bade all who could enjoy it come in spite of their sins, to feed in safety at His breast, and drink till all their wretchedness was cured.

'In that case,' I said, 'all Christians may come and claim admission, first by the precious Blood with which He redeemed us, and then by baptism; for "He that believeth and is baptized shall be saved."[20] And even if a Christian wished to reject his baptism, he could not do so in reason. For the Law will not allow a villein to make a contract or sell his goods without his master's leave. He may run into debt and wander away from home, and roam about heedlessly like an outlaw, but Reason will catch up with him and rebuke him in the end, and Conscience will settle accounts with him; and they will convict him of debt and cast him into prison. For he will burn in Purgatory till the Day of Doom, unless Contrition comes before his death, and he prays, aloud or in his heart, for mercy on his misdeeds.'

'That is true,' said Scripture. 'There is no sin so great, that Mercy and Meekness cannot atone for it. For as our books tell us, "His tender mercies are over all His works." '[21]

'Bah! Who cares about books!' said a man called Trajan,[22] who had once been a true knight, and had broken loose from hell. And now he swore, on the word of a Pope, that he had once been dead and damned for being a pagan. – 'The fact is well known among scholars,' he said. 'Not all the learning of the Church could drag me out of hell, but only love and good faith, and my own just judgements. St Gregory knew this well, and because he saw that my life had been honest, he longed for my soul to be saved. And as he wept and yearned for me to have grace, his boon was granted, and I was saved as you can see, without any prayers or Masses said at all. So by love, by teaching, and by honest living I was brought out of the torments of hell, where no prayer could avail.'

'See, you great men,[23] what good faith has done for a Roman Emperor, who, as the scholars assure us, was not a Christian. It was his perfect honesty that saved him, and not the prayer of a Pope; for St Gregory himself said so. Here is a lesson for

you lords who maintain justice to keep in mind; remember
Trajan's honesty, and deal honestly with the people.

'This matter is still shrouded in mystery to many of you
churchmen; but the story is told in the Lives of the Saints,
much more fully than I can tell it – how true charity and an
honest life were sufficient to draw a pagan of Rome out of
eternal torment. All praise to Truth, who could break open
the gates of hell, and save a heathen from the power of the
Devil – a thing which no learning or skill in the Law could
ever do! For love and truthfulness are a truer learning, one
which fills the Bible with the promise of joy and bliss. And
God wrote the Scriptures with His own finger, and gave them
to Moses on the Mount, that he might teach them to all men.

'For these are Trajan's words, that "Without charity the
Law is not worth a bean! And every branch of learning, and
all the Seven Arts, are a waste of time unless you learn them
for the love of God." So it is wrong to learn in order to make
money, or be called a Master of Divinity; you must study
solely for love of our Lord, and to love the people better. For
St John said truly, "He that loveth not his brother abideth
in death."[24] And he bade all men, whether friends or enemies,
love each other, and give to others as if to themselves; for if
any man does not give, he does not love. And God commands
us to conform our souls to love, and especially to loving the
poor, and after that to loving our enemies, for there is merit
in loving those that hate us, and in giving pleasure to poor
folk; and the prayers of the poor may help us. For our joy and
our healing, Christ Jesus of Heaven, always pursues us in a
poor man's apparel, and looks upon us in a poor man's like-
ness,[25] searching us as we pass with looks of love, and forever
seeking to know us by our kindness of heart; and He sees
which way we cast our eyes, and whether we love the lords
of this earth before the Lord of Heaven.

' "When thou makest a dinner or a supper,"[26] our Lord
directs us in the Gospel, "call not thy friends, nor thy breth-
ren, neither thy kinsmen, nor thy rich neighbours" – but
invite the poor, the wretched, and the deformed. For your
friends would feast you in return, as is the custom, and pay

you back for your fine generosity. "But I shall pay for the
poor," our Lord says, "and reward to the full all the labour
of those who give them food or money, and who love them
for my sake."

'For the best men are sometimes rich, and sometimes poor
and beggars; and we are all Christ's creatures, brothers of one
blood, beggars as well as nobles – every one of us wealthy by
His coffers.[27] For on Calvary the whole of Christendom sprang
from Christ's Blood, and there we became blood brothers,
redeemed by one Body; and "as newborn babes"[28] we all
acquired noble birth. So there is neither beggar nor knave
among us, unless sin is the cause; for "whosoever committeth
sin is the servant of sin."[29]

'In the Old Law, as the Scripture tells us, we were all called
Sons of Men,[30] the issue of Adam and Eve; and so it remained
until Jesus, the god-man, died for us. But after His Resur-
rection He was called Redeemer, and when we had been
bought by Him we all became His brothers, rich and poor
alike. Therefore let us love one another as brothers, and laugh
together as affectionate brothers should; and since we have
only a little while on this earth, let us give all that we can spare
to help our neighbours, and "bear one another's burdens".[31]
And let us not be niggardly with our goods, or with our
talents, for who knows how soon we shall be taken from them?
Nor must you ever find fault with a neighbour – though he
knows more Latin than you do, nor correct another man
abusively, for none are faultless. And whatever the learned say
about Baptism and such matters, Christ himself said[32] to a
prostitute at a public feast, that her faith would save and
absolve her from all her sins.

'So faith is a loyal helper, and above Law and Logic; for in
the Lives of the Saints Logic and Law are little esteemed, un-
less they have faith to support them. It would take Logic a
long time to explain a passage from those Lives; and Law is
always an enemy to Love, unless he can lay his hands on a bag
of silver. So I advise any Christian who wishes to avoid lying
not to attach himself to Logic or to Law. For "With what
measure ye mete, it shall be measured to you again"[33] – these

words truly belong to Faith's teaching, the faith that can save
sinners. And therefore let us learn the law of love, as Christ
taught it, and remember what St Gregory said for the good
of our souls, "that it is better to search out our sins than to
find out the nature of things".

'It is chiefly for the sake of the poor that I insist on charity;
for Our Lord has often been known in their likeness. When He
went to Emmaus[34] in Easter week, Cleophas did not know at
first that He was Christ, because of His poor apparel and pil-
grim's garments; but as soon as He blessed and broke the
bread which they ate, they knew that He was Jesus – not by
His clothing or His speech, but by His actions. And this was
done as an example to us sinners, that we too should be humble
and friendly in speech, and not dress ourselves proudly in fine
clothes, for we are all pilgrims. And in a poor man's clothes
and in the guise of a pilgrim, God has often been met with
among the poor and needy, unseen by any man of the richer
sort. St John and many more of the saints were poorly clothed,
and begged for alms as needy pilgrims do. And Jesus Christ
chose as His Mother a Jew's daughter, who, though she was of
gentle birth, was a poor maid, betrothed to a penniless man.

'When Martha complained aloud against Mary,[35] saying,
"Lord, dost Thou not care that my sister hath left me to serve
alone?" then, as Matthew tells, our Lord answered her
quickly, "Mary hath chosen the better part, which shall not
be taken away from her." So He complied with both their
wishes, yet put poverty first[36] and praised it the more highly
of the two. And as far as I can discover, all the wise men of
the past have praised poverty, and said that, borne with
patience, it is the best life – many times more blessed than
riches. For although it is bitter to the taste, there comes sweet-
ness afterwards; and just as a walnut has a bitter shell, but
when the shell is removed there is a kernel of strengthening
food, so it is with poverty and mortification when taken
patiently. Poverty makes a man mindful of God, and gives
him a strong desire to pray well and weep for his sins; and
from these things Mercy arises, of which the kernel is Christ,
who comforts and strengthens the soul.

'Unlike the rich, the poor man sleeps securely, for he has little fear of sudden death or of thieves in the dark. – "I am poor and full of merriment, while you are rich and weighed down with heavy thoughts." And although Solomon said, "Give me neither poverty nor riches,"[37] men wiser than he have taught and proved that the perfect poverty is to have no possessions, and that this is the life most pleasing to God. For it is written in St Luke, "If thou wilt be perfect, go and sell all that thou hast, and give to the poor."[38] So men who live in the world, if they wish to be perfect, must sell all their possessions, and give the money to those who cry alms for the love of God.

'No man who served God truly ever lacked food; for as David said in the Psalter, "I have not seen the righteous forsaken, nor his seed begging bread."[39] This means that if a man devotes his life to the service of God, he will be able to suffer every mortification gladly, and will never be without food and linen and wool. For "Nothing is impossible with God,"[40] and it is written, "They that seek the Lord shall not want any good thing."[41]

'It follows that if the priests were perfect, they would take no money for their Masses or Hours, nor accept any food or clothing from usurers – not so much as a coat or jacket, even if they were dying with cold. For if they did their duty, they could justly cry with David, "Judge me, O God, and distinguish my cause against an ungodly nation."[42] And the Psalm "Put thy trust in the Lord"[43] also applies to priests without money; for it says that if they do their work honestly and trust in Almighty God, they will never go without a livelihood or lack for clothing.

'The very title of "priest" by which they take Holy Orders, proclaims their new position of authority; so what need have they to take money for saying Masses? If they are worthy of any wages, he who gave them their title should pay them, or else the Bishop who ordained them. No king would ever make a man a knight unless he had the wealth that befits knighthood; or if he did, he would provide him in return for his services, with all that he needed. For a knight without land, or lineage or battle-honours would be a poor wretch indeed – and the king who knighted him, a blackguard! And the same is true of priests who have neither learning nor honest blood – nothing, in fact, but a mere tonsure and the title of "priest" to live on in times of misfortune! But I fancy that most of them are more confident of making their livings by their tonsures alone[44] than by acquiring a proper training or a good reputation. I wonder that the Bishop ordains such priests, to betray ignorant layfolk who know no better.

'A legal contract is open to challenge by a Chief Justice, if the document contains any false Latin. And if any part is left out, or the scrivener has added comments and illuminations between the lines, the Law impugns the contract. So the scribe who defaces manuscripts is thought an ass. And likewise any priest who falters when reading the Gospel or makes mistakes in saying his Mass or Office is an ass! For "Whosoever shall offend in one point, he is guilty of all."[45] And for those who leave passages out, these are the words of David in the Psalter: "Sing praises unto our king, sing praises. For God is the king of all the earth: sing ye praises *with understanding*."[46] So a Bishop who ordains knights of God who can neither sing, nor read Psalms nor say the Mass of the day *with understanding*, will, I believe, be guilty before Almighty God. And not only are the Bishops to blame, but the priests themselves, for they are both indicted by this text: "Ignorance does not excuse Bishops, or ignorant priests."

'But this glance at ignorant priests has made me wander away from my subject, the praise of poverty, which in patient men is more perfect than any riches.'

And as I dreamed, someone disputed with me much further; and I saw all these things in my sleep.

Then Nature approached me, calling me by my name; and he bade me take heed, and gather wisdom from all the wonders of the world. And I dreamt that he led me out on to a mountain called Middle-Earth, so that I might learn from all kinds of creatures to love my Creator. And I saw the sun and the sea, and the sandy shores, and the places where birds and beasts go forth with their mates – wild snakes in the woods, and wonderful birds whose feathers were flecked with many colours. And I could also see man and his mate, in poverty and in plenty, in peace and war; and I saw how men lived in happiness and misery both at once, and how they took money, and refused mercy.

And I perceived how surely Reason followed all the beasts, in their eating and drinking and engendering of their kinds. For when their mating-time was over, they no longer cared for each other as they did when they had coupled together; but presently, all the males drew apart together, and both by morning and evening they left the females alone. And having once conceived, no cow or creature like her would bellow after the bull. And the boar would no longer grunt for the sow, neither would horse nor hound, nor any other beast couple with its mate if she were heavy with young.

And I beheld the birds in the bushes building their nests, which no man, with all his wits, could ever make. And I marvelled to know who taught the magpie to place the sticks in which to lay her eggs and to breed her young; for no crafts-man could make such a nest hold together, and it would be a wonderful mason who could construct a mould for it!

And yet I wondered still more at other birds – how they concealed and covered their eggs secretly on moors and marsh-lands, so that men should never find them; and how they hid them more carefully still when they went away, for fear of the birds of prey and of wild beasts. And there were some birds, I noticed, that trod their mates in the trees, and brought forth their young high up above the ground; while others conceived at their beaks through the act of breathing.[47] And I noted care-fully the way that peacocks breed.[48] And when I saw all these things, I wondered what master they had, and who taught them to rear their houses so high in the trees, where neither man nor beast could reach their young.

Then I gazed out over the sea, and onwards to the stars; and so many were the wonders that I saw, that it would take a lifetime to tell them all. I saw the flowers in the woods, with all their bright colours, growing with so many hues amidst the green grass. And it seemed to me strange that some were rank, while others were sweet, But it would take too long to speak of all their kinds, and of their many different colours.

Yet the thing that moved me most, and changed my way of thinking, was that Reason ruled and cared for all the beasts, except only for man and his mate; for many a time they wandered ungoverned by Reason.

So I reproached Reason to his face, and said to him, 'It amazes me that you, who are thought wise, should be so careless! Why do you not follow man and his mate, and see that they come to no harm?'

Then Reason reproved me, saying, 'Never mind what I allow or do not allow; that is not your business. Do something about it yourself, if you can. But I must wait, for my time is still to come.[49] You should know that forbearance is a great virtue, and also a swift vengeance. What man has ever suffered as God suffers? For if God chose, He could put right all that is wrong in less than a minute; but for the sake of some men, He endures it all, and that is better for us.

'The Scriptures,' continued Reason, 'teach men to suffer likewise – "Be ye subject therefore to every human creature for God's sake."[50] And here is a saying which the French, and the freemen of England, teach their children:

*"*Bele vertue est soffrance . mal dire est petyt veniance;*
Bien dire est bien soffrir . fait lui soffrant a bien venir."[51]

Therefore I advise you to control your tongue, and before you blame others, see how much praise you deserve yourself. For no man on earth can create himself to his own liking; and you can be sure of this, that if men could, everyone would be faultless! You will find very few who are pleased to have their faults brought home to them in all their ugliness.

'The great sage Solomon said in the Bible, "Strive not in a matter that concerneth thee not."[52] For whether a man is handsome or ugly, it is no one's business to criticize the shape and form which God created; for all that God did was done

*'Forbearance is a fair virtue, but cursing is a petty vengeance. Speak kindly and forbear, and you will come to a good end.'

well, as the Scriptures bear witness – "And God saw every-
thing that He had made, and, behold, it was very good."[53]
And He bade every creature increase and multiply, to give
pleasure to man, who must suffer woe through the temptations
of the flesh and the Devil. For man, being made of flesh, is
bound at times to follow the flesh. And as Cato says, "No man
can live without offending." '[54]

Then at once I felt ashamed and began to blush; and with
that I awoke, very distressed because I had not learned more
in my dream. And I began to curse my ill-luck and mutter to
myself, saying, 'By Christ! I should think I ought to know
what Do-well is now' – when suddenly, on raising my eyes, I
saw someone looking at me who said, 'Well, what is it then?
Tell me.'

'Willingly, sir,' I said. 'Do-well is to see much, and to suffer
more!'

'If you had really suffered,' he said, 'you would have under-
stood more of Learning's teaching, although you were asleep;
and with Reason to help you, you would have grasped it better
still. For Reason would have explained to you all that Learn-
ing had to say. But now, because you had to interfere, you are
left alone. "You might be a philosopher," as the saying goes,
"if you could only hold your tongue."[55]

'Adam had all Paradise to enjoy, as long as he held his tongue;
but when he started to talk nonsense about fruit, and tried to
pry into the mind and wisdom of God, he was turned out of
Paradise. And so it was with you and Reason: you, in your
crude way, presumed to judge matters beyond your powers,
and so he was not willing to teach you more.

'And now, in all probability, Pride and Presumption will
inform against you, so that Learning will no longer care to
have you with him. For no amount of chiding and reproach
will chasten a man so quickly as shame, which makes him feel
his disgrace, and inclines him to make amends. If a drunken
fool falls into a ditch, it is best to let him lie there, and ignore
him till he decides to rouse himself. For he does not care how
much Reason reproaches him, and he would not give a straw

for all Learning's advice! So to pitch into him at that moment
would be downright wickedness. But when Necessity drags
him to his feet, for fear of dying, and Shame scrapes the mud
off his clothes and cleans up his legs, then the drunken idiot
knows why he is to blame.'

'You are right,' I said, 'I have often seen it myself. Nothing
stings so sharply or smells so foul as Shame; and people avoid
him whenever he shows his face. I suppose you are telling me
this because I rebuked Reason.'

'Exactly,' he said, and he set off walking; and with that I
jumped up and followed after him, and begged him out of his
kindness to tell me his name.

Book XII

IMAGINATION

THE STORY. *Imagination reminds the poet how he has wasted his life, and he, after trying to excuse himself, asks what Do-well, Do-better, and Do-best are. In his answer, Imagination corrects the dreamer's previous errors and answers some of the questions he had asked long before. He decries riches, shows the dreamer the proper value of Learning and Wisdom, discusses the way of salvation, and assures him that even the heathen may sometimes get to Heaven.*

'I AM Imagination,' he said. 'I am never idle, although I sit and brood by myself, both in health and in sickness. I have followed you now for five and forty years, and stirred you many times to remember your end, and all the years that have vanished away, and the few that are to come. And I have reminded you of your wild and dissolute youth, so that you might make amends in middle age before your strength fails; for old age can ill endure the hardships of poverty and the life of penance and prayer. – "And if He shall come in the second watch, or come in the third, and find them watching, blessed are those servants."[1] So mend your ways now, while you are still able. Often enough you have been warned by outbreaks of Plague, by poverty, and by many afflictions. For God uses these things as sharp rods, to beat the children He loves – "Such as I love, I rebuke and chastise."[2] Therefore David says in the Psalter, of those who love God, "Thy rod and thy staff they comfort me,"[3] which means, "Though Thou strikest me with Thy staff or with Thy rod, yet am I pleased, for it refreshes my soul."

'Yet for all this, you do nothing, but play about with poetry when you might be saying your Psalter and praying for those who give you your daily bread! Are there not enough books already, to expound Do-well, Do-better, and Do-best, and hosts of preachers and pairs of wandering Friars?'

I could see the truth of this; so, partly to excuse myself, I said, 'Cato, who was a man of learning, would please his son from time to time by composing poetry as I do. And did he not say "You should sometimes mingle pleasures with your pains"?[4] What is more, many of the saints, I have heard, would sometimes indulge in amusements, in order to become more perfect. Nevertheless, if someone could really tell me what are Do-well, Do-better, and Do-best, I would never write again, but go to Holy Church and tell my beads all day, when I was not eating or sleeping.'

'St Paul explains what Do-well is,' he said, 'in his Epistle: "And now abideth faith, hope, and charity, these three; but the greatest of these is charity."[5] In other words, all three are great virtues, able to save men, but charity is Do-best for it saves men most quickly.

'For a man who is faithful and follows Loyalty's teaching, truly does well. Thus if you are a married man, you must love your wife, and both live in obedience to the Moral Law. And if you are a Religious, you must not go wandering off to Rome or the shrine of Rochemadour,[6] unless your Rule commands it; for your highway to Heaven is to hold yourself under obedience. And if you are chaste and unmarried, and able to continue so, at all costs do not stray from that path[7] to seek more distant shrines. For what caused Lucifer to fall from the height of Heaven, or robbed Solomon of his wisdom, or Samson of his strength?[8] And consider how dearly Job and Aristotle, Hippocrates[9] and Virgil, and many more paid for their happiness. Even Alexander, who conquered the whole world, came to a miserable end.

'All these men were ruined by their wealth and their intelligence. Likewise the beauty of Felicia[10] brought her to degradation, and Rosamund[11] wasted pitifully all her fairness, and squandered it in a life of wickedness. You may read of many such men and women, whose words were wise, but whose deeds were all the opposite. For "There are plenty of bad men who speak well about virtue."

'In the same way, those who have wealth will pinch and hoard all their lives, only for their worst enemies to spend it in the end; and at last they lose their souls as well, for they see many in need, yet do nothing about them, and refuse to love the poor as Our Lord commanded – "Give, and it shall be given unto you."[12] Therefore so many men are lost through riches and intelligence; and it will go hard with a man who possesses them, unless he uses them well. For "That servant who knew his lord's will . . . and did not do it, shall be beaten with many stripes."[13] And wisdom, the Scripture says, only makes a man's spirit swell with pride – "Wisdom puffeth up, but charity edifieth."[14]

'The same is true of riches, unless they spring from an honest root. The herb of Grace might ease the swellings of the rich, but that Grace can only grow amongst lowly folk. For it flourishes in the soil of patience and poverty, among men of honest and holy life, by the gift of the Holy Ghost, as the Gospel says – "The wind bloweth where it listeth, etc."[15] Intelligence and Learning, on the other hand, spring from sight and teaching, as these words of Scripture prove: "We speak of *that which we know*, and testify of *that which we have seen*."[16] For from "that which we know" arise learning and the knowledge of things Divine, and from "that which we have seen," in other words from the observations of many different men, springs intelligence. But Grace is a gift of God, and it springs from great love; and neither Learning nor Intelligence could ever explain its ways or tell how it comes into being – "Thou knowest not whence it cometh nor whither it goeth."[17]

'Yet learning and intelligence are both worthy of praise, and especially learning, since its root is the love of Christ. And although in the Old Law, which as we know from the testimony of Moses God himself wrote to instruct the Jews, any woman taken in adultery whether rich or poor was stoned to death;[18] yet it was through learning that Christ saved a woman who was guilty of adultery.[19] For by the words which He wrote on the ground, the Jews knew themselves more guilty before God, and in greater sin, than the woman who stood before them; and they departed in shame. And since this

woman was comforted by learning, and Christ saved her by
means of writing, Holy Church follows His example, and uses
learning for the same purpose. So learning brings comfort to
a man who repents, but woe to a hardened sinner who dies
unrepentant.

'Without the use of learning, bread could not be changed
into the Body of Christ, which is a source of healing to the
righteous, but of death and damnation to those that die in sin.
And just as Christ's writing both comforted the woman whom
He thought fit to save, and exposed the guilt of her judges
("Judge not, that ye be not judged"),[20] so the Body of Christ,
if we take it unworthily, will damn us at the Day of Doom[21]
as those Jews were damned.

'Therefore I advise you to love and reverence Learning for
Our Lord's sake; for Intelligence is of his kin, and, truly, they
are both near cousins to Our Lord himself. And like mirrors,
they help us to amend our faults, and are true guides for lay-
folk as well as for clergy. So I counsel you never to reproach
Logic or Law or to mock at their usages, nor ever to contradict
men of learning. For just as a man cannot see without eyes, so
a scholar would be blind unless he learnt from books. Books
were written by men, but their authority came from God, and
the men who wrote them were taught by the Holy Ghost.
And, as the power of sight enables a man to see the highway,
so education leads the ignorant to reason. A blind man may
carry arms into battle and swing his axe, but he has no chance
of hitting the enemy; likewise a man possessed of natural
intelligence who has no scholars to teach him, will never find
the Faith of the Church and attain salvation. For the Church
is the coffer in which Christ keeps His treasure, and the learned
are the keepers of the keys: they may unlock it at their pleasure,
and dispense God's pardon to the layfolk for all their misdeeds,
provided they ask humbly and willingly for grace.

'Under the Old Law, the Levites were the guardians of the
Ark of God,[22] and no one else was permitted to touch it, unless
he were a priest or the son of a priest, a patriarch or a prophet.
And Saul was brought to ruin,[23] together with all his sons,
because he offered a sacrifice without consulting the priests.

Moreover, many of those who followed the Ark of God, and treated it with great reverence and honour, lost their lives because, not being Levites, they laid hands on it to lift it up.[24] Therefore I counsel Christians never to despise priests, nor make light of their learning, no matter what they may practise. But rather let us value their teaching for its own sake, for the things they witness are true. And let us not meddle with them and stir them to anger, lest strife should inflame us to wrath, and we strike one of God's anointed; for it is written: "Touch not mine Anointed: and do my prophets no harm."[25] Thus, under Christ of Heaven, Learning is our protector, and there is no knight in the world but owes his knighthood to Learning.

'Intelligence, on the other hand, springs from men's observations of many things – of birds and beasts, and of experiments both true and false. The men of old used carefully to note all the wonders that they saw, in order to teach them to their sons; and they considered it a high science to read the significance of these things. Yet no one was ever saved by this natural science, nor did their books lead a single soul to Heaven. For it was all a hotch-potch of countless observations. Therefore the patriarchs and prophets denounced their philosophy as frivolous, and despised it as trifling compared with the knowledge of God – "For the wisdom of this world is foolishness with God."[26]

'For the prophets knew how the mighty Spirit of God would cleave Heaven asunder, and Love leap out into this low earth; and how a Virgin should receive it, and Wise Men find it. – "And the shepherds said one to another, Let us now go even unto Bethlehem."[27]

'The story of the Nativity does not mention rich or clever men, nor ignorant lords, but speaks of the most learned men then living – "There came Magi from the East" – so I'll be bound there were no Friars present! Nor was the Holy Child born in a poor man's cottage, but in a place owned by one of the best burgesses of Bethlehem.[28] For it is written, "There was no room for them in the inn,"[29] and, as someone has said, "A poor man has no inn."

'And it was to shepherds and poets[30] that the angel appeared, bidding them go to Bethlehem and honour God's birth. And while the rich lay asleep and snoring in their beds, the shepherds were dazzled by the glory of God, and the herald of Heaven sang them a song of joy – *"Gloria in excelsis deo"*. Yet the Men of Learning knew of all these things, and they came with gifts to pay their homage to Him who was almighty.

'I have told you all this because I noticed how churlishly you opposed Learning, and argued that the ignorant were saved more easily than the educated or intelligent. And in a way you were right about some of them, but notice in what way: Let us suppose that two strong men, of equal weight, are thrown into the Thames stark naked. The one is a skilful diver and swimmer, the other has never been taught to swim a stroke. Which do you think is in the greater danger, the expert swimmer, or the one who is carried along by the flood in terror of drowning?'

'The one who can't swim, I should think,' I said.

'Exactly,' said Imagination, 'and it follows that a man possessed of learning, even if he sins frequently, can climb out of sin if he chooses, and save himself sooner than any ignorant man. For the learned man knows what things are sinful, and he understands how contrition, even without confession, can strengthen the soul. You can read in several of the Psalms how David commends contrition for driving away sin –

"Blessed is he whose unrighteousness is forgiven: and whose sin is covered . . . "[31]

And this comforts the man who can read, and protects him from despair – that flood in which the Devil tries a man most severely. But the ignorant man can only lie there helplessly, waiting till the next Lent comes round; for he has no contrition until he goes to Confession. And even then he can say little, and he trusts and believes whatever his confessor tells him – probably some stupid parish priest incapable of teaching the layfolk at all, like those of whom St Luke speaks – "And if the blind lead the blind, both shall fall into the ditch."[32]

'So a man who must wade the stream with such ignorant

guides, is truly marked out for woe! And well may a child
who is taught to read be grateful to those who sent him to
school, for if he lives by the written word he may save his
soul. – "*Dominus pars hereditatis meae*"* is indeed a cheerful
verse to read, for it has saved dozens of mighty robbers from
Tyburn![33] So where the illiterate thieves must swing for it,
see how Learning saves the ones who can read!

'And as you said yourself, it was because the penitent thief
confessed his faith in Christ on the Cross, and admitted his
guilt, asking our Lord for mercy, that he gained God's grace
and was saved. For God is always merciful to those who ask
humbly, and truly intend to sin no more. But although he
went to Heaven, the thief did not attain the same heights
of bliss as St John or any of the saints, who deserved better
than he. For a rich man may give me food and set me down
in the middle of his hall floor, and I may indeed have plenty
to eat, but I am not honoured like those who sit at the side-
tables, or with the lords of the household on the high dais;
for I sit like a beggar, alone on the bare ground. And so it is
with the penitent thief: he does not sit with St John, St
Simon, or with St Jude, nor with the Virgins and Martyrs,
Confessors and Holy Widows, but is served in silence,
sitting alone on the rushes. For a man that has once been
a thief is for ever in danger and lives all his days at the mercy
of the law. For it is written: "Concerning propitiation, be not
without fear to add sin unto sin: and say not, His mercy is
great; He will be pacified for the multitude of my sins: for
mercy and wrath come from Him, and His indignation resteth
upon sinners."[34] – Nor would it be just or reasonable to serve
a saint and a thief side by side, and to reward them both alike.

'The honest knight Trajan pitched his tent so near the
borders of hell, that our Lord could draw him out quite
easily. And so, I believe, the thief is placed in Paradise –
lounging at ease in the lowest reaches of Heaven. This must be
so if our Faith is true, for the Law of the Church says, "Thou
rewardest every man according to his works."[35]

'And if you ask why one of the crucified thieves accepted

*'The Lord is the portion of my inheritance . . .' (Ps. xvi. 5).

147

the Faith, rather than the other, not all the clergy of Christ
could give you an answer. – "Whatsoever the Lord pleased,
that did He."[36] And so I say to you, when you ask the whys
and wherefores of things. For you cavilled at Reason, and
questioned him about the flowers in the wood and their rich
colours, and the birds and beasts, and their different habits
of breeding. "Where," you said, "did the flowers receive
their hues, so fresh and bright? Why do some birds breed on
the ground and some in the trees?" And you puzzled over the
stones and over the stars and questioned how the birds and
beasts could show such sagacity.

'The cause is known only to Nature himself, and was
never perceived by Learning or Intelligence. For Nature is
the magpie's guide, who whispers in his ear, telling him to
build where the thorn is thickest. And it was he that taught
the peacock its way of breeding, and caused Adam and Eve
to know their privy members and cover them with leaves.

'Laymen often ask men of learning why Adam did not
first cover his mouth, the part that had eaten the apple, rather
than his loins – so simple folk question the theologians. But
only Nature knows why he did so; no other scholar can tell
you.

'Yet the men of old, as we read, used to take birds and
beasts as examples and use them as parables. They said, for
instance, that the most beautiful birds breed in the foulest
manner,[37] and that they are the feeblest in flight of all that
fly and swim. These are the peacocks and peahens, which re-
present the rich and proud. For the peacock is easy to pursue,
as he cannot fly high, and is soon captured, because he trails
his tail on the ground. His flesh, moreover, is repulsive to eat,
his feet are ugly, and his cry is harsh and grating to the ear.
And like the peacocks, the wealthy trail their riches behind
them, refusing to share them until they are overtaken by death,
which is truly the tail-end of all their sorrow. And just as the
wings of the peacock encumber his flight, so the weight of so
many shillings and pence is a plague to all who possess them –
until death plucks off their tails. And then, though the rich
man repent, and bewail that ever he hoarded so much and

gave so little, and though he cry to Christ with the bitterest
longing, his voice will sound in our Lord's ears like the
chattering of a magpie. And when his carcass is cast in the pit
for burial, its foul stench will spread through the soil around,
and poison the others that lie in the graveyard.

'The peacocks' feet, according to the Fables,[38] signify
the rich man's executors, the false friends who ignore the
terms of his will, though they witnessed it and promised to
carry it out to the letter.

'Thus the writer shows that as the peacock is praised
for his feathers alone, so the rich are honoured only for
their goods. The lark, a tiny bird compared with the peacock,
has a far sweeter voice, is much swifter in flight, and its flesh
is many times richer and sweeter to eat; and so the lark is
likened to men of humble life. Some of these comparisons
were made by Aristotle, the great scholar; and thus, in his
Logic,[39] he finds a meaning in the smallest of birds.

'And as to whether Aristotle is saved,[40] Learning, with all
his books, can give you no answer; nor can he tell you of
Socrates, nor of Solomon. But since God is so good, and he
gave these men the wisdom to teach others, and to write
books that help us towards salvation, we must hope and pray
that He will give rest to their souls. For without their writings,
scholars of today would still be in ignorance.'

'But all the clergy of the Church,' I said, 'say in their
sermons that neither Saracens nor Jews nor any other
creature in the likeness of Christ can be saved without
Baptism.'

'I deny it,' said Imagination, frowning, 'for the Scripture
says, "The just man shall *scarcely* be saved on the Day of
Judgement."[41] Therefore he shall be saved. Trajan was an
honest knight, and although he never received baptism, books
tell us that he is saved and his soul is in Heaven. For there is a
baptism by water, a baptism by the shedding of blood, and a
baptism by fire, which means by steadfast faith – "The
divine fire comes not to consume, but to bring light."

'So an honest man that lives by the law that he knows,

believing there is none better (for if he knew of a better
he would accept it) – a man who has never treated any one
unjustly, and who dies in the same spirit – surely the God
of truth would not reject such honesty as this. And whether
it shall be so or not, the faith of such a man is very great,
and from that faith there springs a hope of reward. We
are told that God will give eternal life to His own, and His
own are the faithful and true. For it is written,

> "Yea, though I walk through the valley of the shadow of
> death, I will fear no evil."[42]

And the Commentary on that verse speaks of a great reward
for truthfulness.

'Intelligence and wisdom,' added Imagination, 'were
once considered treasure enough to protect a kingdom; no
better wealth was required, for these were the sources of
pleasure and of courage' – and with those words he vanished.

Book XIII

PATIENCE AND HAUKYN THE ACTIVE MAN

THE STORY. *The dreamer awakes almost frantic with bewilderment, roams about puzzling over his dream and at last falls asleep again. Now he dreams that Conscience invites him to dinner with Scripture, Learning, and a great divine; but while he, with Patience, eats at a side table on meagre rations, the great divine gorges himself on dainties. After dinner the divine briefly answers the dreamer's question about Do-well, etc., but since the dreamer treats him rudely, Conscience as the host turns to Learning and Patience to ask them their opinion. Learning declines to commit himself, but Patience answers with a riddle, saying he possesses a powerful charm that contains Do-well. Conscience is moved by Patience's words, and, despite the protests of the others, goes forth with him as a pilgrim. Before long, Conscience and Patience meet one Haukyn the Active Man, who proudly describes his activities as a baker. But when they point out that his clothes are smeared with sin, he confesses fully how he has soiled his coat of Baptism with all Seven Deadly Sins.*

WITH that I awoke, almost out of my mind; and for many years after this I roamed the earth begging my bread like a pauper. And I puzzled continually over this dream, remembering how Fortune failed me in my greatest need, and Old Age threatened me whenever I met him; how the Friars go after the rich folk, and despise the poor, and no one can be buried in one of their graveyards or churches, unless, while he lives, he bequeaths them some money to pay off their debts; how priests and parsons are swamped in the same covetousness, and how unless God intervenes, simple laymen are led by ignorant priests to incurable torments. And I remembered what Imagination told me of Nature's wisdom – how kind he is to the animals, and how loving to all the beasts on land

and sea; for he never forsakes a living creature, whether great or small, and even the creeping things are among his children. And then I recalled how Imagination said, 'The just man shall *scarcely* be saved,' and how then he suddenly disappeared.

So I lay down absorbed in this thought for a long time, till at last I fell asleep. And now, by the grace of God, Conscience came and strengthened me, and invited me to his castle to dine with Learning. When I heard him speak of Learning, I came eagerly; and there I saw a Master of Divinity – I did not then know what kind of man he was[1] – who bowed low to Scripture and greeted her affectionately.

Conscience knew this Master well, and gave him a polite welcome. And then, having washed and dried their hands, they went in to dinner.

But Patience stood in the courtyard, dressed as a pilgrim, begging his food for charity like a poor hermit. And Conscience called him in and spoke to him courteously, saying, 'Welcome, friend. If you would care to go and wash, dinner will soon be ready.'

The great divine, being the guest of honour, was asked to be seated first, and after him Learning and Conscience, and then Patience. But Patience and I had to keep one another company, for they put us by ourselves at a side table.

Then Conscience called for food, and Scripture came in briskly and served them with many different dishes – dishes of Augustine and Ambrose and all the four Evangelists – 'Eating and drinking such things as they give.'[2] But the Master-Friar and his servant ate no solid meat, but costlier foods, special purées and ragouts. For they were used to living very comfortably with the ill-gotten money left them by wealthy patrons. But their sauce was too tart, for it was pounded into an acrid mess in a mortar called *Post-mortem*[3] – a time of sharp torment for them, unless they say the Masses they promised for their benefactors, and weep bitter tears for their souls. – 'Ye who feast upon the sins of men, unless ye pour out tears for them, shall vomit up amidst torments the food which now ye feast on amid pleasure.'[4]

And then Conscience politely asked Scripture to bring some bread for Patience, and for me, his companion. And she set before us a sour loaf, saying 'Do Penance,'[5] and drew us a draught of liquor which she called *Long-endure*.[6] 'Why, yes, as long as my life and health last out!' I said.

'This is excellent service,' said Patience. 'A prince could hardly fare better.'

Then she brought us a course of the *Miserere*,[7] followed by some 'Blessed-is-he',[8] made by 'Blessed-is-the-man', with a sauce of 'Whose-sin-is-covered', served in a dish of private confession – 'I-said-I-will-confess-my-sins-unto-the-Lord'.

'Bring Patience a little to put in his bag,' whispered Conscience to Scripture. So she gave Patience a pittance of 'For-this-shall-everyone-that-is-godly-make-his-prayer-unto-thee-in-a-time-when-thou-mayest-be-found'.[9] And Conscience cheered us all, and entertained us with pleasant news – 'A broken and contrite heart, O God, shalt thou not despise.'[10]

Patience was truly proud of this excellent service, and he rejoiced over his food; but I was fretting all the time, because the great Doctor at the high table was gulping his wine so greedily. – 'Woe unto them that are mighty to drink wine, and men of strength to mingle strong drink!'[11] And he gobbled up countless different dishes – minced meat and puddings, tripes and galantine and eggs fried in butter. Meanwhile I was muttering to myself, loud enough for Patience to hear me, 'It is less than four days since this fellow was preaching before the Dean of St Paul's about the sufferings of Paul the Apostle[12] – "Of the Jews five times received I forty stripes save one. Thrice was I beaten with rods . . . in perils of waters, in perils of robbers . . . in hunger and thirst, in fastings often, in cold and nakedness, etc." But there is one phrase which these Friars always leave out of their sermons, though St Paul published it to the whole world – "in peril among false brethren".[13] So the Scripture bids us beware – but I will not write it in English, lest it should be repeated too often, and good men also are offended. But Latin scholars may read it – *"Unusquisque a fratre se custodiat, quia, ut dicitur, periculum* *est in falsis fratribus.*'* No friar ever took that for his text, or read it out to the people in English without explanation. They preach about mortification, how profitable it is to the soul, and talk much of the pains Christ suffered for men. But look at this great glutton of God here, with his fat cheeks – he has no pity on the poor, and his life is an abomination; he preaches one thing, and practises another.' – So I spoke to Patience, and wished with all my heart that the dishes and platters surrounding this great Doctor were molten lead in his guts, and the foul fiend among them! 'I will ask this bloated, round-bellied piss-pot' – so I thought to myself – 'to tell me what mortification is; he preached about it only a few days ago!'

But Patience saw what I was thinking, and signed to me to keep quiet. 'You will soon see,' he said, 'when he has stuffed himself to capacity, what a mortification he will have in his belly! He will puff and blow, and belch at every word, and his guts will start to rumble. He has swilled so much wine, he will soon give you a logical demonstration that bacon and brawn, hashed chicken and mincemeat are not meat at all, but a penitent's food – and cite the Apocalypse of Gluttons,[14] and St Aurea's life of penance,[15] to prove it! Then he will preach to you about trinities with a vengeance – Do-this, do-that and the other – and what is more, he will swear, and get his companion to witness, how little food there is in a friar's wallet. And if his very first sentence is not a lie, never believe me again! That is the time to tackle him about Do-well and Do-better, and ask him if Do-best means mortification.'

So I sat still as Patience said. And before very long the Doctor, with a face as red as a rose, rubbed his cheeks, and coughed, and began to speak. Then Conscience suggested to him the threefold subject, and he turned towards us.

'What is Do-well, Doctor,' I said, 'is it some sort of mortification?'

'Do-well?' said the Doctor, taking a gulp from his tankard. 'Do-well is to strive never to injure your fellow-Christians.'

*'Let everyone beware a friar, for as it is written, There is peril among false brethren.'

'Then by Heaven, Doctor,' I said, 'you do not follow Do-well! For you have injured the two of us here, by eating all these puddings and pies and dishes galore, without offering us a morsel! If that is how you treat the sick in your infirmaries, I shouldn't wonder if they were places of strife instead of charity – at least, if the novice-boys dared to complain. But since I am determined to do-well, I will, if you like, exchange my sufferings for yours.'

Then, with a tactful glance, Conscience restrained me, and signalled Patience to ask me to be silent; and, turning to the Doctor, he said, 'If you do not mind, Doctor, we should like you to tell us about Do-well and Do-better. For you theologians understand these things.'

'Do-well,' said the Doctor, 'is to do as the clergy teach; Do-better is to labour in teaching others; and Do-best is to put into practice all that you say and preach; for the Scripture says – "Whosoever shall do and teach the commandments, the same shall be called great in the Kingdom of Heaven." '[16]

'Now, Learning,' said Conscience, 'you give us your opinion about Do-well.'

'I have seven sons,' said Learning, 'who are all servants in a castle; and there lives the Lord of life, to teach them what it is to do-well. But until I see those sons at peace with me again, I dare not try to explain Do-well to anyone. For a certain Piers the Ploughman has taken us all to task, and shrugged aside all the sciences except Love. The only texts he gives to support his words are "Love God" and "Lord, who shall dwell in thy tabernacle, etc. . . . " And he maintains that Do-well and Do-better are two infinites, which, by faith, discover Do-best; and that Do-best is the saviour of man's soul. – So says Piers the Ploughman.'

'I do not understand that,' said Conscience, 'but I know Piers well. I can promise you that he will say nothing which does not agree with Scripture. So let us leave this question till Piers comes, for he will show us Do-well in practice. Patience has been in many places, and perhaps he knows things which no man of learning could tell us; for as Christ said, "The patient conquer." '[17]

'Since you have asked me,' said Patience, 'I am willing to speak, provided no one here will be offended.

'To learn is to do-well; to teach is to do-better; and to love your enemies is to do-best. So I was taught once by a lady whom I loved; and her name was Charity. "As long as you live," she told me, "you must truly love your soul, with all your heart and mind, both in word and deed. And so you will teach yourself, for the love of God, to love your enemy as yourself. Let your kind words," she said, "be as coals of fire upon his head; strive by every word and deed to win his affection; and lay about him so much with your love, that he will be forced at last to smile at you. If such a beating does not bring him to his knees, may he be blind forever!

' "But it would be foolish to treat your friend in this way; for one who truly loves you does not covet your possessions. Natural affection seeks no token but words, with half a line from a Latin inscription – *ex vi transitionis*."[18]

'I carry Do-well about with me,' continued Patience, 'bound fast within these words – in a sign of that Saturday which first set the calendar, and with it all the wisdom of the following Wednesday; and the power of them both springs from the full moon.[19] So long as I have this with me, I am welcome everywhere.

'Undo it, and let this Doctor decide whether it contains Do-well. For I swear by Him who made me, if you take this charm with you, neither pain nor poverty, slander nor misfortune, neither cold nor misery nor the company of robbers, nor hail nor heat nor fire nor flood, neither a fiend from hell nor the fear of your enemies, shall ever trouble you; for "Perfect love casteth out fear."[20] And by the might of this riddle, you shall have at your asking absolute power over Earls and Emperors, Kings and Barons,[21] Popes and Patriarchs – a power not derived from witchcraft, but gained by reason and argument. And you shall cause the King and Queen, and all the people of the realm, to give unsparingly to you as their best protector, and to obey you in all things for as long as they live. For so "The patient conquer." '

'This is an old yarn,' said the Doctor, ' – a mere minstrel's tale. All the arguments under the sun, and all the powers of mighty men, cannot make peace between the Pope and his enemies, [22] or bring to terms two Christian kings [23] to satisfy both their peoples' – and with that he pushed the table away from him, and drawing Learning and Conscience into private consultation, suggested that Patience should take himself off; 'for pilgrims,' he added, 'are notable liars.'

But Conscience raised his voice and said politely, 'Farewell, my friends, for if God gives me the grace, I intend to go with Patience and become a pilgrim, to gain more experience of these things.'[24]

'What!' said Learning, 'Are you hoping this charm will make money for you, and bring you in some New Year Gifts?[25] Or is it that you feel like solving riddles? If that is all, I will fetch a Bible myself, and show you how to unriddle, say, the whole of Leviticus, down to the last detail – which is more than this pilgrim Patience could ever do!'

'Good gracious, no – thank you very much!' said Conscience. 'It is not pride that moves me to go with Patience, in spite of all that he has offered. But it is his strength of purpose and that of these people here, which has stirred my will and made me weep for my sins. A man's will to do good can never wholly be bought by bribes, since an honest purpose is dearer than any money. Did not Mary Magdalen gain more for a box of ointment[26] than Zacchaeus for giving half his goods to the poor?[27] – and the poor widow more for a couple of mites, [28] than all the rich folk that cast their gifts into the Treasury?'

And then Conscience, having said a kind farewell to the Friar, whispered quietly into Learning's ear, 'God knows, I would rather have perfect patience than half your pack of volumes!' Learning would not say goodbye to him, but only answered gravely, 'There will come a time when you will be weary of walking, and then you will be glad to ask my advice.'

'You are right,' said Conscience, 'and if Patience could be friendly with us both, there is no evil in the world that we could not put right; we could make peace between every king and nation, and bring all the Saracens and Syrians and Jews into the one true faith.'

'Yes, I see what you mean,' said Learning: 'that I must continue to do my duty as I now do, establishing children and novices in the Faith, while Patience proves you, to make you perfect.'[29]

Then Conscience went forth with Patience, and they lived as pilgrims together. And Patience carried a wallet as pilgrims do, containing victuals – Sobriety, Simplicity of Speech, and Steadfast Faith – to comfort them both when they came to the hungry lands of Covetousness and Unkindness.[30]

And as they went on their way discussing Do-well, they met a man who seemed to be dressed like a minstrel. And Patience asked him to tell them his trade, and what country he was making for.

'I am a minstrel,'[31] he said, 'and my name is Activa Vita. I hate all folk who are idle, for my name signifies the Life of Business. If you must know, I am a baker, in the service of many lords, though I get no fine robes and fur-lined gowns[32] from them, as their minstrels do! Why, if I could tell tall stories to amuse their lordships, I should rake in plenty of clothes and money. But I can neither play the tambourine nor the trumpet, and I cannot sing ballads, or make vulgar noises or play the fiddle at feasts; neither can I harp or juggle or crack jokes either, nor play the zither, nor pipe to them sweet music; and I am certainly no dancer or acrobat. So I get no tips from these great lords for all the bread I bake them. All I get is a blessing every Sunday, when the priest bids the people say their Paternoster for Piers and all his helpers.[33] And certainly I am one of those – I, the Active Man, the enemy of all idleness; for I supply all honest labourers with waferbread[34] from one year's end to another.

'And all the tramps and loafers beg their bread from me – the rogues and the friars and the men with shaven heads. Why, I provide bread for the Pope himself,[35] and fodder for his palfrey – yet when did he ever give me a nice fat living or a prebend's stall? I've had nothing from him but a leaden-sealed indulgence, stamped with a couple of heads of Peter and Paul! Now if I had a clerk to write me letters, I would send him a petition, and tell him to forward me, under his secret seal, a remedy for the Plague, and issue us with some bulls and blessings to cure cancer! Didn't Christ say, "In my name they shall cast out devils . . . they shall lay hands on the sick, and they shall recover"?[36] If I found that the Pope's pardon could do that – as I believe it should – I would make pastry for the people with a good grace, and do my utmost to get food and drink for the Pope and all his folk! He has the same power that St Peter had, so he must have the magic ointment hidden away somewhere! – "Silver and gold have I none," said Peter, "but such as I have I give thee: In the name of Jesus Christ of Nazareth rise up and walk."[37]

'But it is not the Pope's fault if he can't work miracles; it is because men are not worthy of them. No blessings can ever help us unless we mend our ways; and all your Masses can never make peace among Christians, until the people are purged of their pride. And that will only be when they are short of bread.

'Before oatmeal can be turned into bread, I have to sweat for it; and before the people can have enough food, there is many a cold morning for me. Little do they know what I suffer to provide their wafers! And all London loves my wafers – you should hear how they grumble when there are none to be had. Why, it was not so long ago that they were all beside themselves, for not a single cartload of bread came up from Stratford.[38] And my wafers were so scarce that the beggars were howling, and the workmen were in a panic. They won't forget that for a long time – that was in the dry April of 1370, when Chichester was Mayor.'[39]

Conscience and I took good note of Haukyn the Active Man, and of his clothes. For he wears a coat of Baptism, cut according to the Faith of Holy Church, yet stained and spattered all over with dirty marks: a spot of pride here and of bragging there, smeared in one place with scorn

and in another with scoffing, and soaked right through with
arrogance. For he carries himself haughtily among the people,
shows off expensive clothes as if he were wealthy, and is
always anxious to be thought other than he really is, both
without and within. So he boasts and brags with many a
blasphemous oath, and is furious if anyone finds fault with
him. He is, in fact, unique, a man to himself, in the eyes of the
world; there never was anyone quite like him, so pope-holy
and righteous! And like a hermit without an Order, he forms a
sect by himself, with no Rule and no law of obedience. He
sneers both at the learned and at the ignorant, and pretends to
lead an honest life, though in his soul he is a liar. All his
powers of thought and observation, all his schemes and calcu-
lations, are bent on what is best for his body, and bad for his
soul.

He interferes everywhere where he has no business,
assuming everyone will think him shrewder and cleverer than
they are. He expects them to regard him as the wisest of
scholars, and the mightiest of horsemen, with legs and thighs
like iron; and also as the handsomest of men, and the most
honest in all his dealings. They must believe that there is no
one so pure and holy as he is, none so fine of feature or so
splendidly built; and besides this they must appreciate that
his singing is brilliant, he is most dexterous with his hands,
and so generous to others that he often incurs great losses to
himself!

For if Activa Vita gives money to the poor, he blazes
the fact abroad everywhere; and though his purse and coffer
are empty, he goes about like a lion, and talks like a lord.

He is truly the boldest of beggars, this penniless braggart.
He spins yarns in every town and tavern, holding forth about
things he never saw, and swearing black and blue that they
are so; bragging of deeds he never did, and proclaiming his
own good works from every housetop. 'If you don't believe
me,' he says, 'ask so-and-so and so-and-so, and they will tell
you. No, I wouldn't lie to you: they know how much I
suffered – what things I saw – how much I possessed – the
astonishing things I could do – what a lot I knew – who I am

related to – etc., etc.' So he means his words and deeds to be
the talk of the town, the wonder of all men, and a glory to
himself.

'Do I seek to please men? for if I yet pleased men, I should
not be the servant of Christ.' And 'No man can serve two
masters.'[40]

'Good heavens, Haukyn!' said Conscience. 'Your best coat
is very marked and stained – it needs washing.'
'Yes,' said Haukyn, 'I am afraid, if you look closely,
you will find wrinkles and dirty patches inside and out,
both back and front and on the sides.' With that he quickly
turned round the other way, and I saw that his coat was
many times filthier than it had seemed at first. It was all
bespattered with anger and ill-will, and smirched with envy
and malicious talk and the stirring up of quarrels; and the
cloth was mouldy with lies and with scornful laughter. For
Haukyn's tongue was always ready to wrangle; and he would
repeat all the ill that he knew of others, accusing men behind
their backs and praying for their destruction. Whatever he
heard about Will, he would tell to Walter, and whatever
Walter told him, he repeated to Will; and his evil-speaking
turned even his best friends into enemies. 'I revenge myself,'
he said, 'by the power of the tongue, if I can't do it by other
men's muscles; and if I fail, I chafe and fret like a rusty pair of
shears.'

Such are those evil wretches of whom the Psalmist speaks –
'Whose mouths are full of cursing, deceit, and fraud: under
whose tongues are ungodliness and vanity.'[41] And again,
they are 'the children of men that are set on fire: whose teeth
are spears and arrows, and their tongue a sharp sword.'[42]

'I love no one for long,' continued Haukyn. 'I tell so many
tales that nobody trusts me. And if I cannot get the better of
someone, I become liverish and have attacks of heartburn, or I
am crippled with rheumatism; and sometimes I am so exas-
perated, that it brings on an ague or a fever lasting a whole

year. And then I begin to despise the Christian doctors, and
resort to witches; and I say quite openly that no trained
doctor, not even Christ himself, can cure diseases as well as the
old cobbler-woman of Southwark, or Dame Emma of Shore-
ditch![43] "The word of God never healed me yet," I say,
"All the health and good luck I ever had, came from magic
charms!" '

Then I looked more carefully at Haukyn's coat, and
noticed that it was splashed with lustful desire, and smeared
with lecherous glances on every side. For to every girl that
he met he made some lewd sign, tempting her to sin; and
sometimes he would press her mouth to his, and begin to
fumble under her clothes, till their lusts were aroused and
they would set to work – no matter if it were a Friday, a
fast-day, or one of the forbidden nights; for all times were
alike to them, and such works were never out of season, even
in Lent. And when they were past it, they would tell one
another dirty stories, and laugh and joke about sex, gloating
in middle age over their youthful dissipations.

Then Patience noticed how parts of his clothing were
rotten with covetousness, and moth-eaten with unnatural
greed. For he loved his goods more than he loved God,
and his mind was crawling with schemes for getting more,
by false measures, false weights, and false witnesses. He
despised plain dealing, and was ever on the watch for ways of
cheating his customers. He would lend money in the hope of
keeping their pledge, and mix his wares to make a fine show,
while hiding the worst within. 'I thought this was a splendid
trick,' he said, 'and if my neighbour had a servant, or a beast,
or anything more valuable than mine, I would rack my brains
for a means of getting it from him. And if I could get it no
other way, in the end I would steal it, or secretly empty his
purse or pick his locks. So I was busy night and day heaping
up all my wealth by crooked means.

'If I went ploughing, I would skirt my neighbour's strip
so closely, that I filched a foot or a furrow's breadth of his
land; and if I were reaping, I would tell my men to reach over
with their sickles, and take in grain that I never sowed.

'And if one of my debtors wanted extra time for repayment, he would either have to bribe me secretly, or else pay a large sum cash down; so that willy-nilly I was always the gainer. Even towards my own relations I was niggardly. And I quarrelled with my customers unless they offered me more than a thing was worth, and swore by heaven and earth that it cost me far more than it did.

'When I heard Mass on holy-days, I never thought of begging God's mercy for my sins, but repented my losses much more than my lusts. For when I had lent some money and then lost it, or it was a long time being repaid, I was more disturbed than if I had committed a mortal sin. And if ever I gave any money away for charity, I would be stabbed with cruel pangs of remorse. But worst of all was when I had sent my apprentices overseas, to barter goods or exchange money in Bruges or in Prussia; for in the interval of waiting, neither Mass nor Matins, nor any kind of diversion, could comfort me; and though I performed penances and said Paternosters, my mind was always on my goods, and I could not think of the grace of God or His great providence. – "For where your treasure is, there will your heart be also." '[44]

Moreover this Glutton had spattered his garments with great oaths, and drabbled them in the slime of deceitful talk, throwing the name of God about idly, and swearing till the sweat drenched his jacket. And he had eaten and drunk more than his belly could take, and made himself so sick with surfeiting, that he was in terror of dying in mortal sin. Then he would fall into despair, and give up all hope of salvation – a sloth so deadly that no medicine can cure it, and even the infinite mercy of God cannot help such a man on his deathbed.

What are the branches of sloth that lead to despair? – When a man ceases to sorrow over his sins, and performs badly the penance which the priest has set him; when he gives no alms, and fears sin no longer, and lives against the Faith, keeping no Law; when he treats every day as a holy-day or as a major feast, and will listen to nothing but the loose talk of jesters – for it irks him to hear the name of Christ, or anything to do with holy living, and he will listen only to what is light and frivolous; and most of all when he hates those who talk of mortification or poverty, or the sufferings of the saints – these are all the branches of sloth that lead to despair. Take heed of this, you lords and ladies, and dignitaries of the Church – you who keep professional fools and flatterers and liars, laughing at their jokes and revelling in their conversation; for it is written, 'Woe unto you that laugh now! for ye shall mourn and weep.'[45] Since you give food and money to fools, and refuse the poor, I fear that when you die these jesters and tattlers will bring you much sorrow. – 'Those who connive at evil shall be punished equally with the doers thereof.'[46] And just as the patriarchs and prophets and preachers of God's word save men's souls from hell by preaching them sermons, so these flatterers and fools are the Devil's apostles, enticing men to sin by their tales and ribaldry. David said of them – and priests who know the Scriptures should tell this to their masters – 'Those whose works are proud and who speak iniquity shall not dwell in my house.'[47] So, in the halls and chambers of wise men, no ribald may have audience, nor may any vain man be allowed in their company.

Knights and scholars welcome the king's minstrels, and out of love for the king, their lord, they listen to them at their feasts. How much more, then, should the rich entertain beggars, who are the minstrels of God. For Christ says, in the Gospel of St John, 'He that despiseth you despiseth me.'[48]

So you rich men, I counsel you, at your banquets, to refresh your souls with minstrels like these: to have a poor man sitting at your high table, in place of a foolish 'wit', and a priest to sing you ballads of the sufferings of Christ, and so to save your souls from your enemy Satan; and let him, without flattering your vanity, fiddle for you the story of Good Friday. And for your jester, you should have a blind man or a bed-ridden woman, who would cry to our Lord for alms for you, and sing your praises to God. Such minstrels as these might make you truly merry, and if you would listen to them and appreciate their music, they might bring you great comfort at the hour of death. For your soul would be full of hope, knowing that you acted so towards God's holy ones.

But these flatterers and fools of yours, with their foul talk, will lead all their admirers to the banquet of Lucifer, with a song of woe sung to Obscenity, Lucifer's own fiddle.

Thus did Haukyn the Active Man soil his coat, until Conscience took him politely to task, and asked him why he had not washed or brushed it.

Book XIV

PATIENCE TEACHES HAUKYN
THE MEANING OF POVERTY

THE STORY. *Conscience tells Haukyn how to clean his suit of Baptism with Contrition, and Patience offers him spiritual food. But Haukyn, chary of their advice, asks certain questions, and in answer Patience teaches him a great deal about the virtue of poverty and its advantages over wealth. Then Haukyn, still not fully satisfied, asks for the real meaning of poverty. He is answered in a Latin quotation which has to be explained to him phrase by phrase – each one enlarging on the graces that spring from poverty. Then at last Haukyn is moved to repentance, and the poet awakes.*

'IT is the only suit I have,' said Haukyn, 'so you can hardly blame me if it is often dirty. I even have to sleep in it at night. And what is more, I have a wife and children and servants ("I have married a wife, and therefore I cannot come"),[1] who keep messing it up in spite of all I can do! It has been washed dozens of times, in and out of Lent – scrubbed with the soap of Sickness which penetrates very deeply, and so cleansed by the loss of money, that I've shuddered at the very thought of offending God or any righteous man, so far as I could help it. I've been shriven by the priest too, and he gave me as a penance, patience, and the task of feeding the poor, and told me to keep my coat clean if I wished to keep my baptismal faith.

'But, by God, I never could manage to, not for a single hour, without soiling it with some lustful glance or idle remark; and either by words or deeds or impure thoughts, I would go slobbering foully all over it from morn till night.'

'But I will teach you an act of Contrition,' said Conscience, 'that will scrape every kind of filth off your coat. First you

must use Contrition of Heart,[2] and Do-well will wash and
wring your coat through a wise confessor. Then use Contri-
tion by Word of Mouth, and Do-better will boil and beat it
till it is as bright as scarlet, and dye it with a pinch of goodwill,
with the grace of God to help you make amends. And then
he will send you to Do-best, which is Satisfaction,[3] who will
mend all the tears and make it look like new.

'And after this, the fog will never soil it again, nor the
moths destroy it, nor devils or treacherous men defile it, while
you live. And no herald or harper shall have a handsomer
garment than Haukyn the Active Man, if he follows my teach-
ing; nor any minstrel be more honoured amongst rich and
poor, than the wife of Haukyn Activa Vita, the baker.'

'And I will supply you with dough, even when the soil lies
fallow,' said Patience, 'and give you the flour that is best for
the people's souls, when there is no grain in the fields or grapes
on the vine. I will find food for all living people, and none
shall lack the things that they need most. For we should not
be too busy about our livelihood – "Take no thought for your
life, what ye shall eat, etc. . . . Behold the fowls of the air.
Your heavenly father feedeth them":[4] and again, "The patient
conquer." '

Then, with a feeble laugh, Haukyn answered lightly,
'Good gracious, anyone who relied on you would be in for a
thin time!'

'No,' answered Patience patiently, and he took from his
wallet victuals of great sustaining powers, for all kinds of
creatures. 'See, here is food enough,' he said, 'if our faith is
true. For God never gave life to any creature, without pro-
viding it with food and the means to live. There is the wild
worm beneath the wet earth, and the fish in the sea, and the
cricket in the fire; and the curlew, that lives on air, and has the
sweetest flesh of all birds, and the beasts that live on grass
and corn and on green roots. And these things teach us that
men should trust God likewise, and live through steadfast
faith and through love, as Christ bore witness –

"Whatsoever ye shall ask in my name, that will I do," and

again: "Man shall not live by bread alone, but by every word
that proceedeth out of the mouth of God." '5

But, looking to see what food it was that Patience praised so
highly, I found it was a piece of the Paternoster, *Thy will be
done*.

'Take it, Haukyn,' he said, 'and eat of it whenever you
are hungry, or numb with cold, or parched with thirst. And
then neither fetters nor the wrath of mighty lords, nor pain
nor prison can ever trouble you, for so "The patient triumph."
And if you are sober in eye and in tongue, in eating and
touching and in all your five senses, you will never trouble
yourself about corn, or wool and linen, or what you have to
drink. Nor will you fear death, but will gladly die as God wills,
through heat, or hunger or any means that He chooses; for if
you live by His law, the shorter your life the better – "He who
loves Christ has no care for this world."

'For through His Breath the beasts came forth to roam
the earth: "He spake the word, and they were created."6
Therefore men and beasts can also live by His Breath, as
the Scripture bears witness in the words that we use for a
grace –

"Thou openest thine hand:
    and fillest all things living with plenteousness."7

And it is written that for forty years the Children of Israel
lived without tilling the soil, and that out of the hard rock
there gushed a flood of water, for men and beasts to drink.
And in the time of Elijah Heaven's gates were closed and
there was no rain; yet for many years the people lived without
grain or crops. You can also read how the Seven Sleepers of
Ephesus slept for seven hundred years,8 and at last awoke,
having lived all that time without food. And again, the word
of God assures us, that if men lived in moderation there would
be no more famine in Christendom. For dearth leads Christ-
ians to treat one another cruelly, and over-plenty gives rise to
pride among rich and poor; but moderation is a virtue so
great that you cannot prize it too dearly. The sins and miseries
of the men of Sodom grew from abundance of bread and from

pure sloth – "Idleness and abundance of bread fostered the foulest sin."[9] And because they used no moderation in eating and drinking, they committed that deadly sin which so delighted the Devil. And so, for their vileness, God's vengeance fell upon them, and each of those cities sank into hell.

'Therefore let us exercise moderation, and make our faith our shield; for from faith springs contrition, as Conscience will tell you; and contrition drives away mortal sin, and converts it to venial sin. If a man were unable to speak and make his confession, contrition alone might yet bring his soul to Heaven – provided Faith witnessed that during his life he had believed the teaching of Holy Church. So Contrition, Faith, and Conscience are properly Do-well, and the surgeons for deadly sin when there is no confession.

'But for a man who is inwardly contrite, spoken confession is worth more than contrition alone. For confession to a priest will slay any sin, no matter how deadly; whereas contrition by itself can only beat down mortal sin, and reduce it to venial sin. That is why David, in Psalm 32, uses the word "covered" – "Blessed is he . . . whose sin is *covered*." But Satisfaction does more than cover sin, it seeks out its root, tears it out and destroys it, as if it had never been. And then it is like a wound completely healed, leaving no mark and causing no more pain.'

'But where does Charity live?' said Haukyn. 'I've done a good deal of travelling in my time, but I've never met a single man who has spoken with him.'

'Wherever there is perfect truth,' answered Patience, 'and patient speech and poverty of spirit, there you will find Charity, the Lord Chamberlain to God's own household.'

'Then tell me,' said Haukyn, 'is patient poverty more pleasing to our Lord than wealth honestly earned and put to good use?'

'Well, show me such a rich and just man,' answered Patience, 'and I will be the first to praise him. But I think you can read of wealthy men till Doomsday, and never find one who was not in terror at the approach of death, and who did not fall into debt at the last reckoning.

'Yet when a poor man comes to Judgement, he dares to plead with God, and give reasons why he should be treated kindly. And he claims by right, before a just Judge, the joy that he never tasted while on earth, saying: "Look at the birds and beasts, for whom there is no paradise, and the wild snakes that live in the woods: in winter-time You afflict them grievously, and make them almost tame and gentle through lack of food. But then You send them the summer, their sovereign joy, which is the Heaven of all living creatures, wild or tame."

'So like the beasts, the beggars may wait for a time of relief – men who have lived all their lives in want and sickness. For if God did not send them some kind of joy at last, Nature herself would rebel against it. For who was ever so doomed that God did not create him for joy? The angels who are now in hell were happy once, and Dives[10] once lived on the fat of the land and lapped himself in luxury. And so with all rich men and their ladies – their days on earth were spent in revelry.

'But to human reason it seems strange that God should wish to give some men their payment before they have earned it. For that is how He treats the wealthy. And it is pitiful to think how they have had their wages on earth, and that this is their Heaven – the great pleasure of living without bodily labour. For when they die they are rejected, as David says in the Psalter:

"The proud are robbed, they have slept their sleep:
    and all the men whose hands are mighty have found nothing . . ."[11]

and again, in another place:

"Yea, even like as a dream when one awaketh:
    so shalt thou make their image to vanish out of the city."[12]

Alas! that at his last end, riches should snatch away man's soul from the love of our Lord!

'For those servants who take their wages in advance are continually in need, and the man who eats before he has earned his food seldom dies out of debt. He should first do his duty, and complete his day's work; for until a workman has finished his job, no one can see what he deserves for it. If he takes money in advance, how can he be sure that his work will not be rejected? – And so I say to you rich men: it is wrong to expect heaven in your present life, and another heaven here-after, like a servant who first takes his payment in advance, and then claims it again afterwards as though he had never received it before. Such a thing cannot be – witness these words of St Matthew: "It is difficult to pass from one delight to another."[13]

'But if you rich folk have pity on the poor and reward them well, and live by the law of God and act justly to all men, then Christ in His courtesy will comfort you in the end, rewarding with double riches all who have pitying hearts. And just as a servant who has received his wages beforehand is sometimes given a further reward, a coat or a jerkin, for doing his duty well, so Christ gives Heaven both to rich and to poor, if they lead lives of mercy. And all who do their duty well shall have double pay for their labours, the forgiveness of their sins and the bliss of Heaven.

'But according to the writings of the Saints, God seldom rewards a rich man with double ease. For amongst the rich there is much revelry, with plenty of food and fine clothing; they are like the wild beasts that make merry in the May-time, their happiness lasts only as long as the summer. But the beggars sup without bread even in mid-summer, and the winter time is far more terrible for them; for then they trudge about with wet feet, famished and parched with thirst, and so foully abused that it is pitiful to hear how the rich folk spurn them and kick them out of the way. O Lord, send them their summer, and let them know some happiness, that they who suffer such want in this world may find Heaven when they leave it. For if it had so pleased You, You could have made all men equal, no man poorer than any other, and all alike clever and wise.

'And have pity, O God, on the rich, who do not reward your captives – those who are so often ungrateful for all the wealth You give them. Send them, of Your goodness, Lord, the grace to make amends. For nothing can harm such men if they have good health, neither famine nor drought, heat nor flood nor hailstorm, nor do they lack anything they could wish for on earth.

'But the poor folk, O Lord, Your prisoners, in the pit of misery – comfort these who suffer so much pain, through famine and drought, all the days of their lives; who are wretched in winter-time for want of clothing, and in summer-time can rarely get a good meal. Comfort the sorrowful ones, in Your Kingdom, O Christ, for the Scripture tells us how You comfort Your creatures –

"Come back and keep still, and all shall be well with you: in quietness and in confidence lies your strength."[14]

Such was the promise which Jesus Christ, in deigning to be born in human flesh, made to all men – robbers and thieves, rich and poor alike. And He taught us to receive Baptism in the name of the Trinity, and be cleansed by this christening from all kinds of sins. And if, through folly, we fall into sin again, then by confession and acknowledging our faults and craving His mercy, we may be restored as many times as we wish. But if the Devil should plead against this absolution and torment us with scruples, then Christ will at once take our Reprieve[15] and show it to the Evil One – "Let it be known unto all men, that through the Passion of Christ . . . etc." – and so drive off the tempter and prove our ransom.

'Yet the parchment of this Reprieve must be made of our poverty, our spotless patience, and our perfect faith; for it slips away from Pride and Ostentation, and is lost to all men but the poor in spirit. Without that virtue, all we ever wrote on it was worthless – all our Paternosters, our penances and pilgrimages to Rome; for unless we give and spend from honest motives, then all our labour is lost. See how men have their names engraved in Friary windows,[16] when the whole foundation of their giving is false! Christians should hold their riches in common,[17] and none covet anything for himself.

'There are seven sins which attack us unceasingly, and the Devil goes with them all and tries to help them; yet it is by Wealth that the old Serpent beguiles us most easily. For wherever Wealth reigns, Prestige follows and gratifies pride in rich and poor. And so, while the rich man is honoured for his riches, the poor man is pushed to the wall; though the poor may be more gifted with sense and wisdom, which are far better gifts and sooner heard in Heaven than wealth or royal blood. For the wealthy have much to account for, and they creep like snails along the highway to Heaven, weighed down by their riches – "A rich man shall hardly enter the Kingdom of Heaven."[18] But the poor on that road press forward ahead of the rich, and swing along with their bundles on their backs – "and their works do follow them."[19] And boldly and rowdily, like beggars round an almsgiver, they clamour for perpetual joy, the reward of their poverty and patience. – "Blessed be ye poor: for yours is the Kingdom of Heaven."[20]

'For Pride reigns among riches rather than poverty, and keeps his state with the master sooner than the man. But where poverty is borne with patience, Pride has no dominion, nor may any of the Seven Sins dwell there for long: they lose their power in the presence of patient poverty. For the poor man is always eager to please the rich, and will obey his wishes for a few crusts of bread. And Obedience is forever at war with Boasting, for the pair of them clash in every action of life.

'And if Anger wrestles[21] with a poor man, he gets the worst of it. If they go to law together, the poor man only speaks mildly, for by quarrelling and arguing he would get into worse trouble. A man who is forced to beg food and money from others, is always soft-spoken and obliging in his manner.

'And if Gluttony gets hold of Poverty, he gains nothing by it, for a poor man's income will not stretch to rich food. And though he longs for good ale, he must go to his chill bedding, and lie uncomfortably huddled with his bare head askew; and when he tries to stretch his legs, he finds only straw for sheets. So he suffers a heavy penance for gluttony and sloth – the wretchedness of waking up crying with the cold, or weeping perhaps for his sins. And so there is no happiness for him that is not mingled with grief and soured by misfortune.

'And if Covetousness would grapple with a poor man, the two cannot come to grips – let alone seize each other by the throat. For it is well known what a long reach Covetousness has, and what lanky arms, springing as it does from an eager craving. But Poverty is only a *petit* fellow, who hardly comes up to his navel – and there's no fun in a fight between long and short!

'And if Avarice tries to injure a poor man, he has little power, for Poverty has only sacks to keep his possessions in, while Avarice keeps them in ambries and iron-bound coffers. And which is the easier to break open, a beggar's wallet or an iron-bound chest? The wallet would surely make less of an outcry!

'And Lechery is not fond of poor men, for they have little silver to give, and do not eat rich food or drink much wine. What use are they to the whorehouses? If the only customers were poor men, the brothels would soon be roofless and fall to pieces.

'And if the poor man is pursued by Sloth and fails to serve God well, then Adversity is his teacher, reminding him that his greatest helper is not man, but God, and that Jesus is truly his servant (for He said so Himself)[22] and wears the poor man's livery. And even if God does not help him on earth, yet he knows that Jesus bears the sign of poverty, and saved all mankind in that apparel. So, at their life's end, all poor folk who are patient may ask and expect the bliss of the Kingdom of Heaven.

'And much more boldly may a man claim that bliss who, though he might have all he could wish for on earth – land and power and bodily pleasure – yet for the love of God abandons it all and lives as a beggar. He is like a maiden[23] whose love for a man causes her to forsake her mother and father and all her friends to follow her husband; – and any man who marries such a maiden should love her dearly; for she deserves more than one who is married through a broker by an agreement between parties, with money into the bargain. Such marriages are the fruit of avarice, not of mutual love; – so, like a true lover is he who forsakes his possessions and sets out to learn patience, and marries Poverty. For she is akin to God himself, and sister to his saints.'

'Well, I must say you praise poverty in good earnest,' said Haukyn. 'But what exactly *is* patient poverty?'

'*Paupertas*,' said Patience, '*est odibile bonum, remotio curarum, possessio sine calumnia, donum dei, sanitatis mater; absque solicitudine semita, sapientiae temperatrix, negotium sine damno; incerta fortuna, absque solicitudine felicitas.*'*

'I can't translate all that,' said Haukyn. 'You must teach me it in English.'

'It is very hard to explain it fully in English,' answered Patience, 'but I will teach you some of it, as far as you can understand it.

'In the first place, there is nothing on earth more hateful to Pride than Poverty, and anything which shocks Pride is bound to be good. Conscience will tell you how Contrition, though a sorrowful thing in itself, strengthens a man and gives consolation to his soul. And so Poverty, if you seek it with joy as a penance, is pure spiritual health to the body. Therefore *Paupertas est odibile bonum*, just as Contrition is the comfort and the cure for souls.

'Next, Poverty seldom sits in a bench of jurymen, and is never asked to be magistrate or mayor or an officer of the king, to judge his fellowmen. So he is rarely forced to punish others. Therefore Poverty is *Remotio curarum*, and poor men obey the commandment, "Judge not that ye be not judged."[25]

'Thirdly, a poor man seldom gains a fortune unless by rightful inheritance; nor does he make a profit with false weights or uncertified measures, nor borrow from his neighbours what he cannot easily pay back. So Poverty is *Possessio sine calumnia*.

---

*'Poverty,' said Patience, 'is a hateful blessing, the putting off of cares, possession without fraud, the gift of God, the mother of health; a narrow way without disquiet, the nurse of wisdom, business without loss; an unsettled fortune, yet a happiness without anxiety.'[24]

'Fourthly, Poverty is indeed a handsome fortune, for it restrains us from the extravagance of sin, and so makes our souls flourish. Moreover, it holds back the flesh from a host of follies, giving in return an equal comfort, which is Christ's own gift. – So it is *Donum Dei*.

'The fifth title of Poverty is Mother of Health – a friend in all trials, the country's physician at all times, and a lover of innocence. – *Sanitatis Mater*.

'The sixth is Path of Peace – and indeed, Poverty could walk even through the Alton Pass[26] without fear of robbery. For when Poverty walks, Peace follows after, and the less a man carries with him, the less is he afraid. And so Seneca says:[27] "*Paupertas est absque solicitudine semita,*" and he adds: "A poor traveller sings lightheartedly in the face of robbers."[28]

'The seventh name is Well of Wisdom, for Poverty has few words to offer, and noblemen give him little praise and seldom heed his sayings; but he trains his tongue to speak the truth, and scorns riches, and so is called *Sapientiae temperatrix*.

'Eighthly, Poverty is an honest labourer, loath to take more wages than he truly deserves, in summer or in winter. And if he buys or sells he does not mind what he loses, provided he can increase in charity. Therefore Poverty is called *Negotium sine damno*.

'The ninth gift of Poverty is sweeter than honey[29] to the soul; for patience is the bread of poverty, and sobriety is a sweet drink and an excellent medicine for sickness. Thus did the learned St Augustine[30] teach me, for the love of our Lord – that Poverty is a life without anxiety, blessed for both body and soul: *Absque solicitudine felicitas*.

'And now may God, the giver of all good, grant eternal rest to the soul of him who first wrote these things, and taught us the meaning of Poverty.'

'Alas!' said Haukyn, 'that I was not dead and buried after my Baptism, for Do-well's sake! For how wretched it is to live and commit sin. Yet sin pursues us every day of our lives' – and he grew sorrowful and wept bitterly, and bewailed every deed by which he had displeased God. And falling on his face

he sobbed, and heaving many sighs said: 'If only I had pos-
sessed no land or had no position in the world – if only I had
owned nothing, with no more control over others than I had
over myself! God knows, I have made this suit of mine so
foul, I do not deserve to have any clothes at all, not so much
as a shirt or a pair of shoes, beyond what modesty compels me
to wear.' Then he cried out earnestly for God's mercy, weeping
and wailing over his sins. And with that I awoke.

Book XV

THE PROLOGUE TO DO-BETTER:
ANIMA'S DISCOURSE ON CHARITY

THE STORY. *The poet is almost beside himself, but mercifully he falls asleep again, to meet with a ghostly creature, Anima, who has many names. Over-eager to learn from him, he is rebuked for his vain thirsting after knowledge. This leads Anima to preach against proud clerics, and show the great evils that spring from a corrupt priesthood. When he mentions charity the dreamer breaks in to ask him what this virtue is. There follows a discourse on charity, in which Anima says that only Piers, who is Christ, can make it visible. He also praises the asceticism of the Desert Fathers, laments the decay of learning, and impresses on the dreamer the responsibilities of the priesthood, especially towards the heathen.*

AFTER I awoke, I continued for many long years trying to grasp the meaning of Do-well, till I became half-crazed, and my fuddled wits would come and go like the moon. People were shocked at the life I led and rebuked me for it, looking on me as an idler and good-for-nothing. For I would not pay respect to lords and ladies, or take off my cap to the fur-clad priests in their silver trappings; and I walked past Sergeants-at-Law and other important officials without so much as a nod or 'God save you, sirs.' No wonder they took me for an idiot! And so I went raving on, till at last Reason took pity on me and rocked me gently to sleep.

Then, as if by magic, I saw a strange thing – a creature with neither tongue nor teeth, who told me exactly where I was going, where I had come from and what sort of person I was. It was some time before I could find my tongue, and then I begged him, for Christ's love, to tell me whether or not he was one of God's creatures.

'I am God's creature,' he said, 'and am known for a true

Christian in many different places. I am well known in Christ's
Court, and am one of His kin. Neither Peter, the doorkeeper
there, nor Paul with his falchion[1] will ever shut me out, how-
ever late I knock. Both at noon and midnight they know
my voice, and every member of His Court will give me a
welcome.'

'Well, what do the Christians call you up there?' I asked.

'While I animate the body,' he said, 'I am called Life;[2] but
when I will and choose, my name is Soul; and since I can
know and understand, I am also called Mind; and when I
complain to God, my name is Memory;[3] and when I make
judgements and obey the dictates of Truth, they call me
Reason; and when I hear what others say to me, my name is
Sense – and that is my first name, since intelligence and wisdom
and all the arts spring from the senses; and when I claim some-
thing or do not claim it, or when I buy or refuse to buy, then
I am called Conscience, God's scribe and notary; and when I
truly love our Lord and all my neighbours, then my name is
True Love, or in Latin, Amor; and lastly, when I flee from the
flesh and forsake the body, then I am called Spirit. Both
Augustine and Isidore[4] have given me these names – and now
that you know them all, you can choose which you prefer to
call me. All this is written in Isidore:

"The soul has different names according to its different
functions: while it animates the body, it is Life; while it wills,
it is Soul; while it knows, it is Mind; while it recollects, it is
Memory; while it consents or refuses, it is Conscience; while
it breathes and lives, it is Spirit." '

'Why, you must be a Bishop,' I said in jest, 'for they have
dozens of different titles – Ordinary, Pontiff, Metropolitan,
Diocesan, Pastor, and Lord knows how many more!'

'True enough,' he said, 'and now I see what you're after.
You would like to know the reason for all those names, and
mine too, if you could – is that what you want?'

'Yes, sir,' I said, 'as long as no one takes it amiss. Why, if
it were possible, I would like to master all branches of learn-
ing, and be skilled in every one of the fine arts.'

'Then you are an impious man!' cried he, 'and a knight in Pride's army. It was just such a craving for knowledge that caused Lucifer to fall from Heaven: "I will exalt my throne (he said) above the stars of God: I will sit in the sides of the North . . . I will be like the most High."[5] It is against Nature, and contrary to all Reason that anyone but Christ should know all things. Solomon has a word to say about men like you – he despises their wisdom –

"It is not good to eat much honey:
 so for men to search their own glory is not glory."[6]

And in plain English, that means that too much honey cloys a man's stomach, and the more good matter he hears without practising it, the more harm it does him. "Blessed is he," says St Bernard,[7] "who reads the Scripture and does his utmost to turn its words into deeds." It was a longing for knowledge and understanding that drove Adam and Eve out of Paradise – "The lust for knowledge robbed mankind of the glory of immortal life." And as honey is hard to digest and gorges the stomach, so does a man gorge his soul and lose God's gifts by seeking to grasp the source of God's power by Reason. For there is a pride lurking in this lust for knowledge, a fleshy craving opposed to the teaching of Christ and all the Fathers – that we should "not be more wise than it behoveth to be wise".[8]

'So, all you Friars and theologians who preach to the lay-folk, talking abstrusely about the Trinity[9] and stirring up questions beyond the reach of Reason, little wonder that the ignorant people are led to doubt their Faith! Most of you had far better give up teaching such stuff, and preach instead about the Ten Commandments and Seven Deadly Sins and all the branches of them that lead men to hell; and point out how men squander their senses on vanities – how Friars and other churchmen foolishly waste God's gifts, on their houses, on clothes, and on displays of learning, more to show off than for charity's sake.

'For this is the plain truth, and the people know it: you dance attendance on lords and flatter the wealthy, only for their silver. – "Confounded be all they that worship carved images, and that delight in vain gods,"[10] says the Psalmist and again:

> "O ye sons of men, how long will ye blaspheme mine honour: and have such pleasure in vanity, and seek after lying?"[11]

See what the Commentary says[12] on that verse, you great scholars, and if I've got it wrong, you can burn me at the stake! For you will refuse alms from no one, so it seems, not even from usurers, swindlers, and whores; and against your Rule and your calling, you bow and scrape to any man with money. Yet these are the words of Jesus to His disciples: "Thou shalt not respect persons, neither take a gift."[13]

'I could write volumes on this theme – the responsibility of priests for Christian souls. But at least, for Truth's sake, I must tell you what the Fathers of the Church say about it. So if you choose to listen, take heed now.

'Whereas Holy Church is the source of all holiness and truth, which spring from her through honest men who teach God's Law, yet equally, when she has a corrupt priesthood and time-serving preachers and teachers, she can also be the source of all manner of evils. For the Church is like the trees in summer-time – some boughs are covered in leaves, while others are bare; and if the boughs are bare, you know the roots of the tree are diseased. So the parsons and priests and preachers of Holy Church are the roots of the true faith, on whom the people depend; and where the roots are rotten, clearly the flowers, the fruits, and leaves will never be healthy.

'If you clerics would only have done with your passion for fine robes and would use Christ's gifts kindly and generously, as churchmen should – if you would only keep your tongues from lying and your bodies from uncleanness, and despise foul talk, and refuse to take tithes from men's wrongful gains in farming or business – then the layfolk would shrink from disobeying your words, and take upon themselves to correct wrong-doers. – And all this because you set them an example, instead of preaching what you do not practise, which looks

like hypocrisy! For in the Latin proverb[14] hypocrisy is com-
pared to a dunghill full of snakes, beneath a shroud of snow,
or to a whitewashed wall that is filthy underneath. That is
what many of you churchmen are like – whitewashed[15] with
fair words and surplices of linen, whilst underneath your
words and doings are foul.

'And therefore St John Chrysostom[16] says of priests and
clerics: "*Sicut de templo omne bonum progeditur, sic de templo omne
malum procedit. Si sacerdocium integrum fuerit, tota floret ecclesia;
si autem curruptum fuerit, omnium fides marcida est. Si sacerdocium
fuerit in peccatis, totus populus convertitur ad peccandum. Sicut cum
videris arborem pallidam et marcidam, inteligis quod vicium habet in
radice, Ita cum videris populum indisciplinatum et irreligiosum, sine
dubio sacerdocium eius non est sanum.*"**

'It would no more surprise me to find laymen translating
this Latin and naming the author, than it would to see priests
going about with Rosaries in their hands and books under
their arms, instead of wearing short-swords[17] and trinkets!
For it is quite the thing nowadays for Father John, and Mon-
signor Geoffrey, to wear silver girdles and carry daggers and
sheath-knives studded with gilt. And as for their Breviaries,
the weapons they should use for saying the Office, they wait
for someone to offer them silver before they would dream
of using them. Alas! you ignorant laymen, what vast sums of
money you squander on these priests! God in His wisdom
would never allow it if it weren't that you got your money by
fraud in the first place, and all ill-gotten gains should go to
the wicked – to worldly priests and men who preach for silver,
to all these executors, and sub-deans, and summoners and
their mistresses. So what was got by swindling goes on wick-
edness, and whores and brothel-keepers reap the benefit, while
for want of money God's people are ruined and perish.

*'Just as all good springs from the Temple, so out of the Temple
issues all that is evil. If the priesthood is sound, the whole Church will
flourish; but if it is corrupt, the faith of all men will be rotten. Likewise
if the priesthood is full of errors, the whole people turns to error. When
you see a tree mouldy and rotten, you know that it has a disease in the
roots; and so when you see a people undisciplined and irreligious, you
can be sure the priesthood is unsound.'

'And frequently, when some miserly priest has hoarded up money, he leaves it to profligates to grab as they like after his death. Or the priest dies intestate, and then the Bishop and all his henchmen enter the house and make merry with his wealth, saying, "To hell with the old skinflint! He never gave a penny away to friend or stranger, and always kept a wretched table. Now we can enjoy ourselves on his scrapings and hoardings!"

'Whenever a miser gives up the ghost, whether he's a cleric or a layman, this is always what happens to his property. But upon the death of a good man who has given food to the poor the people mourn and remember him in their prayers and penances with perfect charity.'

'What is charity?' I asked him then.

'A child-like thing,' he replied, 'for "unless you become as little children, you shall not enter into the kingdom of heaven."[18] It is a frank and generous goodwill, without folly or childishness.'

'But where can you find such an open-hearted friend?' I said. 'I have lived all over the land, and men call me Long Will,[19] but, search where I would, I have never yet found perfect charity. Folk are kind to beggars and to the poor, and will lend money where they think they will get it back. But as to the charity that is most pleasing to our Saviour and which St Paul praises above everything else, that which "vaunteth not itself, is not puffed up, and seeketh not her own"[20] – I swear to God I have never met the man who would not claim back what belongs to him, and sometimes cast a covetous eye on things not his, thinking, "I'd take that, if I got half a chance!"

'I have been told by the theologians that Christ is everywhere; yet I have never seen him in person – only His reflection in myself, as in a mirror: "For now we see through a glass, darkly; but then face to face"[21] – and from what I hear, I should think the same is true of charity. At any rate, I am sure of this, that he is not to be found in the tournaments of knights, or in the dealings of businessmen.'

'Charity never bargains,' said Anima, 'nor does he challenge

his opponents or assert his rights. He is as proud of a penny
as of a gold sovereign, and as pleased with a grey home spun
coat, as with a tunic of Tartary silk or finest scarlet. Charity
rejoices with those who rejoice, returns good for evil and trusts
and loves all whom our Lord created. He never curses and he
bears no malice, and takes no delight in slander or making fun
of others. For he trusts whatever men say and accepts it
cheerfully, bearing patiently all manner of injuries. Nor does
he covet any earthly goods, but seeks only the bliss of the
kingdom of Heaven.'

'But has he no sort of income?' I asked. 'No money, or
wealthy patrons?'

'He never gives a thought to money or income, for he is
never without a friend to provide for him in need. *Thy-will-be-
done* always helps him out, and the only supper he eats is a bowl
of *Trust-in-the-Lord*.[22] Besides, he is a skilful illuminator, and
can paint illustrations of the Paternoster and embellish it with
Ave Marias.[23]

'At other times he makes pilgrimages to the places where
poor men and prisoners lie awaiting their reprieve. And though
he takes them no bread, he brings them sweeter food, and loves
them truly as our Lord commanded, caring for their well-
being.

'And when he is tired of such work, then he will toil for
long stretches in a laundry.[24] For he plunges into the thoughts
and desires of his youth, vehemently seizes on Pride with all
its appurtenances, squeezes them together and pummels them
at his breast till they are beaten clean. Then he wrings them
for a long time with groans of penitence, crying:

"I am weary with my groaning; every night I bathe my bed:
and drench my couch with my tears."[25]

And so, with the hot tears from his eyes, he rinses them,
weeping and singing this Psalm:

"A broken and a contrite heart, O God:
shalt thou not despise." '[26]

'O God! If only I knew him!' I cried. 'He is the one I seek above all others!'

'Unless Piers the Ploughman helps you,' he said, 'you will never see him truly, face to face.'

'But surely,' I said, 'the priests who rule the Church can find him out?'

'A priest only knows men by their words and actions,' he answered. 'But Piers sees more deeply;[27] he understands the reasons and motives which make so many folk assume an air of charity – "And God saw their thoughts."[28] For there are haughty men who yet speak patiently, and whose manners are gracious towards noblemen and burgesses, but they grow peppery when they meet the poor, and glare like lions if anyone criticizes them.

'There are also beggars and tramps who look like saints, as meek as lambs and godly in their manner; yet the poverty they so glibly assume is intended rather for getting food than for mortifying the flesh and seeking perfection.

'So you will never recognize Charity by appearances,[29] or by learning, or by words and actions – but only by knowing the heart. And no one on earth, not even a priest, can know that, but only Piers the Ploughman – *Peter, that is, Christ*.[30]

'For Charity does not dwell with vagrants or with roving hermits, nor with anchorites who carry alms-boxes. These are all impostors – away with such men and all who encourage them! But Charity is God's knight-errant, as gentle in manners as a well-bred child, and full of good cheer when he takes his place at the table. For the love that is in his heart makes him sociable and friendly, as Christ himself bade us when He said, "Be not, as the hypocrites, of a sad countenance."[31]

'I have seen Charity sometimes in silk, sometimes in homespun; in sober grey, and in rich furs with trappings of gold – yet even these he gave away gladly to men who needed them. And Edmund[32] and Edward the Confessor were both kings, yet were reverenced as saints because of their charity.

'I have seen Charity singing the Psalter and reading the Gospel, I have seen him on horseback and wandering about in rags, but I have never seen him wheedling like a beggar.[33]

Most of all he prefers to walk in clean rich robes,[34] of cobweb lawn and cloth of Tartary, with tonsured head, a skull-cap and a fringe of crimped hair.[35] Once he was seen in a Friar's frock, but that was a long time ago, in St Francis's time, and since then he has seldom been known in that Order.

'He has a high esteem for the rich who lead guileless lives, and accepts their gifts of clothing, for it is written, "Blessed is the rich man that is found without blemish, and hath not gone after gold."[36] And when there are honest Councillors, he often comes to the king's court; but he keeps well away if Covetousness is among them. He also avoids the Court jesters, for they backbite and bear false witness and stir up trouble.

'You will rarely find him in the Consistory Courts pleading before the Bishop's Officer; for unless you use bribes a lawsuit there lásts for ever. Moreover, the Doctors of Canon Law make and unmake marriages,[37] dishonestly breaking the bonds that Christ and Conscience have knit.

'At one time, Charity consorted with great prelates, with Bishops and Archbishops, and shared out Christ's patrimony among the poor. But nowadays Avarice keeps the keys, reserving all the treasure for his kinsmen, his servants, and his executors – not to mention the Bishop's own offspring!

'Yet for all this I blame no one, but pray God to reform us all, and give us grace to follow Charity. For if anyone met him, they would find he shrank from condemning others. Blaming and cursing, boasting and adulation, carping, flattering, frowning and glaring, coveting and clamouring for more – all these are unknown to him, for his watchword is:

"I will lay me down in peace, and take my rest:
    for it is thou, Lord, only, that makest me dwell in safety."[38]

So he lives on the food of love, united to the Passion of Christ – neither begging nor borrowing, nor harming nor speaking ill of any man.

'Such mildness should be constant among Christians, and in all their afflictions they should lay this to heart – that whatever they suffer, God suffered more for us, and shewed us by

His example that we should take no vengeance on the foes
that deceive us, for such is the will of our Father. For it is
clear that, without God's will, Judas and the Jews could never
have crucified Jesus, nor martyred Peter and Paul or put them
in prison. But Christ suffered to show us how we too should
suffer, and He assures those who are willing to suffer like Him
that "The patient conquer."

'And this is proved many times in the Lives of the Saints,
by their poverty and mortification, and by the pain they en-
dured in hunger and heat and all manner of torments. St
Anthony, St Giles, and many more of the holy Fathers lived
their lives in the desert among wild beasts; and monks and
lay-brothers dwelt in solitude, making their homes in caves and
dens, and seldom speaking to one another. And Anthony
and Giles[39] and all the hermits of those ages (so we read in
their Legends) received their food from the birds of the air –
though not from lions and tigers! Once, however, St Giles
called a hind to his cell, and nourished himself with the milk
from that gentle creature; yet he did not call her to him every
day, but only at long intervals, to satisfy his hunger – for so
the book tells us.

'St Anthony received his bread from a bird, which brought
it to him every afternoon. And on one occasion when he had a
guest, God provided for them both.

'St Paul,[40] the first hermit, fenced himself in so thickly with
leaves and mosses, that no one could see him, and for many
years he too was fed by the birds; and later he founded the
Order of Augustinian Friars. And St Paul the Apostle, after
his day's preaching, would weave baskets[41] and earn enough
with his hands to stave off hunger. Moreover St Peter and his
companion St Andrew would go fishing for their food; some
they sold, and some they grilled for themselves, and so made a
living. And St Mary Magdalen[42] lived on roots and had only
dew to drink – but her chief food was her devotion to God
and the memory of Christ. And if I went on for a whole week,
I could not recount the names of all those who lived in this
way for many long years out of love for our Lord. And every
lion and leopard that stalked the forests, the bears and the

wild boars and all the other beasts, would fall at these hermits'
feet and caress them with their tails. And if these beasts could
have spoken, I swear they would have fed the hermits even
more readily than the birds did. For they showed them all the
gentleness that animals know, and as they roamed the forests
they would stop to lick the saints' hands and crouch down
before them.

'Yet God chose the birds to feed them, and not the beasts
of prey, in order to teach us that only gentle creatures should
feed such peaceful men; and likewise just men should provide
for men of Religion, and only the righteous give food to God's
holy ones. For noblemen and their ladies would shrink from
injustice and cease to overcharge their tenants when they
found Friars refusing to accept their money, and telling them
to take it back where they seized it from. For we are God's
birds, always depending on other birds to bring us our food.
And a simple meal, with soup and bread and thin ale to drink,
is quite enough for you monks and friars – I have read as much
in your Rule. – "Doth the wild ass bray when he hath grass?
or loweth the ox over his fodder?"[43] – those are the words of
Scripture, and here is the Comment on that verse: "The
nature of brute beasts condemns you, for they are satisfied
with their common fodder, while you, through living on the
fat of the land, are full of iniquity."[44]

'If laymen were familiar with this text, they would take
more care where they doled out their money, and think twice
before signing away all their property to monks and canons.
Alas! you lords and ladies, how ill-advised you are to deprive
your heirs of their ancestral heritage, and hand it over, for the
sake of their prayers, to men who are rich already, and specially
endowed to pray for the souls of others!

'I put it to you, who is there living today who still fulfils
this prophecy, "He hath dispensed abroad, and given to the
poor"?[45] If anyone, it must be the poor Friars! For what they
beg on their rounds they spend on their own buildings, and it
all goes to themselves and their fellow-labourers. So they
take from the haves, and give it to the have-nots!

'To what then shall I compare you wealthy clergymen and

knights and commoners? Many of you are like a man with a forest of beautiful trees, who plots and schemes to plant more trees among them! For you clothe the rich, help those that help you and give to folk who have plenty of everything. It is as though you filled a cask with river-water, and then went off with it to wet the Thames! You go to great lengths to comfort the comfortably-off, and to clothe and feed people who have as much as you have.

'But wealthy Religious are more strictly bound to feed beggars than wealthy laymen are. For it is written: "If you do not give to the poor what belongs to them, you commit sacrilege; and likewise, if you give to sinners, you are sacrificing to demons. When a needy monk accepts gifts, he must always give away more than he receives; and it is robbery for him to accept more than he needs. Moreover a monk is never truly in need so long as he has enough to satisfy nature."[46]

'So my advice to all Christian people is to build their lives on charity; for Charity, most certainly, frees the spirit, and releases many souls from Purgatory by its prayers. But today there is a great flaw in those who guard the Church, so the layfolk waver and are feeble in faith. For coins that are false may look like sterling and be stamped with the king's stamp, yet they contain a base alloy and their metal is defective. And many men are like that nowadays – they are well-spoken, they wear the tonsure and have received the sign of the King of Heaven in Baptism, yet the metal of their souls is foully debased by sin. And this false alloy is found in clergy and laymen alike, for it seems that no man loves either God or his neighbour.

'For there are so many wars and calamities and sudden tempests that weatherwise seamen have lost all faith in the skies, and scholars distrust the teaching of scientists. Moreover the astrologers, who once used to warn us of things to come, fail every day in their art. And at one time, sailors and shepherds had only to look at the sky to foretell the weather and warn men of coming storms and tempests; and the land was so dependable that farm-workers could estimate the yield of the soil from the seed they sowed, and advise their masters how much to keep, and how much to sell and give away. But now, seamen and landsmen – shepherds and sailors and farmers – are all wrong in their predictions, and can no longer choose between one course and another. And astronomers are at their wits' end, for they make a calculation from the stars, only to find things turn out the opposite.

'What is more, even Grammar, the basis of all education, baffles the brains of the younger generation today. For if you take note, there is not a single modern schoolboy who can compose verses or write a decent letter. I doubt too whether one in a hundred can read a Latin author, or decipher a word of any foreign language. – And no wonder, for at every level of our educational system you'll find Humbug in charge, and his colleague Flattery tagging along behind him. And as for dons and Divinity lecturers – the men who are supposed to master all branches of learning, and be ready to debate every question and answer every argument – I am ashamed to say that if you were to examine them tomorrow in the Arts and Sciences, they would all be ploughed!

'So there is reason to fear that the priests, like other readers, may skip over parts of the Mass and Office. But if they do (as I sincerely hope not), then our faith will make up for it, for in the Corpus Christi hymn[47] are the words "Sola fides sufficit" – faith alone is sufficient to save the ignorant.

'And that being so, many Jews and Saracens may be saved, perhaps before we are. What a pity, then, that our teachers set such a bad example, and so the layfolk go on offending God! For the Saracens have something resembling our Faith: they believe in and love one Almighty God, just as we do. But a certain man, Mohammed, led them into heresy, and this is how he did it:[48] He was originally a Christian, and since he was thwarted in his ambition to become Pope, he made his way into Syria, and there cunningly tamed a dove, feeding it by day and by night; and the corn which the dove ate he always placed in his ear. So, when he went about preaching to the people, the dove, conjured by its master, would come to his ear for food. Then he would swear that the dove was sent to him as a messenger from God to tell him what to preach, and the people would fall on their knees. So, by means of a white dove and a little ingenuity, Mohammed led men and women into heresy, and in those countries learned and ignorant still follow his doctrines.

'But since God allowed the Saracens to be led astray by a reprobate Christian priest – yet it's as much as my life is worth to tell the truth, how English priests also feed a dove, whose name is Avarice, and behave so like Mohammed that no one knows what honesty means any more.

'Every anchorite or hermit, monk or Friar, if he follows the way of perfection, is on a level with the Twelve Apostles. Surely then, the God of truth would not wish his chosen ministers to accept alms from the oppressors of honest Christians; He would wish them rather to emulate their founders, St Anthony, Dominic, Francis, and Bernard, who taught them to live on very little, in humble dwellings, with the alms that good folk gave them. For if they lived holy lives, God's grace would flourish in the world and put forth leaves,[49] and the sick would find themselves the better for their prayers, in body and soul. And besides, if they were true Religious, their prayers and mortifications would bring peace between all who were at enmity. For it is written, "Ask, and it shall be given to you; seek, and ye shall find; knock, and it shall be opened unto you."[50]

'Salt, so a good housewife will tell you, is a preservative. So, when our Lord said, "Ye are the salt of the earth,"[51] He meant that if the leaders of Holy Church were truly holy, they would be the salt to preserve Christian souls; but "if the salt have lost its savour, wherewith shall it be salted?" For fresh meat and fish, whether you boil or roast it, is tasteless without salt; likewise the soul of man is savourless when churchmen fail to set a good example. For they should be our guides, to lead us along the highway and go before us as good standard-bearers, encouraging the laggards by their own strength of character.

'If eleven holy men could convert the whole world to the true Faith, how much easier should it be with the vast army we have now – tens of thousands of divines and priests and preachers, with a Pope to rule them, all set apart to be the salt of the earth and preserve the souls of men!

'The whole of England and Wales was once heathen, until St Gregory sent missionaries to preach here. And then St Augustine, after baptizing the king at Canterbury, converted all that part of England to Christianity by his miracles, so the Histories tell us. He explained the Faith, taught them to honour the Cross and baptized men by the thousand. And his miracles and good deeds did more than his holy words; yet he did not neglect to instruct them in the meaning of Baptism and faith.

'Before newly-woven cloth is fit to wear, it has to be cleaned in fulling-mills or trodden underfoot in water; and it does not come to the tailor until it is combed with teazles, fluffed out, and thoroughly stretched. So also a new-born child, until it is christened in the name of Christ and confirmed by the Bishop, is still a heathen, for its soul is helpless and as yet unfitted for Heaven. And the word "heathen"[52] is derived from *heath*, meaning untilled land. So the heathen are like the beasts that flourish in the forests, galloping about unsaddled, wild and lawless.

'You remember the parable in St Matthew[53] about a man who prepared a feast. Well, it was not with venison or roast pheasants that he fed his guests, but with the flesh of hand-fed birds that would come when he whistled. "My oxen and fatlings are killed," he said, "and all things are ready."[54] And it was fitting that he should feed the folk whom he loved on calves' meat, for the calf is a symbol of innocence[55] in those who keep God's Laws. And as the cow feeds the calf on its own milk till it becomes an ox, so honest men are fed on love and obedience; and just as a calf hungers for sweet milk, so do men and women who are good and gentle hunger after mercy and truth.

'By hand-fed birds is meant those of God's folk who are slow to love Him unless they are taught by parables. For when poultry in a yard hear a man whistle, they follow him looking for food; and likewise simple men, who cannot reason much for themselves, only love and believe in God through the example of educated men, and trust implicitly in all their words and actions. And as poultry hope to find food by following a man's whistling, so these simple men hope to gain Heaven by running after the chirrupings of their priests.

'But the man who makes the feast is really God, inviting all men to share in His bliss. And when He chooses to honour us in this way, He warns us with the whistling of tempests and by signs from Heaven to come and feast and feed with Him for ever.

'But who are the men that excuse themselves from the feast? – they are the priests and parsons, leaders of Holy Church, who have all they could wish for on this side of the grave without working for it. For they get a tenth of the wages of every honest man's toil. I don't doubt they will be angry with me for saying this, but I have Matthew and Mark to back me up, as well as the Psalm, "Lord, remember David" – "Lo, we heard of the same at Ephrata: and found it in the wood."[56]

'For what Pope or what prelate is there today who carries out Christ's command, "Go ye into all the world, and preach the Gospel to every creature"?[57] Alas! that men should so long follow Mohammed, while the Pope ordains hundreds of prelates to preach the Gospel, and there are men with the titles Bishop of Nazareth, Bishop of Ninevah, Nephthali, Damascus, and so forth! Well then, since they enjoy such titles, why don't they go there as pastors, preaching the Cross of Christ and obeying His command – to live and die as "good shepherds that give their lives for their sheep"?[58] For those are our Lord's words, and they apply to the salvation of the Saracens as well as others. "Go ye into my vineyard,"[59] He said to His preachers, which does not mean only the Christian countries, but the heathen as well. And since Saracens, Scribes, and Jews share part of our Faith, it would be all the easier to convert them, I think, if someone would make the effort and teach them about the Three Persons of the Trinity. – "Ask, and it shall be given you."[60]

'It is piteous to read how righteous men used to live – how

they chastised their flesh, and surrendered their wills to God, and went about ill-clothed, far from their friends and kindred, with scarcely a bed to lie on and no book to read but Conscience, rejoicing in the Cross as their only riches. – "But God forbid that I should glory, save in the cross of our Lord Jesus Christ, whereby the world is crucified unto me, and I unto the world."[61]

'In those days, there was peace and plenty among rich and poor. But now – and this is still more pitiful – the cross on the back of a gold coin is worshipped above the Cross of Christ, and reverenced more than the Rood which overcame death and mortal sin. And so there is war and misery everywhere. And why? – because all we covet is the cross on the gold pieces, and the only Rood that rich men and wealthy priests worship is the one stamped on florins and threepenny-bits! One of these days, these churchmen will come to grief through their love of that cross, as the Templars[62] did before them. – Tell me, you wise men, have you never heard how those men honoured riches above truth? I dare not tell you about it, but it is enough to say that their Order was condemned by Reason and Rightful Judgement. And your avarice will be punished too, before long, and your endowments taken from you and all your pomp scattered to the four winds. For "He putteth down the mighty from their seats, and exalteth the humble and meek."[63]

'Believe me, you Bishops, if Knighthood and Public Conscience hold firmly together, you will soon lose all your lands and dominions for ever, and live as the Levites did in the Bible, "through your tithes and heave offerings."[64]

'For when Constantine endowed the Church[65] so generously, and gave it lands and vassals, estates and incomes, an angel was heard to cry in the air over the city of Rome, saying: "This day the wealth of the Church is poisoned, and those who have Peter's power have drunk venom."

'So we need an antidote strong enough to reform these prelates who should pray for peace but are hindered by their possessions. – Then take their land from them, you nobles, and let them live on their tithes! For surely, if property is a deadly poison that corrupts them, it would be good for Holy Church's sake to relieve them of it, and purge them of this poison before it grows more dangerous.

'If the priesthood were sound, all those people that oppose Christ's Law and despise Christendom would be converted. For the Saracens all pray to the same Almighty God, fully believing in Him and asking His grace; only they beseech Mohammed to intercede for them. Thus they live with a true faith, but a false mediator, and this is a sad thing for the righteous ones who belong to God's Kingdom, as well as a threat to the Pope and the prelates he makes – the so-called Bishops of Bethlehem and Babylon!

'When the King of Heaven sent His Son to this earth, He wrought many miracles to convert mankind. In this way He showed us that we can never be saved by sober reason, but only by grace and mercy, by mortification, suffering, and perfect faith. So God took man's nature by a Virgin, and became our great Archbishop, baptizing and confirming with His Heart's Blood all who would believe in Him in their souls. And since then, many saints have suffered martyrdom to establish this Faith, dying terrible deaths in India, Egypt, Armenia, Spain, and many other lands. And St Thomas à Becket was martyred to save the Faith, dying among treacherous Christians for the love of Christ, and for the rights of this and every other Christian land. And Holy Church is honoured by his death, for he is a pattern and a bright mirror for all Bishops – especially those with the titles of pagan cities, who have nothing better to do than to gallivant around England, consecrating altars and creeping in amongst the parish priests to hear folk's confessions, which is against the Law of God, "Thou shalt not move a sickle into a neighbour's standing corn."[66] And at Rome, many people were martyred before ever the Cross was honoured there, or the Church established.

'Every Bishop who carries a crozier is thereby bound to travel through his diocese and show himself to his people. And he must teach them to believe in the three Persons of the Godhead, and feed them with spiritual food and provide for the poor. For it is to men like you Bishops that Isaiah and Hosea are referring, when they say that no one should be a ruler unless he has both bodily and spiritual food to give to the needy: "In my house is neither bread nor clothing: make me not a ruler of the people."[67] And for the sake of the sick and feeble, Hosea says, "Bring ye all the tithes into the storehouse, that there may be meat in my house."[68]

'God forbid that we Christians, who believe in the Cross, should ever waver in our beliefs, or lack priests to keep us and our children firm in the Faith. For the Jews possess a true Law, which God himself engraved on stone so that it should be steadfast and last for ever. "Love God and your neighbour" is the perfect Law of the Jews, and God gave it to Moses to teach to men until the Messiah came. So to this day the Jews follow that Law and believe it to be the best.

'The Jews, moreover, acknowledged Christ as a true prophet, although He taught them the Christian Faith, for He cured people of many diseases. And they saw for themselves all His signs and miracles, how He feasted five thousand people with five loaves and two fishes; and by that feast alone they could see He was like the Messiah they awaited. Why, before their very eyes He raised Lazarus from the grave, whose body lay under a tombstone, dead and stinking, and called him with a loud voice, saying, "Lazarus, come forth,"[69] and the dead rose and walked in the sight of the Jews. Yet they swore that Christ did it by sorcery, and they planned to destroy Him – and so to destroy themselves also, for His patient endurance brought their power to nothing – "The patient conquer."

'The prophet Daniel had already prophesied their undoing, for he said, "When the holy of holies shall come, your anointing shall cease."[70] Yet still those poor wretches think that Christ was a false prophet and His teaching lies, despising it all, and expecting that their Saviour, whether Moses again or Messiah, is still to come – for so their Rabbis continue to prophesy.

'But Pharisees, Saracens, Scribes, and Greeks all have this faith at least – that they worship God the Father. And since they know the first clause of our Creed, "I believe in God the

Father Almighty," the Bishops of Christian countries should try hard, step by step, to teach them the second, "And in Jesus Christ His only Son" – and so on, until they can spell out "I believe in the Holy Ghost," and read and remember it together with "The forgiveness of sins, the resurrection of the body, and the life everlasting. Amen." '

Book XVI

THE TREE OF CHARITY AND THE
DREAMER'S MEETING WITH FAITH

THE STORY. *The dreamer is told that Charity is a precious tree, growing under Piers' direction in the garden of man's body. On hearing the name of Piers, he faints with joy, and falls into a deeper dream in which Piers himself shows him the tree and explains it to him. At the dreamer's request, Piers knocks down some of the fruit, and as it falls the Devil snatches it up and carries it away. Piers pursues the Devil, and the dream dissolves into a vision of the life of Christ, from the Annunciation to His victory over the Devil on the Cross. Then the dreamer awakes from his deeper dream, and sets out eagerly to look for Piers. He soon meets with Abraham, or Faith, who is searching for Christ, and who explains to him the doctrine of the Trinity. But as the dreamer is staring in wonder at the souls of the patriarchs playing in Abraham's bosom, he notices another man running in the same direction as himself, and turns to question him.*

'MAY Heaven reward you for your excellent teaching,' I said. 'I shall always love you now, for Haukyn's sake. But I am still in doubt about the meaning of Charity.'

'Charity,' said Anima, 'is a precious tree,[1] with a root of Mercy and a trunk of Pity. Its leaves are the steadfast words of the Church's Law, and its blossoms are humble speech and gentle looks. The tree itself is called Patience or Poverty of Spirit, and, by the labour of God and of good men, it bears the fruit of Charity.'

'I would gladly go on foot through half the world,' I said, 'to have a sight of that tree, and I would eat dry bread for the rest of my life, if only I could have my fill of its fruit. Great God, is there no one who can tell me where it grows!'

'It grows,' he replied, 'in a garden planted by God, for its root springs from man's body and its soil is the Heart. The land is leased to one Free Will, whose job is to hoe and weed it under Piers the Ploughman.'

'Piers the Ploughman!' I cried, and fainted with sheer joy on hearing his name. And so I lay for a long time in a lonely dream, till at last it seemed that Piers the Ploughman came himself and showed me the whole garden, bidding me examine the tree from its roots upwards. And noticing that it was supported by three props, I said to Piers, 'Piers, what are these three props doing here?'

'They are to keep it from falling in windy weather,' he said. 'For it is written, "Though a good man fall, he shall not be cast away: for the Lord upholdeth him with his hand."[2] But for the help of these three staves, the flowers would all be nipped off in blossom-time. For the World, an evil wind – for so it is to those that seek after Truth – breeds in the tree a worm of Covetousness, which creeps about among the leaves and, alluring men with countless attractions, eats away at the tree close to the fruit. So I then seize the first stave, the power of God the Father, and knock down Covetousness with it.

'The Flesh is also a fierce wind, laden with lust and pleasure – a wind which blows so loud in blossom-time that it breeds lustful glances and lascivious words, which break out into evil deeds or worms of sin; and these will eat the blossoms down to the bare leaves. Then I rely on the second stave, the Wisdom of God the Father, which is the Passion and the power of our Lord Jesus Christ. So, through prayers, through penance, and through thinking on the Passion of Christ, I keep the tree safe until it is partly fruited.

'But as soon as the fruit begins to ripen, the Devil, with all the wiles that he knows, will strive to destroy it. He will give the tree a violent shake from beneath, or throw up at the fruit anything he can lay hands on – unkind neighbours, brawlers and wranglers, backbiters out to make trouble – and will set up a ladder against it, with rungs made of lies, and will sometimes carry off my flowers before my very eyes. For a time, my deputy Free Will, whom I have appointed to guard the tree, resists the Devil single-handed. For it is written, "Whoever speaketh against the Holy Ghost, it shall not be forgiven him,"[3] and to speak against the Holy Ghost means to sin of one's own free will, making no effort to resist the temptation. So when the Devil, side by side with the World and the Flesh, threatens to steal my fruit behind my back, then Free Will seizes the third stave, the grace and strength of the Holy Ghost, beats down the Devil and gains the victory for me.'

'God bless you, Piers,' I said, 'for explaining the uses of these staves so clearly. But I still have many questions to ask about them. Where did they grow originally – what forest have they come from? For it looks to me as if they sprang from the same root:[4] they are all of exactly the same length and thickness, and have the same fresh colour.'

'You are right, it may well be as you say,' said Piers. 'I will tell you about it briefly – the ground where it grows is called Goodness,[5] and as for the tree itself – haven't I told you its name already? – it is a symbol of the Trinity' – and with that he looked at me so keenly that I dared not question him any further about it. So I asked him politely if he would describe the tempting fruit that hung from its branches.

'Here, on the lowest branches,' said Piers, 'within my reach whenever I need it, is a fruit named Marriage[6] – a very juicy one too. Nearer the top, some sweet pears have been grafted on, and they are called Continence. At the very top is the purest fruit of all, a part of the natural stock, and its name is Virginity (for virgins are as high as the angels of Heaven). It is the quickest to ripen, and is very sweet although it never swells, and will never go sour.'

Then I begged Piers to pluck down an apple, if he would, and let me try its taste. So he threw something at the top of the tree, and at once it began to weep; and he shook the branches where Widowhood grew, and they also wept. But when he stirred the lowest branches, Marriage made such a fearful cry and wailed so bitterly that I began to pity it. For as the fruits kept dropping down, the Devil stood waiting to carry them all off. He heaped them together, big ones and small indiscriminately – Adam, Abraham, Isaiah the prophet, Samson, Samuel, and St John the Baptist – and carried them boldly away, for there was no one to stop him. So he made a hoard of holy men in the Limbo of Hell,[7] where there is darkness and terror and only the Devil is master.

Then Piers, in sheer rage, seized the middle stave (the one which, by the Father's will and the grace of the Holy Ghost, is called the Son), and, going in pursuit of the Devil, hit out at him recklessly – determined to rob the coward and snatch the fruit from him.

And then the Holy Ghost, through the mouth of Gabriel, spoke to a humble virgin named Mary, saying: 'One Jesus the son of a Judge, must sleep in your room for a while, to await "the fullness of time"[8] when Piers' fruit has flowered and ripened. Then he will fight for the fruit, and force of arms shall decide whether he or the Devil shall have it.'

The virgin humbly gave her consent, and said courteously to God's messenger: 'Behold me His handmaid, free from all sin and ready to do His will – *Ecce ancilla domini*; *fiat mihi secundum verbum tuum.*'[9]

When He had been in her womb for forty weeks, Jesus was born of her flesh, and became a child; and He grew so skilled in arms that He could have fought with the Devil long before the appointed day. But Piers the Ploughman,[10] knowing that Jesus must await the fullness of time, taught Him the art of healing, so that He might be able to cure Himself and save His own life if He were wounded by His enemies. And he made Him test His powers on those that were sick, until He became perfect in the art of healing and fully equipped for every peril. So He sought out and healed the sick and the sinful, cured the blind and deformed, and converted even the common whores to goodness – 'For they that be whole need not a physician, but they that are sick.'[11] And though He cured so many – of leprosy, of dumbness, and of issues of blood – He thought little of His own skill and made light of it, save only once, when he raised Lazarus to life, a man who had lain four days in the grave. For then, as He began to exert His power, He was overpowered with grief[12] and the bystanders saw the tears fall from His eyes.

And of those who witnessed this miracle, some hailed Him as the Physician of Life and the Lord of Heaven. But the Jews refuted them, and quoted their laws to prove that He did it by sorcery and the power of the Devil. 'He hath a devil,'[13] they said, 'and He is mad.'

'Then you, and all your children, are slaves,' answered Jesus. 'Satan is your Saviour[14] – you have just admitted it yourselves. For it is I that have saved you and your children – saved your bodies, saved your beasts, given sight to your blind, and fed you so well with five loaves and two fishes that whole baskets-full were left for the scavengers' – And He abused the Jews to their faces, fearlessly, and threatened them with a whip and lashed them, knocking over the stalls of the money-changers[15] and those who bought and sold in the Temple. And openly, in the hearing of them all, He uttered these words: 'I shall dash this Temple to the ground and destroy it entirely, and build it again completely in three days, larger and more spacious than it was before. I command you therefore to call this place a house of prayer and perfection: "My house shall be called a house of prayer." '[16]

Then the Jews, filled with envy and malice, planned to destroy Him as soon as they got a chance; and they waited day after day till at last, on the Friday before the Feast of the Passover, they saw their opportunity.

On the previous day, Maundy Thursday (the day on which He washed His disciples' feet), Jesus had spoken to His disciples as He was sitting at supper, saying, 'I have been sold by one of you – one who will live to curse the day that he bartered his Saviour for silver.' And though Judas argued with Him, Jesus told him plainly that he was the one – '*Tu dicis* – Thou sayest it.'[17] So the traitor went out and, meeting with the Jews, gave them a sign by which they could recognize Jesus – a sign that is used to this day only too often, the smile and flattering kiss[18] that hides an evil motive. So this wretch Judas betrayed his master: 'Hail, Rabbi!' he said, and went right up to Him and kissed Him in order that the Jews might seize and kill Him.

Then Jesus said to Judas and the Jews, 'I see only falsehood in your flattery, guile in your pleasant looks and gall in your laughter. Your flattery shall be like a mirror,[19] and deceive many who think as you do; but it shall be the worse for you, Judas, and all your wickedness shall fall upon yourself. "For it must needs be that offences come; but woe to that man by whom the offence cometh!"[20] But now that you have your wish and I am captured by your treason, leave my apostles in peace and let them leave me.'[21]

So, after dark on that Thursday, He was taken by Judas and the Jews – the same Jesus who, on the following Friday, fought for us in the lists at Jerusalem, and brought joy to all mankind. For on the Cross on Calvary Christ did battle against Death[22] and the Devil, and broke the power of both; and by dying He destroyed Death, and turned night into day . . .

With that I awoke, rubbed my eyes, and stared all about me looking for Piers the Ploughman. I searched for him eagerly East and West, and set out like a madman to scour the country for him. But on mid-Lent Sunday,[23] after searching in many places, I met a man as white as a hawthorn, and his name was Abraham. So I asked him where he had come from, where he lived, and where he was making for.

'I am Faith,' he said. 'I would not deceive you. I am a herald-of-arms of the house of Abraham, and am looking for a man whom I have seen once before – a bold, young novice-in-arms whom I knew by his coat-armour.'

'What coat-of-arms does he bear?' I said. 'Tell me, I beg you!'

'It consists of three persons in one body, all of the same height and breadth and power. What one of them does, they all do, yet each acts of his own accord. The first possesses power and majesty: He is the Creator of all things, and by himself He is called the Father. The second, who is the Son of that Father, is called Truth, the guardian of His Father's wisdom,[24] and He too is without beginning. The third is called the Holy Ghost, and He is also a separate Person – the light of all that lives on land or sea, the Comforter of God's creatures, and the source of all happiness.

'Three things are necessary[25] for a lord who claims men's allegiance: the first is power, the second is a medium through which to show forth his power (and also that of his servant), and the third is that which he and his servant suffer.[26] So God, who had no beginning (for that could only have been when He himself chose), sent forth His Son for a while in the form of a servant, to engage himself here on earth until children were born – that is to say, children begotten by Charity, and whose mother was Holy Church. These children were the patriarchs, the prophets, and the apostles, and also Christ, the Christian Faith, and the Christian people of Holy Church. These groups of three are types of the Trinity[27] and of the true Faith. And this means that men must believe in one God, but a God who, whenever He fashioned a thing in his own likeness or loved any creature, revealed himself as three persons. The nature of man himself proves this, for the three different states of life, wedlock, widowhood, and virginity, all proceed from one man, Adam; and so mankind is in himself a type of the Trinity. Or again, Adam was the father of us all, Eve proceeded from Adam, and their issue sprang from them both – thus, on earth as in heaven, there are three separate persons, each the delight of the other, and yet having one, single nature. Manhood, therefore, springing as it does from marriage, betokens the Trinity.

'And marriage,[28] since its function is to multiply the earth, is a symbol of God's power, and denotes (if I dare say such a thing) God the Father of Heaven, the Creator of all things. And furthermore (if I may say so), God the Son resembles the state of a widow. For when He said: "My God, my God, why hast Thou forsaken Me?"[29] He spoke in His human nature, or in other words, as the Creator changed into the creature, to experience the lives of both. And just as there could be no widow without wedlock, so God could never have become a man unless He first had a mother.[30] By the same token, any marriage without lawful issue is scarcely worthy of the name of marriage – "Accursed is the man who has not left seed in Israel."[31] So manhood, in its completeness, consists of three persons, a man, a wife, and their lawful children; but in heaven there is only one source of generation. The Father begets the Son, and Free Will springs from them both – "The Holy Ghost proceeding from the Father and the Son." Yet they are all but one God.

'And that is how I saw Him once,[32] as I sat in my porch on a summer's day. I arose, bowed down to Him, greeted Him with every courtesy, and entertained Him as well as I could. Yet it seemed to me that there were three men present, not one. I washed and wiped their feet, and they ate some veal and milk loaves with me, and were aware of all that I was thinking.

'Sure tokens have passed between God and myself, which I may speak of freely. First, He tested me to see whether I loved Him or my son Isaac better, and He found out what was my true mind towards Him. I am sure in my soul that He will commend me, and my son too, for this. Then it was for His sake that I circumcised my son Ishmael;[33] and I too, with all the male members of my household, shed my blood for the love of God, hoping in His promises. All my trust and faith are fixed on this hope, for He promised,[34] to me and all my issue, not land and dominion merely, or eternal life, but a further thing – the forgiveness of all our sins as many times as we asked.

' "As He spake to our fathers, to Abraham, and to his seed for ever."[35]

'Then He sent me a message that I must do Him sacrifice[36] and worship Him with bread and wine; and He called me the first stone of His Faith – a faith that would save the people and preserve those who put their trust in me from Satan. So I have always been His herald, on earth and in hell, and have comforted many suffering souls[37] that wait there for His coming.

'And that is why I am seeking Him,' Abraham said. 'I have heard recently that a man, John the Baptist, has baptized Him. And this man has told the souls in hell,[38] the patriarchs and prophets, that he has seen the Lord, who will save us all, walking on this earth. – "Ecce agnus dei – Behold the Lamb of God, which taketh away the sin of the world." '[39]

I was amazed at his words, but even more at his ample garments. For there was something which he carried in his bosom and blessed continually as he spoke. So I had a look, and saw a leper lying there, with a host of prophets and patriarchs all making merry together.

'What's the matter?' he said. 'Is there something you are after?'

'I should like to know, if you please, what you've got in your lap.'

'Then look!' he said, and showed me.

'Good heavens! that must be a priceless gift. What king are you intending it for?'

'It certainly is a precious gift,' he replied, 'but alas, the Devil has claimed it for himself! – Yes, and me with it! What is more, he won't accept any pledge to buy us back, nor let anyone get us out of his power by standing bail. No ordinary ransom can buy us out of the Devil's pound, not until the Christ of whom I was speaking comes to fetch us. But one day He will deliver us, and lay down a better pledge than we could ever deserve – His life for ours. But unless such a Lord comes to fetch us, these folk will lie like this, lolling about in my lap for ever.'

'Alas!' I said, 'to think that sin should hinder the power of God's mercy for so long, that mercy which is enough to make amends for us all!' – and I wept at Abraham's words. Then suddenly I saw another man, running quickly in the same direction as ourselves. So I asked him what he was called, where he had come from, and where he was going, and he readily answered me.

Book XVII

THE DREAMER MEETS WITH HOPE
AND CHARITY

THE STORY. *The second man whom the dreamer meets is Hope, or Moses, carrying the Tables of the Law; and he also is seeking for Christ. While the dreamer is hesitating whether to believe in Abraham or Moses, they are overtaken by a Samaritan riding a mule, and at the same moment, they all notice a wounded man lying by the roadside. Faith and Hope hurry by on the other side, but the Samaritan stops to help him and takes him to an inn. Then as the Samaritan spurs on towards Jerusalem, the dreamer catches him up and offers himself as his servant. He tells the dreamer the meaning of the events on the road, explains Faith's doctrine of the Trinity more clearly and says that he must believe in both Faith and Hope. Then the dreamer awakes.*

'I AM Hope, a scout,'[1] he said, 'and I am searching for a knight who gave me a Law on Mt Sinai, and told me to use it in ruling all nations. I carry the document here.'

'Is it sealed?' I asked. 'May one see what the writing says?'

'No,' he replied, 'but I am looking for the man who keeps the great seal – the seal whose impress is Baptism and Christ hanging on the Cross; and as soon as this writ is sealed with that seal,[2] Lucifer's power will come to an end.'

'Let us see your parchment,' I said, 'and learn what is contained in the Law.'

So he pulled out his charter, which was a piece of solid rock; and on it were inscribed two short precepts – 'Love God and love your neighbour' – and that was the whole text, for I took careful note of it. But beneath it, splendidly inscribed in gold lettering, was this commentary: 'On these two commandments hang all the Law and the prophets.'[3]

'Are these, then, all your lord's laws?' I asked.

'Yes, indeed they are,' he replied, 'and I promise you, you

need not fear the Devil, and Death will hold no perils for you if you live by these laws. I have saved tens of thousands of men and women with this charm – though I say it myself.'

'He is telling the truth,' said the herald; 'I have often witnessed the fact myself. See, here are some of those who believed in his charm, sitting in my lap here – Joshua, Judith, Judas Maccabaeus – and sixty thousand more whom you can't see.'

'Your words astound me,' I said. 'How can I tell which of you to believe – which of you to trust to save one's soul? Abraham says that he saw the Holy Trinity – three distinct persons who are all one God – and that is what he taught me to believe. And you can't deny that he has saved thousands, simply because they believed what he taught them and repented of their sins – far more than he can count; and some of them are here in his lap at this moment. So why is there any need to start a new Law, if the first is enough by itself to bring men to Heaven and its bliss? Yet this Hope comes along claiming to have discovered the Law, and tells us nothing about the Holy Trinity who gave him his Law – the Law which tells us to love and trust one Almighty God, and on top of that to love all men as ourselves!

'A man who walks with one stick obviously gets along better than one with two. So it follows that an ignorant man, who can scarcely grasp the simplest of lessons, will not take so easily to two. It is surely hard enough to believe in Abraham, without having to love one's neighbours, rogues and all! That is expecting too much of any man. So for goodness' sake be off with you!' I said to Hope. 'Those who learn your law won't practise it for long!'

As we went on our way arguing together, we saw a Samaritan[4] sitting on a mule. He was riding the same way as we were, as fast as he could go – from Jericho to a tournament in Jerusalem.

At the place where he caught up with Hope and the herald, there was a man who had fallen among thieves, lying wounded. He was stretched out prostrate, unable to stir hand or foot to help himself, more dead than alive, and as naked as a needle, with no one to help him. Faith, the first to see him, ran by on the other side, careful not to go within twenty yards. Then Hope came jogging along – the man who had just boasted of all the folk he had saved through the Law of Moses – and catching sight of the wounded man he started aside in panic, like a duck from a falcon.

But the Samaritan, as soon as he saw him, jumped down from his horse and, leading it by the bridle, went up and looked at his wounds. He felt his pulse, and found that unless he could be brought round quickly he might never stir again. So he rushed for his two bottles, opened them hastily, and washed the man's wounds[5] with wine and oil, then anointed him and bandaged up his head. And laying him across his lap he mounted his horse and carried him to an outlying hamlet called Lex Christi, six or seven miles from the New Market-town. Here he lodged him at an inn, and called out to the inn-keeper, 'Take this man and look after him until I return from the tournament. Here is some money to buy ointment for his wounds.' Then he gave him twopence more for the man's keep, adding, 'If he spends anything over and above this, I will make it right with you when I come back. I can't stop now' – and with that he bestrid his horse and dashed off along the road that leads straight to Jerusalem.

Faith, who hoped to meet him, went in pursuit at once, and Hope dashed after him too, for he was anxious to talk with him before they reached the town. And when I saw this, I could not wait, but ran full tilt and caught up with the Samaritan who was so full of compassion, and offered myself as his servant.

'Thank you,' he said, 'but you will find in me a friend and a companion in need rather than a master.'

Then I thanked him, and told him how Faith and Hope had fled away at the sight of the poor man who was robbed.

'You must excuse them,' he said. 'Their help would have been of little use. No medicine on earth, not even Faith and Hope, can heal that man; his wounds are so festered. The only cure is the blood of a child born of a virgin. Once he is bathed or baptized in that blood, and treated with plasters made of the penance and passion of that child, he will stand and walk again. But still he will never be strong, until he has eaten the whole child and drunk its blood.[6]

'No one on earth, whether on foot or horseback, has ever passed[7] through this wilderness without being robbed, save only Faith, Hope, and myself – and now you too, and others who follow our example. For there are outlaws lurking in the woods and hiding under the banks, who can see every man who passes. They note carefully who goes in front and who follows behind, which men are riding on horseback and which are on foot – for a man on horseback is bolder than one on foot. That is why, when their chief saw me, a Samaritan, following Faith and Hope on my horse named the Flesh (I took it from mankind), the scoundrel took fright and hid himself in hell. But I promise you he will be in fetters in less than three days from now, and will never again molest those who pass this way. – "O Death, I will be thy death."[8]

'Then Faith will be the keeper here,[9] and will walk through this wood showing the way I went to common folk who do not know the country; he will direct them on the path to Jerusalem. And Hope will be the inn-keeper's man, at the hostel where I took the wounded man to be healed. He will look after all the faint-hearted and feeble whom Faith cannot teach, leading them gently on by the love that his own Law commands. He will give them lodging, and heal them through the faith of Holy Church, until I return with a cure for all the sick. Then I shall come through this country again, bringing comfort to all who crave and cry out for my medicine. For the child of whom I spoke is already born in Bethlehem – He whose blood will save all who live in Faith and follow the teaching of Hope.'

'Ah! my dear Master!' I said, 'Must I then believe what both of them taught me, Faith and his companion? For according to Abraham, I must believe in three eternal persons, all distinct and yet one God, and Hope taught me to love one God above all things, with my whole soul, and then to love all men as I love myself.'

'Fix your faith firmly,' he said, 'on Abraham's teaching, but obey Hope's commandments as well; for I also command you to love your fellow-Christians as you love yourself. And if Conscience, or Common Sense, or heretics with their arguments should speak against your Faith, then show them your hand; for God is like a hand. Listen now, and learn in what way.

'The Father, in the beginning, was like a fist, with one finger folded. Then, at His choosing, He unfolded His finger, putting it out by the power of His palm in the direction He wished it to go. For the palm is really the hand itself; it puts out the fingers to give or make such things as the power of the hand approves. The palm, therefore, signifies the Holy Ghost. The fingers, which are free either to fold themselves up or to serve the hand, betoken the Son, who was sent to the earth to touch the Virgin Mary and so take human flesh – "Who was conceived by the Holy Ghost, born of the Virgin Mary."

'So the Father is a fist, having a finger with which to touch all that the palm chooses to handle – "I will draw all things unto myself."[10] Thus they are all three but one, as a hand is one – three different manifestations in one appearance. And just as the palm puts forth fingers and fist, so also the Holy Ghost shows forth the Father and the Son. And just as the hand, with its four fingers, thumb, and palm, holds everything hard in a tight grip, so the Father, the Son, and the Holy Ghost grasp the whole, wide world between them – sky and wind, water and earth, heaven and hell and all that they contain.

'Thus it is clear (and there is nothing contrary to reason in this) that our Lord of Heaven has three different forms, each of them a separate Being, yet never apart, any more than my hand can move apart from my fingers. And as my fist is really a whole hand folded up, so the Father alone is a whole God, a shaper and a creator – "the maker of all things", whose power consists entirely in works of creation. The fingers also form a complete hand, and their special skill is in drawing and painting, carving and making designs. So the Son is the skill of the Father, and is himself fully God like the Father, neither weaker nor stronger than He. The palm is the hand itself, and it has a power of its own, independent of that of the closed fist and fingers. For it has the power to open all the joints and unfold the knuckles; and when it feels the fist and the fingers grasp anything, it can either hold it or let it fall. So the Holy Ghost is also God, neither greater nor lesser than the Father and Son, and having the same power as they. Yet all three are but one God, just as my hand – fingers, fist, and palm, folded or unfolded – is but one hand, whichever way I turn it.

'But a man who is hurt in the middle of his hand can grasp nothing; for the pain in his palm causes the fingers, which should be able to clench and form the fist, to lose their power, so that they cannot clutch or grip. If, then, my hand were maimed or pierced in the middle, I could retain nothing that I tried to grasp. But if, on the other hand, my thumb and fingers were torn to shreds, I could still help myself in many ways, provided the middle of my hand was unhurt – I could move and gradually recover, though all my fingers were throbbing. I see in this evidence of the fact that whoever sins against the Holy Ghost will never be forgiven on earth or hereafter – *"Qui peccat in Spiritum Sanctum, numquam . . . etc."*[11] For he who "blasphemes against the Holy Ghost" pricks God as it were in the palm. – For God the Father is like the fist, the Son is like the finger, the Holy Ghost like the palm; so whoever sins against the Holy Ghost injures God in the place where He grips, and deliberately murders His grace.[12]

'The Trinity can also be compared to a torch or taper, which consists of wax and wick twined together, and a flame that flares from them both. And just as this wax, wick, and flame are used to light a fire, so the Father, the Son, and the Holy Ghost kindle among Christian people a fire of love and of faith which cleanses them from their sins. And as you sometimes see a torch whose flame is suddenly blown out, yet whose wick continues to smoulder without setting fire to the matchwood, so the Holy Ghost is a God without mercy, and a Grace without life, to all those so depraved as to wish to quench true love,[13] or destroy the very life which our Lord created.

'Workmen who stay awake on winter nights are not cheered so much by glowing embers as they are by a blazing torch, or by a candle, or anything that gives out a flame. So, the Father, the Son, and the Holy Ghost do not grant men grace or forgiveness of sins, till the fire of the Holy Ghost begins to burn and to blaze. For the Holy Ghost glows but as an ember until true love lies down by His fire and blows it into flame; and then He flares out like a living fire, and warms the Father and the Son and melts their power into mercy. - So, in winter, you can see icicles on the roofs of houses, which, once they feel the heat of the sun, melt in a minute into mist and water; and in the same way the grace of the Holy Ghost melts into mercy the great might of the Trinity - but only for those who practise mercy themselves.

'And as wax alone will flare up into a blaze when it is put on a glowing ember, and gladden the hearts of men who sit in darkness, so the Father alone will forgive folk of humble heart provided they sorely repent and pay all they can in restitution. And if any man dying in such a mind cannot pay enough to make satisfaction, then Mercy will take his meekness into account and pay the rest for him.[14] And again, just as a lighted wick alone will make a warm flame and cheer men who sit in darkness, so Christ also, if we beg for His mercy, will graciously forgive and forget, and furthermore pray to the Father of Heaven for our forgiveness.

'But you can go on striking a light from a flint for ever, and all your labour will be wasted unless you have some tow or tinder or sticks to catch the sparks. For a spark cannot kindle a flame without something akin to itself, something inflammable, to catch on to. So also the Holy Ghost is a God without mercy and a dead grace, to all vicious natures; Christ himself bears witness of this - "Verily, I say unto you, I know you not."[15] For though you pray, and give alms, and do penance day and night without ceasing, and though you gain every available indulgence and purchase all the pardons of Pampeluna[16] and Rome, yet if you are unkind or ungrateful towards your fellowmen, it will profit you nothing: the Holy Ghost will never hear or help you. For unkindness quenches His light so that He cannot shine or burn or blaze at all. St Paul the Apostle proves me right in this: "Though I speak with the

tongues of men and of angels, and have not Charity, I am be-
come as sounding brass, or a tinkling cymbal."[17] Beware,
therefore, you wise men whose business is with the world, you
who are rich and intelligent – rule your souls well and do not
be callous to your fellow-Christians! For many of you, they
say, are like beacons that give no light: you burn, but you do
not blaze. – "Not everyone that saith unto me, Lord, Lord,
shall enter into the kingdom of heaven."[18]

'When Dives[19] died he was damned for his heartlessness in
not giving food and money to men in need. So I counsel all
rich men to remember Dives, and give their wealth back to
God from whom all our gifts come. He who is unkind to
God's people may expect to spend eternity with Dives. For
unkindness is the contrary of God; it quenches the grace of
the Holy Ghost, which is God in His very essence. What Nat-
ure creates, unnaturalness or unkindness destroys. What can
we say, then, of those cursed, vicious thieves who, out of
covetousness and envy, will slay a man for his goods – no
matter whether they do it with their own hands or by the
slander of their tongues? For they destroy that which belongs
to the Holy Ghost – life and love and the flame of man's body.[20]
For every good man may be compared to a torch or a taper,
offered, in adoration, to the Holy Trinity. My conscience is
clear on this point: that if anyone murders a good man, he
destroys the light that our Lord loves most dearly.

'There are many other ways in which men sin against the
Holy Ghost, but this is the worst – to destroy deliberately, for
the sake of any kind of gain, that which Christ bought so
dearly. How can a man ask for mercy, or how can mercy help
him, who would wickedly and wilfully extinguish mercy?
For Innocence, which is the thing closest to God, cries out
night and day: "Vengeance! Vengeance! May it never be for-
given, the sin which shed our blood, destroyed and almost
unmade us! 'Avenge the blood of the righteous!' "[21] Then
even Charity cries out for vengeance. And since Holy Church
and Charity enforced this so strongly, I cannot believe that
our Lord could show love to a man without charity, or have
pity on him when he begs for mercy.'

'But supposing I had sinned in just that way,' I said, 'and were now on the point of death and sorry for having offended the Holy Ghost, and supposing I made my confession and humbly begged for God's grace and mercy – would it be impossible for me to be saved?'

'No,' said the Samaritan, 'you might repent so well that justice would be converted to mercy. But how often does it happen that a man, after being found guilty by honest witnesses before a king's Justice, is pardoned merely because he repents – in a case where all reason condemns him? For when the injured party is prosecuting, the accusation is so grave that even the king cannot grant pardon – not until both parties agree, and both are satisfied that they have been treated justly. For the Scripture says: "The sin is never forgiven, till restitution is made." It is the same with those who live sinful, deceitful lives and only cease from sin on the point of death. The fear of despair drives away all grace, so that mercy cannot penetrate their minds. Even Hope, that should support them, turns to despair – not through any impotence on the part of God, nor because he lacks the power to put right all that is amiss (for, as the Bible says, his mercy is greater than all our wickedness – "His mercy is over all His works")[22] but because some measure of restitution is necessary before His justice will turn to pity; yet if a man cannot pay at all, his sorrow alone is sufficient payment.

'According to Scripture, there are three things[23] which force a man to flee from his home. The first is a shrewish wife who will not be corrected, and whose husband flees from her for fear of her tongue. The second is a leaking roof through which the rain drips on to his bed, so that he has to search high and low for a dry place to sleep. The third and worst is a wood fire, that fills the house with smoke. The smoke gets in his eyes and well nigh blinds him, and the fumes make him hoarse, till he coughs and curses his servants, "Confound them all! Why can't they bring in better wood, or blow the fire till it burns up clearly!"

'These three things are to be understood as follows: The wife is our stubborn flesh that will not be corrected, for nature clings to us continually and wars against the soul. Yet when the flesh leads us into sin, we have a good excuse in our natural frailty, so that if we ask for mercy and truly intend to do better, this sin is easily forgiven and forgotten.

'The rain that rains in on our beds is the sickness and the sorrows that come upon us so often – those which St Paul had in mind when he said: "My strength is made perfect through weakness."[24] And though some men moan and fret at such times, and show impatience in enduring their penance, their sickness clearly gives them good reason to grumble. And when they die, our Lord does not treat them harshly because they bore their suffering badly.

'But the smoke and fumes that get in our eyes are covetousness and unkindness, and these extinguish God's mercy completely. For unkindness is against all reason: no one is ever so sick, sorrowful, or wretched that he cannot love others if he chooses, and intend well towards them: to say a good word to someone, to desire God to have mercy on all men, and so amend our lives – these things are never impossible.

'But I have stayed too long,' added the Samaritan, and then he spurred his horse and rode away like the wind. And with that I awoke.

Book XVIII

THE PASSION AND HARROWING OF HELL

THE STORY. *After further wanderings, the poet falls asleep again and dreams of Christ's entry into Jerusalem, His Passion and death. Fleeing from these sights in awe, he comes to the borders of hell, where the four daughters of God, Righteousness, Truth, Mercy, and Peace are debating the meaning of a strange light which has appeared near hell gate. This proves to be Christ himself, who breaks his way into hell to proclaim to Lucifer the justice of the redemption, binding him in chains and bringing out of hell all the souls of the righteous. Then the four daughters of God are reconciled, and dance and sing for joy; and the poet, awakened by the bells of Easter morning, calls his wife and children to come to Mass and adore the Cross.*

ONCE again I set out, with wet feet, and the rough wool chafing my skin. I wandered on heedlessly throughout my life, regardless of pain and misery, living as a beggar, till at last I grew tired of the world and longed to sleep. So I drowsed away till it was Lent, and slept for a long time, and lay there snoring heavily until Palm Sunday.[1] I dreamt a long dream about children;[2] – I could hear them chanting 'Gloria, laus,'[3] and the old people singing 'Hosanna in excelsis' to the sound of the organ; and then I dreamt of Christ's Passion, and of the penance which He suffered for all the people.

A man came riding along barefoot on an ass, unarmed and without spurs. He looked like the Good Samaritan – or was it Piers the Ploughman? He was young and lusty, like a squire coming to be dubbed knight and receive his golden spurs[4] and cut-away shoes.

Then Faith, who was standing at a window, cried out, 'See! The Son of David!' – like a herald proclaiming a knight who comes to the tournament. And the aged Jews of Jerusalem sang for joy, 'Blessed is he that cometh in the name of the Lord.'[5]

So I asked Faith the meaning of all this stir – 'Who was going to joust in Jerusalem?'

'Jesus,' he said, 'to win back Piers' fruit, which the Devil has claimed.'

'Is Piers in this city?' I asked.

He looked at me keenly and answered, 'Jesus, out of chivalry, will joust in Piers' coat-of-arms, and wear His helmet and mail, Human Nature; He will ride in Piers' doublet, that no one here may know Him as Almighty God. For whatever blows He receives, they cannot wound Him in His divine nature.'

'Who will fight with Jesus?' I said. 'The Jews and Scribes?'

'No,' said Faith, 'the Devil, False Judgement, and Death. For Death vows to destroy all living creatures, both on land and water; but Life has branded him a liar, and pledged His life that within three days He will fetch Piers' fruit from the fiend, carry it where He chooses, bind Lucifer and vanquish Sorrow and Death for ever. – "O Death, I will be thy death; O grave, I will be thy destruction." '[6]

*

Then Pilate came with a great crowd, and sat down in the judgement seat[7] to see how bravely Death would fight, and judge between the rival claims. The Judge himself and all the Jews were against Jesus, and the whole Court cried out against Him with shrill voices, saying, 'Crucify Him!' Then a robber, pushing himself forward before Pilate, cried, 'This Jesus mocked at and despised our Jewish Temple; He said He would destroy it in a day and rebuild it again in three – there He stands, the very man himself! And He boasted He would make it as wide and tall and spacious as it was before, every detail the same.'

'Crucify Him!' cried an officer, 'I'll swear He's a sorcerer.'

'Off with him! Take Him away!' yelled another, and seizing some sharp thorns, he made a wreath and rammed it on His head, mocking Him with cries of, 'Hail, Rabbi!' and thrusting reeds at Him. Then they nailed Him, with three nails, naked, to the Cross. and putting poison to His lips on the end of a pole they told Him to drink His death-drink, for his days were over. 'But if you're a magician,' they said, 'come down from the cross; then we'll believe that Life loves you so much, he won't let you die!'

Christ said, 'It is finished,' and began to grow fearfully pale, like a prisoner on the point of death. And so the Lord of Life and of Light closed His eyes. Then at once the daylight fled in fear and the sun became dark; the wall of the Temple shook and split, and the whole earth quaked.

On hearing this dreadful sound, the dead came forth from their deep graves and spoke to the living, to tell them why the storm raged for so long. 'For in this darkness,' said one of the dead, 'Life and Death are waging a grievous battle; one is destroying the other, and no one will know who has won, until daybreak on Sunday' – and with those words he sank back into the earth.

When they saw how nobly He died, some said that Jesus was the Son of God – 'Indeed, this was the Son of God' – but others still believed Him a sorcerer and added, 'We'd better make sure He is really dead before He is taken down.'

On either side of Christ two thieves had also been put to death on crosses (for this was the common practice of that time), and an officer came and broke their arms and legs. But not one of those wretches had the nerve to lay hands on the body of God; for since He was a true knight and the Son of a king, Nature, for once, saw to it that no common fellow should touch Him. Yet the Book tells of a knight with a sharp spear, whose name was Longinus,[8] who had been blind a long time. And as he was standing near the crosses before Pilate and others, they forced him, in spite of his protests, to take his spear in hand and tilt against Christ. For all who stood about waiting on foot or on horseback were scared to handle Him and take Him down from the Cross. So this blind, young knight pierced Jesus through the heart; and as the Blood spurted down the steel, it unsealed his sight. Then he fell on his knees and cried for mercy, saying, 'It was against my will,

Lord, that I dealt you this grievous wound' – and he groaned and said, 'I repent bitterly for what I have done, and cast myself on your mercy. O just Jesus, have pity on me,' and with those words he wept.

Then Faith turned fiercely on the Jews and cursed them saying, 'May God's vengeance fall on the lot of you, cowards that you are! For this vileness you shall be accursed for ever. What fouler trick than to force a blind knight to strike a man bound to the stake! Did you think it was chivalrous to maltreat a dead body, you damnable wretches?

'But Christ has won the day, in spite of this gaping wound. For at this very moment your chief knight and champion is yielding in the lists to Jesus' mercy. And as soon as this darkness is over, Christ's life shall be avenged, Life himself shall conquer, and you, my lords, will have lost your battle. Then all the liberties that God has given you shall turn to slavery; you shall become serfs, and all your children with you; never again shall you prosper, never have land or dominion or plough the soil again. But you shall lead barren lives, and make your money by usury, a livelihood condemned by God in all His commandments. For now, as Daniel prophesied, your good days have come to an end – "When the Holy of Holies shall come, your anointing shall cease." '[9]

Appalled by this miracle and the treachery of the Jews, I drew back in the darkness and went down into the depths of the earth. And there, in accordance with Scripture,[10] I dreamt that I saw a maiden come walking from the west,[11] and looking towards hell. Mercy was her name, and she seemed a very gentle lady, courteous and kind in all that she said. And then I saw her sister come walking quietly out of the East, and gazing intently westwards. She was very fair, and her name was Truth; for she possessed a heavenly power that made her fearless.

When these ladies, Mercy and Truth, met together, they asked each other about the great wonder that had come to pass – the noise and darkness and then the sudden dawn.[12] Why this light and radiance before the gates of hell? 'The whole thing amazes me,' said Truth; 'I am now on my way to find out what it all means.'

'Do not be surprised,' said Mercy, 'for these are signs of great joy. There is a maiden called Mary, who has conceived and grown big with child without any knowledge of a man, but through the word of the Holy Ghost alone; and she has brought Him into the world without sin, as God himself can vouch. It is thirty years now since the child was born, and at midday today he was put to death. That is why the sun is eclipsed – to show us that men are to be drawn out of darkness, while Lucifer is blinded by the dazzling light. The patriarchs and prophets have often preached about this – that mankind should be saved through the help of a virgin, that a tree should win back what was lost by a tree,[13] and a death should raise up those whom Death has cast down.'

'What a lot of clap-trap!' said Truth. 'How could that light raise up Adam and Eve, Abraham and all the patriarchs and prophets who lie in pain? What power has it to draw them out of hell? Hold your tongue, Mercy, and stop talking nonsense! I am Truth, and I know the truth. Once in hell, no man ever comes out again; the patriarch Job condemns all these sayings of yours – "He that goeth down to the grave shall come up no more." '[14]

Then Mercy answered mildly and said, 'Yet from what I have seen, I have good reason to hope they will be saved. For poison is an antidote to poison – I can show you that by examples. A scorpion's sting is the most poisonous of all, and all remedies are useless against it. Yet if you apply the dead scorpion to the sore place, all the ill effects are cured, and the poison is dispelled by its own poison. So this death will destroy all that Death destroyed first, enticed by the Devil – I would stake my life on this. Just as man was deceived through the Devil's guile, so Grace, which was with man in the beginning, will beguile the Devil in turn – "*Ars ut artem falleret* – Art to deceive art." '[15]

'Now let's wait patiently a moment,' said Truth, 'for I think I can see Righteousness not far off, hurrying this way from the freezing North. Let us wait till she comes, for she

knows more than we do; she was alive before we were born.'
'Yes,' said Mercy, 'I agree. And look, here comes Peace
from the South, dancing gaily along in her garments of
Patience. Love has set his heart on her for such a long time
that I am sure he will have written to tell her what this
light means that is hovering over hell. So she will be able to
tell us.'

When Peace, dressed in Patience, came up to the two
maidens, Righteousness looked at her rich attire and greeted
her politely, asking her where she was off to in these gay
clothes.

'I am on my way to welcome all the lost souls,' she said,
'whom I have not seen for many a long day now, because of
the darkness of sin. For Adam and Eve and Moses and many
more of those in hell are to have a pardon. And oh, how I shall
be dancing with joy when I see them – and you, dear sister,
must come and dance too. Jesus has fought well, and joy is
dawning at last – "Weeping may endure for a night, but joy
cometh in the morning."[16] For Charity, my lover, has sent me
a letter to say that my sister Mercy and I are to save mankind –
God has given us permission to stand bail for them for ever.
See, here is the warrant, and these are the actual words –
"I will both lay me down in peace," and, to make sure the deed
is lasting, "and rest secure."[17]

'Have you gone off your head?' said Righteousness, 'or had
too much to drink! Do you really suppose that this light can
unlock hell, and save the souls of men? Don't you believe it!
God himself pronounced this Doom in the beginning, that
Adam and Eve and all their seed should surely die, and
after death live in torment, if ever they touched the fruit of a
certain tree. In spite of this command Adam ate the fruit; so,
in effect, he refused God's love as well as His law, and chose
instead the word of the Devil and his wife's greed, out of all
reason. I am Righteousness, and I tell you this for certain: that
their suffering will never cease, and no prayer can ever help
them. So leave them to the fate they chose and let us stop this
argument, my sisters. The fruit which they ate was deadly
poison and there's no remedy for it.'

'But,' said Peace, 'I can prove that their pain must come to an end, and suffering is bound to turn to happiness in the end. For if they had never known any suffering, they could never know happiness. – No man can grasp what pleasure is who has never suffered, or understand hunger who has never been without food. I am sure that if there were no night, no one would know for certain the meaning of day! And a rich man living in ease and comfort couldn't have any notion of misery, if nature did not force him to die. That is why God, the creator of all things, of His goodness became a man and was born of a virgin to save mankind. He allowed himself to be sold so that He might feel the bitterness of death, which unravels all sorrow and is the beginning of rest.

'For until we meet with Scarcity no one knows what it is to have enough. And so God of His goodness placed the first man, Adam, in a state of contentment and perfect happiness, and then allowed him to sin and experience sorrow, so that he might learn for himself what real happiness was. And then God ventured himself and took Adam's nature to experience what he had suffered, not only on earth but in three different places, heaven, earth, and hell. For now He means to go into hell, so that, as He knows infinite bliss, He may also know infinite misery.

'And so it shall be with these folk: their folly and sin will show them what pain is, and then endless bliss. For no man living in times of peace can imagine war, nor can a man really know happiness till troubles come to teach him.'

Then there appeared a man with two broad, open eyes – a Reverend Father by the name of Book, who was very out-spoken. 'By the Body of Christ, I bear witness,' said this Book, 'that when this Child was born a star blazed in the sky, and all the wise men in the world agreed what it meant – that a child was born in Bethlehem who would save man's soul and destroy sin. And all the four elements, air, water, fire, and earth bore witness to it. First the air and the sky proclaimed Him to be the God who created the world; for the spirits in heaven took a comet and kindled it for a torch to honour His birth; and the light followed its Lord down into the lowly earth.

'The water also witnessed that He was God, for He walked upon it; and Peter the Apostle, seeing Him coming, recognized Him as He walked on the water, and cried, "Lord, bid me come to Thee upon the waters."[18]

'And now look how the sun itself, on seeing Him suffer who made the sun and the sea, has locked up her light within herself – while the earth, in anguish for His pain, quakes like a living thing and shatters the rocks. Behold, when God suffered, even Hell itself could no longer hold together, for when it saw Him hanging on the Cross it opened and let the sons of Simeon out.[9] And now even Lucifer shall believe the truth of this, however he may hate it. For the Giant Jesus[20] has forged a weapon with which to break and beat down all that stands in His way.

'And I, Book, will gladly be burnt if Jesus does not rise and live again with all the powers of a man, to bring back joy to his mother and comfort to all his kin, and to dash to pieces all the triumph of the Jews. For unless they adore His Cross and His Resurrection and believe in a New Law, they shall be lost both body and soul.'

'Let us wait,' said Truth, 'for I can hear a spirit speaking to hell – Now I can see him. He is commanding them to unbar the gates: "Lift up your heads, o ye gates; and be ye lift up, ye everlasting doors." '[21]

Then, from within the light, a loud voice cried out to Lucifer: 'Princes of hell, unbar and unlock the gates, for there comes here a crowned monarch, the King of Glory.'

Then Satan heaving a great sigh, spoke thus to all the fiends: 'It was a light like this which fetched Lazarus away without our leave, so we may as well be prepared for trouble. If this king comes in, He will seize mankind and carry them off where He likes, and it won't take Him long to bind me in chains. This has long been talked of by the patriarchs and prophets – that such a king and a light should lead them all away.'

'Listen to me,' said Lucifer, 'I know this lord and this light – I met Him long ago. Death cannot hurt Him, nor any of your Devils' tricks: if He chooses to do a thing, He'll have His way. But he'd better consider the risks: for if He deprives me of my right, He is robbing me by force. The men who are here, both good and evil, are legally mine, body and soul of them. The ruler of Heaven said so himself – that if Adam ate the apple all men should die and live with us here. That was His threat, and He is the Truth that made it. I have been in possession now for seven hundred years, so I don't see how the Law can allow Him anything.'

'That may be true enough,' replied Satan,[22] 'but I still dread what will come of this; for you took them by guile, Lucifer – you broke into His garden disguised as a serpent, twined yourself round an apple-tree, and enticed Adam and Eve to eat the apple. And you went to Eve when she was alone, and told her a tale loaded with lies. That was how you had them banished from the garden, and got them here at last. But nothing is won for sure if it is founded on guile.'

'You can't catch God out that way. He won't be fooled,' said an ugly demon. 'We haven't a leg to stand on – they were damned through treachery.'

'Exactly,' said the Devil, 'and I'm afraid Truth is going to carry them off. He has been going about on the earth and teaching men for a good thirty years now, I think. I have tried to tempt Him with sin, and I once asked Him if He was God or God's Son,[23] but only got snubbed for my pains. So He has wandered at large these thirty-two years, which is why I went to Pilate's wife in her sleep,[24] to warn her what make of man this Jesus was. For though the Jews hated Him and put Him to death, I would rather have prolonged His life – Why? Because I knew that, if He died, His soul would never endure the sight of sin like ours. For while He went about in a human body He was busy all the time absolving all who chose to be saved from their sins.

'And now I can see a soul sailing towards us, blazing with light and glory – I am certain it is God. Quickly, we must escape while we can; it would be more than our lives are

worth to let Him find us here. It is you, Lucifer, with your lies,
that have lost us all our prey. It was all your fault that we fell
from the heights of heaven in the first place; not one of us
would have leapt out after you, if we hadn't swallowed your
talk. And now, thanks to your latest invention, we have lost
Adam, and, more than likely, all our dominion over land and
sea – "Now shall the prince of this world be cast out." '25

Then again the light bade them unlock the gates, and
Lucifer answered, saying, 'What lord art thou? – "Who is this
King. . . ?" '26

'The King of Glory,' answered the Light at once; 'the
Lord of power and might, and king of every virtue. Unbar
the gates quickly, you lords of this dreary place, so that Christ,
the Son of the King of Heaven, may enter.'

With that word, Hell itself, and all the bars of Belial, burst
asunder, and the gates flew open in the face of the guards.
And all the patriarchs and prophets, 'the people that sat in
darkness',27 sang aloud the hymn of St John the Baptist –
'*Ecce agnus dei* – Behold the Lamb of God.'28 But Lucifer
could not look to see, for the Light had blinded his eyes. And
then our Lord caught up into His Light all those that loved
Him; and turning to Satan He said:

'Behold, here is my soul as a ransom for all these sinful
souls, to redeem those that are worthy. They are mine; they
came from me, and therefore I have the better claim on them.
I do not deny that, in strict justice, they were condemned to
die if they ate the apple. But I did not sentence them to stay
in hell for ever. Your deceit was the cause of what they did;
you won them by guile, without a semblance of justice. – You
stole into my palace of Paradise in the form of an adder, and
took away by treachery the thing that I loved; and disguised
as a reptile with a woman's face,29 you crept in and robbed
me like a common thief.

'The Old Law says that he who deceives shall be deceived,
which is good reason – "An eye for an eye, and a tooth for a
tooth."30 So I offer you soul for soul; sin shall counter sin,31
and I, as a man, will make amends for all that man has done

wrong. Member for member, life for life [32] – that was the old law of restitution. And it is by that law that I claim Adam and all his issue, to do what I wish to do with them from now onwards. What Death has destroyed in them, my death shall restore; it shall raise them to life, and pay for all whom sin has slain.

'Justice demands that grace should destroy guile.[33] So do not think, Lucifer, that I take them away unlawfully. It is right and just that I should ransom my own subjects. "I came not to destroy the Law, but to fulfil."[34] You, by falsehood and crime and against all justice, took away what was mine, in my own domain; I, in fairness, recover them by paying the ransom, and by no other means. What you got by guile is won back by grace. You, Lucifer, like a slippery adder, got by guile those whom God loved; while I, that am Lord of Heaven, have come like a man, and graciously repaid your guile – guile against guile! And as a tree caused Adam and all mankind to die, so my gallows-tree shall bring them back to life.

'So Guile is beguiled, and fallen in his own guile – "He made a pit, and digged it, and is fallen into the ditch he made."[35] At last your guile begins to turn against you, while my grace grows ever wider and greater. The bitterness that you have brewed, you shall drink yourself; you that are doctor of death, shall swallow your own medicine!

'For I, the Lord of Life, drink no drink but love, and for that drink I died today on earth. I have fought so hard for man's soul that I am still thirsty, and no drink can ever refresh me or quench my thirst, till the vintage fall in the valley of Jehoshaphat,[36] so that I may drink the ripe new wine of the resurrection of the dead. Then I shall come as a king crowned with angels, and draw all men's souls out of hell. All the fiends, both great and small, shall stand before me, ready to do my bidding and go wherever I send them.

'And how can I, with my human nature, refuse men mercy on that day? For we are brothers of one blood, though we are not all of one baptism. And none who are wholly my brothers, in blood and in baptism, shall be condemned to eternal death; for it is written, "Against thee only have I sinned."[37]

'When on earth a criminal is put to death, it is not the custom to hang the man again[38] if the first hanging fails, even though he may be a traitor. And if the king of the country comes to the place of execution at the moment when the man is about to die, the law says that the king can grant him his life, if he but looks at the condemned man. So I, the King of kings, shall come at the moment when all the wicked are under sentence of death; and if the Law lets me look upon them, then it rests with my mercy whether they die or not, no matter what crimes they may have committed. And if their sin of pride against God has already been paid for, I can grant them mercy without offending justice, and all my words remain true.

'And though the words of Scripture require that I should take vengeance on the wicked, and say that "No evil will go unpunished,"[39] yet I have a prison called Purgatory, where they shall be thoroughly cleansed and washed from their sins, until I give the word of command to spare them. And then my mercy will be shown to many of my brethren. For a man may suffer his kind to go cold and hungry, but he cannot see them bleed without pitying them.'

"And I heard secret words which it is not granted to man to utter."[40]

'My righteousness and my justice shall rule over hell, and my mercy over all mankind before me in Heaven. I should be an inhuman king if I refused help to my own brethren, especially when they will need help so sorely. – "Enter not into judgement with thy servant, O Lord."[41]

'Therefore, by lawful right,' said our Lord, 'I shall lead from this place the men who loved me and believed in my coming. And you, Lucifer, shall grievously pay for the lies you told to Eve' – and having said this He bound him in chains.

Then Ashtoreth [42] and all the rout of devils scuttled away into the corners. Even the boldest dared not look upon our Lord, but left Him to do His will and lead away whom He chose.

Many hundreds of angels harped and sang –

> *'*Culpat caro, purgat caro;*
> *Regnat deus dei caro.'*[43]

Then Peace played on her pipe, singing this song –

'*Clarior est solito post maxima nebula Phoebus,*
Post inimicitias clarior est et amor – [44]
After the sharpest showers the sun shines brightest;
No weather is warmer than after the blackest clouds,
Nor any love fresher nor friendship fonder
Than after strife and struggle, when Love and Peace have
    conquered.
There was never a war in this world, nor wickedness so
    cruel,
That Love, if he liked, might not turn to laughter,
And Peace, through Patience, put an end to its perils.'

'I give way,' said Truth. 'You are in the right, Mercy. Let us make our peace together, and seal it with a kiss.'

'And nobody shall know that we ever quarrelled,' said Peace, 'for nothing is impossible with Almighty God.'

'I agree,' said Righteousness, and she solemnly kissed Peace, and Peace kissed her – world without end.

'Mercy and Truth are met together:
Righteousness and Peace have kissed each other.'[45]

Then Truth blew on a trumpet and sang the *Te Deum Laudamus*, and Love played on a lute, singing aloud –

'Behold, how good and joyful a thing it is:
brethren, to dwell together in unity!'[46]

*'The flesh sins, the flesh atones for sin; the flesh of God reigns as God.'

And so these maidens danced till daybreak, when the bells of Easter morning rang out for the Resurrection. And with that sound I awoke, and called out to my wife Kitty and my daughter Kate, 'Get up, and come to honour God's Resurrection. Creep to the Cross[47] on your knees and kiss it as a priceless jewel! For it bore God's blessed Body for our salvation, and such is its power that the Devil shrinks from it in terror, and evil spirits dare not glide beneath its shadow.'

Book XIX

THE FOUNDING OF HOLY CHURCH

THE STORY. *The poet falls asleep in the middle of Mass, and dreams that he sees Christ, carrying His Cross, coming in before the people. Conscience, who is by his side, explains this vision by relating the main events of Christ's life under the forms of knight, king, and conqueror. After the Resurrection, Christ gives to Piers (who now represents St Peter) and the apostles the power of bishops, so that they may lead the life of Do-best. The dreamer then sees the Holy Ghost descending upon them, distributing gifts to all the Christians, and equipping Piers as His Ploughman, to plough the field of the world. Antichrist then prepares to attack, and Conscience directs all the Christians to build a fortress, Unity or Holy Church. When this is done and the Church seems secure, Conscience offers them the Eucharist as a reward. But some refuse to prepare for it by paying back what they have taken from others, and the dreamer learns through the mouth of an 'ignorant vicar' how unprepared the Christians are.*

THUS I awoke, wrote down my dream, put on my best clothes, and went to church to hear the whole Mass and receive Communion.

But in the middle of Mass, just as the people were going up to make their offerings, I fell asleep once more, and suddenly dreamt that Piers the Ploughman, all stained with blood[1] and bearing a cross, came in before the people. Yet in form and figure, he looked exactly like Jesus. So I called to Conscience to tell me the truth about it – 'Is this Jesus,' I said, 'the knight whom the Jews put to death, or is it Piers the Ploughman? And who stained him so red?'

'These are Piers' arms,' said Conscience, kneeling, 'and his colours and coat-armour. Yet he that comes in them, so drenched in blood, is Christ with His Cross, the Christians' Conqueror.'

'Why do you call Him *Christ*?' I said. 'For the Jews called Him *Jesus*, and no name can compare with the name of Jesus.[2] It is the one name we need to call on, by day and night. All the powers of darkness tremble to hear it, and sinners are saved by it and comforted. Why, then, do you give Him the name *Christ*? Is it a more worthy and more powerful name than that of *Jesus* or *Jesu*, which brought all our joy?'

'You know, if you stop to think,' said Conscience, 'that a knight, a king, and a conqueror[3] may be one and the same person. And though it is an honour to be called a knight, and men kneel before you, it is finer still to be called a king, for a king can make knights; but to earn the name Conqueror you need special gifts, a rare mixture of firmness and chivalry. For a Conqueror takes young men from the lands he subdues, and makes lords of them; and if freemen refuse to obey his laws, he can turn them into vassals.

'The Jews were once men of rank, but since they despised the teaching and law of Jesus, they are now no better than serfs. For throughout the whole world they are subject to tribute and taxation like bondmen. But the few who followed John the Baptist's advice and became Christians are now freemen and noblemen with Jesus, by virtue of Baptism. For Jesus was himself baptized, and was crowned King of the Jews on the Cross of Calvary.

'It is the duty of a king who conquers kingdoms to defend his laws, and to deal out gifts to his liegemen. That is what Jesus did for the Jews. He taught and showed them the law of eternal life, and defended them from all kinds of foul evils – from fevers and fluxes, from possession by devils, and from false beliefs. So they called Him *Jesus*, the great prophet and king of their kingdom – and He bore a crown of thorns.

'Then on the Cross He overcame His enemies, and became a great conqueror. Death itself could not destroy Him or lay Him low, but He rose again, became a king and took hell by storm. Then He was called the Conqueror of the living and the dead, for He led forth Adam and Eve and numberless others who had lain for many long years in Lucifer's power, and gave them all the bliss of heaven.

'And since He gave unsparingly to all His loyal liegemen – gave them places in paradise when they left this life – He may well be called a Conqueror; and that is the meaning of *Christ*.

'But the reason for His coming to us in this way, with the Cross on which He suffered, is that the Cross may teach us a lesson. For we must learn to use it when we are tempted, to fight with it, and so prevent ourselves from falling into sin. And He means to show us by His suffering, that whoever desires happiness must first choose penance and poverty, and be willing to suffer much misery in the world.

'But to speak more of the name *Christ*, and how He acquired it. – The truth is that His first name was simply *Jesus*. And when He was born in Bethlehem, as the Scripture tells, and came to take human nature, kings and angels worshipped Him with the riches of the earth. First there came the angels from heaven, who knelt and sang: "Gloria in excelsis Deo." Then came the three kings, kneeling and offering Him myrrh and abundance of gold. They did not ask for thanks, or for anything in return, but came to acknowledge Him sovereign of sun and earth and sea; and then they returned to their royal kinsmen, guided on their way by angels. Thus the words which you quoted were fulfilled – "That at the name of Jesus every knee should bow, of things in heaven, of things on earth, and things under the earth."[4] For all the angels of heaven kneeled at His birth, and all the wisdom of the world was in those three kings. And the gifts they offered were Reason, Righteousness, and Pity.[5] Therefore the wise men of that time, the Doctors and men of learning, called them the *Magi*.

'The first king came with the gift of Reason, symbolized by incense. The second offered Righteousness, the counterpart of Reason, which seemed like red gold. For gold is like perpetual Loyalty, and Reason like rich gold,[6] which stands for Righteousness and Truth. And the third king who came and knelt before Jesus offered Him Pity, signified by myrrh. For myrrh is a symbol of mercy and mildness of speech. So these three gifts, of equal worth, were offered together by the kings of three different peoples, all kneeling to Jesus.

'But despite all these precious gifts, our Lord and Prince Jesus was neither king nor conqueror until He began to grow to manhood and show His great wisdom. For a man who would be a Conqueror and leader of men must be a master of many skills and wiles, and possess great wisdom – as Jesus did in His life, if I had time to tell it. Sometimes He suffered, and sometimes He went into hiding; sometimes He fought for His life, and sometimes He fled. At other times, He dispensed gifts and granted men healing as well, and restored life and limb to folk as He chose. So He set to work as a Conqueror does, and did not cease until He had won all those for whom He shed His Blood.

'When he was a young man, according to Scripture, He turned water into wine, at a feast of the Jews. It was then that God, of His grace, began to do-well. For wine is a symbol of law[7] and of holy living, and at that time the Law was imperfect, for it did not teach men to love their enemies. Therefore Christ counselled and commanded us all, clergy and laymen, to love our enemies. So at this feast, as I said before, God of His grace and goodness began to do-well. And at that time, being still a young man (though full of shrewdness and wisdom), He was not called *Christ* but only *Jesus*, the Son of Mary.

'He performed this miracle in the presence of His mother Mary, so that she, before all others, should firmly believe Him to be begotten by Grace, and not by any mortal man. For He did this, not by some clever trick, but by His word alone, in accordance with the nature from which He had sprung. And so He began to do-well.

'When he had grown more to manhood, and no longer lived with His mother, He made lame men jump for joy, gave sight to the blind, and fed the five thousand famished people with five loaves and two fishes. And since He comforted the sorrowful wherever He went, He earned a greater name, *Do-better*.[8] He made the deaf hear and the dumb speak, and helped and healed all who asked for His grace. Then, when they saw what great things He did, the common folk throughout the country called Him *Son of David*. For David in his time performed such mighty deeds that the maidens used to sing of him: "Saul hath slain his thousands, and David his ten thousands."[9] So wherever Jesus went they called Him *Jesus, Son of David,* and gave Him the title *Jesus of Nazareth,* for they thought no man worthier than He to be king of Judah and Chief Judge of the Jews.

'That is why Caiaphas and others of the Jews envied Him, and day and night planned to put Him to death. And at last they killed Him on a cross, at Calvary, on Good Friday. And when they had buried His body, they gave orders that it should be guarded at night by armed soldiers, to prevent any of His friends from fetching it away. For the prophets had told them that His blessed body would rise from the tomb, and He would go into Galilee and bring joy to His mother and the apostles – so it was believed beforehand. And afterwards, the soldiers who guarded the tomb confessed the truth themselves: that before dawn, angels and archangels came and knelt before the body singing: *"Christus resurgens* . . . Christ being raised from the dead dieth no more"[10] – and that He rose as a living man before them all, and went forth with the angels.

'Then the Jews begged the soldiers to keep silent about it and to tell the people another tale – that a company of His apostles had come and bewitched them as they were guarding the tomb, and stolen the Body away. But Mary Magdalen met Jesus on His way towards Galilee, alive, both as God and as man. And she cried out to everyone she met, "Christ is risen!" So the secret that Christ had now conquered, had recovered from death and lived, came to be known (for a thing that is known to a woman cannot be hidden!). – "Thus it behoved Christ to suffer, and to rise from the dead the third day."[11]

'Now when Peter heard these things, he went forth with James and John in search of Jesus, and they were followed by Thaddaeus, Thomas of India,[12] and ten others. Then, when all these wise men were together, shut up safely in a house, and all the gates and doors were locked and barred, Christ himself came in and said to them, "Peace be unto you".[13] And taking Thomas by the hand, He told him to touch Him and feel the flesh of His heart with his fingers. And when

Thomas had touched it, he cried out: "*Deus meus et Dominus meus*[14] – Now I believe that you are Jesus, my Lord and my God – that you suffered death and are now alive again, and will live for ever and be the Judge of us all." Then Christ spoke gently to him and said, "Thomas, because you have faith and believe this truly, I bless you now and will bless you for ever. But even more blessed are they that shall never see me with their eyes, as you do now, and yet shall truly believe all this; I shall love them and bless them for it. – *Beati qui non viderunt, et crediderunt* . . ."[15]

'And after this, Christ taught his apostles how to live the life of Do-best, and gave Piers authority to dispense pardon and mercy and forgiveness to all men. He granted him power to remit all kinds of sins, but only on condition that men gladly acknowledged his Pardon and fulfilled its condition, "*Redde quod debes* – Pay back that which thou owest."[16] So, provided that condition is carried out, Piers has the power to bind and unbind both on earth and in heaven, and absolve men from every sin except debt.

'As soon as these things were accomplished, Christ ascended into heaven, to dwell there until the Last Day, when He will come again and reward to the full whoever "pays back that which he owes" – and pays it honestly and completely. And those who do not pay their debts He will punish. For on that day of Doom our Lord will be Judge both of the living and of the dead, and will send the good to dwell with God in perfect joy, and the wicked to dwell in pain for ever.'

So Conscience spoke to me of Christ and His Cross, and bade me kneel before it. And as I dreamed, I thought I saw the Paraclete coming down upon Piers and his friends, descending on them all like forked lightning, and giving them the power to speak and understand many languages. But I was frightened by the light, and wondering what it could be (for the Holy Ghost in the likeness of fire was hovering over them all), I gave Conscience a nudge to attract his attention.

Then Conscience knelt down and said: 'This is Christ's Messenger whose name is Grace, and He comes from God on High. Kneel now (he said), and if you know how to sing, welcome and worship Him with *Veni Creator Spiritus.*' So together with many hundreds of others, I sang that hymn, and we all cried out with Conscience, 'Help us, thou God of grace!'

From that time, Grace began to accompany Piers the Ploughman, and He commanded Piers and Conscience to call the people together. 'For today,' said Grace, 'I shall distribute my gifts of grace to all God's creatures who can use them. I will give them treasure to live by till the end of their days, and weapons to fight with that will never fail. For it is not long now before Antichrist and his followers[17] will come to ravage the whole world, and unless Christ helps you, Conscience, you may be overwhelmed. For a swarm of false prophets, flatterers, and glib theologians will come and make themselves the confessors of kings and earls; and Pride shall become Pope and Prince of the Church, and Covetousness and Unkindness shall be the Cardinals who direct him. Therefore (said Grace), I will give you treasure before I go, and provide you with weapons to fight with when Antichrist attacks you.'

Then He gave each man a gift with which to govern his life, so that Idleness, Envy, and Pride should never get the better of him.

'Now there are diversities of gifts, but the same Spirit.'[18] – So He gave to some men Intelligence, with the gift of words to express and explain things, and Wits by which to earn their living as life demands – preachers and priests, for example, and students of Law. Such men as these were required to live truthfully by the labour of their tongues, and, under the direction of Grace, to teach others through their wisdom. He also taught some men to trade, giving them a keen eye, to earn their bread by buying and selling; – some to labour – an honest and fine way of life; – some, to till the soil, to ditch and to thatch, and so to earn their living; – some, to understand figures and make calculations; – some, to draw plans and mix colours; – some, like astronomers, astrologers, and clever philosophers, to foresee and predict the future, for good or for

ill. Some He taught to ride out on horseback and recover
unlawful gains, winning them back from treacherous men
by a rough justice, with speed and strength of arm; – and
some to live in penance and poverty, longing for heaven and
praying for all Christians.

And He told them all to be faithful to their trust, saying
that each craft must love the other, and forbidding all strife
between them. 'Some occupations are cleaner than others,'
said Grace, 'but you can be sure that the man who works at
the pleasantest job could just as easily have been put to the
foulest. So you must all remember that your talents are gifts
from me. Let no profession despise another, but love one
another as brothers. Whoever has the most talents should be
the mildest in bearing. Conscience must be your king, and
Skill your steward, and by his instructions you must clothe
and feed yourselves. Piers the Ploughman is my manager, my
bailiff, and my treasurer, and he will receive the payments due
for his pardon. Piers, then, shall be my purveyor as well as
my ploughman on earth; and I shall give him a team of oxen
to plough the field of Truth.'

So Grace gave Piers a team of four great oxen. The first
was Luke, a large, meek-looking beast; then there were two
mighty beasts called Mark and Matthew; and lastly, He yoked
with them one named John, the gentlest of them all and the
chief ox of Piers' plough.

Besides these, Grace generously gave Piers four bullocks,
whose work was to harrow over all the land that his oxen
had ploughed. Their names were Augustine, Ambrose,
Gregory the great scholar, and the good Jerome.[19] These four
followed Piers' team and taught men the Faith. They used
two harrows, an old and a new one (that is to say, the Old
and New Testaments), and before very long they had harrowed
the whole of the Scriptures.

Grace also gave him some seeds of corn called the Cardinal
Virtues,[20] to sow in the souls of men. And this is how He
explained their names: The first seed was called the Spirit
of Prudence, and whoever ate this grain would learn to think
and consider the consequences before he took any action.

In other words, if you want to prevent a pot from boiling over and save the fat that floats on top, you must buy a ladle with a long handle!

The second seed was called the Spirit of Moderation. Whoever ate this grain would never grow fat through over-eating or drinking, he would keep his judgement in the face of spite or scolding, and whatever wealth or riches he won, he would never waste an idle word or say an evil thing. No costly cloth would grace his back, nor the chef's rare spiced dishes enter his mouth.

The third seed Piers sowed was the Spirit of Fortitude. The man who ate this grain would always have the courage to endure all that God sent, both sickness and trouble. Neither slander nor loss of this world's goods could ever make him grieve, for he would always remain happy in soul and strong and patient when suffering insults. For he would pass them off lightly with patience, saying the Psalm 'Spare me, Lord,'[21] and would protect himself with wise Cato's saying: 'Be strong in mind when thou art blamed unjustly.'[22]

The fourth seed that Piers sowed was called the Spirit of Justice. If anyone ate this grain he would always be honest with God, and fear nothing but guile. For Guile moves about so stealthily in defiance of Justice, that Honesty sometimes disappears completely.

The Spirit of Justice does not spare the guilty, or fear to correct even the king himself if he breaks the Law. For when Justice gives sentence as a Judge in court, he cares nothing for a king's wrath, nor does he tremble before a Duke. He is willing to face death, provided only that the Law is carried out – regardless of bribes, petitions, or letters from princes. And as far as it lies in his power, he deals justice to all men.

When Piers had sown these four seeds, he harrowed them with the Old and the New Law, so that Love might grow up among the four virtues, and destroy the vices. For it often happens in the country that ragwort and weeds choke the crops in the field, as the vices choke the virtues. 'We must harrow all men capable of reason,' he said, 'with the teaching of these four Doctors, and cultivate in them the Cardinal Virtues.'

'But before your grain begins to ripen, Piers,' said Grace, 'you must build yourself a barn to hold your corn.'

'Then you will have to give me the timber yourself, Grace,' said Piers, 'and prepare the building for me before you go.'

So Grace gave Piers the Cross – that on which Christ suffered for mankind on Calvary – and with it His Crown of Thorns; and He made a kind of mortar out of Christ's baptism and the blood that He shed on the Rood, calling it Mercy. With these He made a firm foundation, and then He walled and wattled the house with Christ's pains and Passion. The roof He made entirely of Holy Scripture, and He called the house Unity, which in plain English means Holy Church.

Having completed this, Grace constructed a cart to carry Piers' sheaves, and named it Christendom. He then gave him two horses for his cart, which were Contrition and Confession. And when He had appointed a hayward, whose name was Priesthood, He went off with Piers far and wide over the world, to grow the seed of Truth.

When Piers had gone to the plough, Pride saw his chance, and gathered a great host with which to attack Conscience and all the Christians and the Cardinal Virtues – to smash and flatten the corn, and break the roots asunder. So he sent out his sergeant-of-arms, one Arrogance, and his spy, Kill-love, sometimes known as Speak-evil-behind-your-back. And these two came to Conscience and the Christians, and threatened them, and told them that they would lose the seeds that Piers had sown (the Cardinal Virtues), and that Piers' barn would be broken down, and all the people in Unity be dispersed. – 'And your two horses,' they said, 'Confession and Contrition, not to mention your cart of the Faith, will be so cleverly camouflaged and painted over with our sophistry, that Conscience will no longer be able to distinguish Christian from a heathen, so confused will Confession and Contrition appear; and business men will not know what is usury and what is not, or whether their profits are just or unjust. For Pride comes armed with such subtle cloaks and pretences, and with him the lord that lives for the lust of his body; and helped by our wits, they will waste away the whole world in ease and riotous living' – so said Arrogance.

Then Conscience spoke to all the Christians, and said, 'I think we should get inside Unity as fast as we can, and stay there together, and pray that there may be peace in the barn of Piers the Ploughman. For I am sure that without the help of Grace we have not the strength to go out against Pride.'

Then Common Sense came to advise Conscience, and gave out a command that all the Christians should dig a deep moat around the fortress, so that Holy Church would stand united and firm, like a solid pier in the water. So Conscience commanded all the Christians to dig this huge dyke, to fortify Holy Church and help those who guarded her.

Then Christians of all ranks repented and turned away from sin – all except the prostitutes[23] and others like them – the liars and flatterers, usurers and thieves, and those shifty coroners who were always perjuring themselves for money, and wilfully sided with falsehood.

Every Christian of sound mind, except for those few wretches of whom I spoke, played his part in deepening the moat of Holiness. Some did it by telling their beads, some went on pilgrimages, some did private penance, and others gave what little money they had. And then, as they wept for their wicked deeds, the water began to well up, streaming sorrowfully out of men's eyes; and the pure lives of the layfolk, and the clean living of the clergy, united Holy Church in a bond of Holiness.

'What do I care if Pride comes now?' said Conscience, 'I am certain the lord of lust will make no progress this Lent. So come, all you Christians that have laboured so faithfully through Lent, and let us dine together. Here I have the blessed bread that contains God's body – the Bread which Grace, through the word of God, gave Piers the power to make. And all men are invited, for their help and healing, to eat it once a month or as often as they have need, provided they have paid their debts as Piers' pardon lays down.'

241

'How do you mean?' said all the people. 'Are you telling us to pay everyone all that we owe, before we go to Communion?'

'That is my advice,' said Conscience. 'The Cardinal Virtues teach the same – that every man must forgive his neighbour. Even the Paternoster requires it: "Forgive us our debts, as we also forgive our debtors" – only then may you have absolution and make your Communion.'

'Come off it!' said a pub-keeper. 'I shan't be ruled by any Spirit of Justice – not for all your jabber, by Christ! – nor by you, Conscience! – not while I can sell my dregs and hogwash, by Jesus! and draw thick and thin at the same tap! That's always been my way – I certainly shan't go grubbing round after holiness. So shut your trap, Conscience!'

'You vile wretch!' answered Conscience, 'unless God comes to your aid, you will certainly be damned! For I tell you, if you do not live by the Spirit of Justice, that fourth seed that Piers sowed, you can never be saved. The people must either be fed by Conscience and the Cardinal Virtues, or else, believe me, they are lost, body and soul.'

'Well in that case there will be thousands lost,' said an ignorant vicar.[24] 'Speaking as a parish priest of the Church, I can tell you this: that in all my time as a priest, I haven't met a single man who'd even heard of the Cardinal Virtues, or who cared a cock's feather for Conscience! The only Cardinals I've ever known are those that come from the Pope – and whenever they come, we parsons have to pay for their keep, including their fine furs and their palfrey's fodder[25] – and the same for all the robbers that come in their train. Every day I hear the people crying out against them, and saying to each other, "It was a bad day for the country when cardinals first came here. Wherever they stay for long, the place stinks of lechery!" And for my part, I would to God that no cardinal ever came among the common folk. – Why can't their holinesses stay quietly at Avignon,[26] with their friends the Jews – as the Scripture says, "With the holy they shall be holy"? – or else in Rome, as their Rule says, looking after the relics! And as for you, Conscience, you should be at the king's court, and stay there for good; and Grace, whom you shout so much about, He should be the leader of all the clerics; and Piers, with both his ploughs, the new and the old, should be Emperor of the whole world – and then perhaps all men might be Christians!

'He's a poor sort of Pope who sends armies to kill[27] the very folk he's meant to save. For if anyone ought to be the people's protector, he is the man. So good luck, I say, to Piers the Ploughman, who follows the example of God himself; for God "sends rain at the same time on the evil and on the good,"[28] and makes the sun shine just as brightly on the wicked man's crops, as on those of the best man on earth – and so does Piers the Ploughman. He takes as much trouble to grow food for a good-for-nothing or a brothel-wench, as he does for himself or his own servants (although it's true that they get served first). He never ceases to sweat and toil, and works as hard for traitors as he does for honest men. – And all praise to God himself, who created all men, bad and good, and lets the sinners go on living to give them time to repent! Let's hope that some day He may even improve the Pope, who claims, even more than the king, to be the defender of all Christians, yet robs the Church, and thinks nothing of letting Christians be killed and plundered. For he fits out armies to fight, and spills Christian blood, in defiance of both the Laws, Old and New – witness the words of St Luke: "Thou shalt not kill," and these also: "Vengeance belongs to me, saith the Lord."[29] But as long as the Pope gets his own way, it seems he cares nothing about the rest of the world. – And may Christ, in His mercy, save the Cardinals too, and turn their wits into real wisdom and health of soul.

'So I assure you (the vicar said) that the layfolk take no notice of Conscience or the Cardinal Virtues, except when they see they can gain something by it. They make no bones about deceiving or telling lies; for with them, the Spirit of Prudence *is* deceit, and all those fair virtues show up as vices. For everyone invents some clever scheme to hide his sin, and dresses it up as an honest business.'

Then a nobleman who heard this speech burst out laughing and said: 'By this light! I always accept from my Reeve just as much as my auditor or my steward puts down in his account – and quite right and proper it is too! Am I to question what my clerks write in their rolls? Why, they're fine fellows – they search through the rolls with the true Spirit of Wisdom, while I, with the Spirit of Fortitude, rake in the money!'[30]

Then a king came forward, and swore by his crown, saying: 'I am an anointed king and it is my duty to rule the people, and defend the Church and the clergy from traitors. If I have not enough to live on, the Law lets me seize what I want, wherever I can get it most quickly. In fact, I am the head of the Law[31] – you are only the members, and I am above the lot of you. And since I am head of you all, I am also the guardian of you all – the chief support of the Church and leader of the Commons. Whatever I take from either, I take with the sanction of the Spirit of Justice; for I am the Judge of you all. Therefore I can receive Communion without any scruple; for I never beg or borrow from the Commons, except as my status requires.'

'You may certainly take what you need, within reason,' said Conscience. 'Your Law allows it – but only on condition that you rule your kingdom well, according to reason and truth. – "All things are yours for defence, but not for spoil." '[32]

The vicar had a long way to go home, so he politely took his leave. Whereupon I awoke, and wrote down my dream.

Book XX

THE COMING OF ANTICHRIST

THE STORY. *Will continues his wanderings, hungry and miserable, until he meets Need, who rebukes him for being so faint-hearted and praises the virtue of poverty. Then he falls asleep again and dreams of the coming of Antichrist. Conscience summons his few loyal supporters to defend the castle of Unity, and Nature helps him by sending Old Age, Death, and the Plague against his enemies. But as soon as the Plague ceases, men return to lives of recklessness and pleasure. Then Old Age attacks the dreamer himself, who takes refuge in Unity. The battle against the forces of Antichrist continues, until Conscience makes the mistake of letting a Friar into the castle to hear confessions, and the Friar makes penance so easy that the people lose all fear of sin and fall into a stupor. Then Conscience, unable any longer to resist Antichrist without help, sets out on a final pilgrimage in search of Piers, and the dreamer awakes.*

WHEN I was thus awakened, I went on my way lonely and miserable, and looking glum because I did not know where to find food. And when it was nearing midday,[1] I met with Need, who hailed me with insults and called me a beggar.

'Could you not have excused yourself,' he said, 'as the king and the others did, and explained that you took food and clothing out of necessity, as you learnt from the Spirit of Moderation? – and took no more than Need taught you – Need, who knows no law[2] and is indebted to no one? For to keep alive, there are three things which Need takes without asking. The first is food; for if men refuse to give him any, and he has no money, nothing to pawn, and no one to guarantee him, then he seizes it for himself. And there he commits no sin, even if he uses deceit to get it. He can take clothing in the same way, provided he has no better payment to offer; Need is always ready to bail a man out of prison for that. And thirdly, if his tongue is parched, the law of his nature compels him to drink at every ditch rather than die of thirst.

'So in great necessity, Need may help himself, without consulting Conscience or the Cardinal Virtues – provided he keeps the Spirit of Moderation. For no virtue can compare with this, not even justice or fortitude. The Spirit of Fortitude constantly does men wrong, going beyond the bounds of moderation – flogging men too harshly (or else not enough!) and injuring them more severely than he need in fairness. And the Spirit of Justice is bound, willy nilly, to judge according to the king's policy or the people's pleasure. And the Spirit of Prudence, in attempting to foresee the future, cannot help but fail in many points, for it depends entirely on a man's wisdom; and opinion is not wisdom, nor is clever conjecture. "Man proposes, but God disposes," and He controls all true virtues.

'But Need resembles God in this, that it humbles a man in a moment; for when he lacks the things he needs he becomes as meek as a lamb. That is why the wise men of old gave up prosperity and refused riches, preferring to be needy and dwell in the wilderness. And so God himself, forsaking all the spiritual riches of Heaven, came and took man's nature, and became needy. He was so poor (as the Scripture tells us in many places) that He spoke these words in His agony on the Cross:

"The foxes and birds can creep and fly to their coverts,
  And the fish have fins swiftly to dart to their rest;
  But Need has held me here; here must I needs abide,
  And suffer sorrows most sore, that shall turn to joy."[3]

So do not be ashamed to beg and be needy, for He who created the world chose to be so; no one was ever so needy as He, or died in such poverty.'

When Need had thus reproached me, I at once fell asleep, and had a most wonderful dream of the coming of Antichrist – how he came in the form of a man and overturned all the crop of Truth, tearing it up by the roots, and causing Falsehood to spring up and spread and supply all men's needs. In every district where he came he cut down Truth, and grew Guile instead, disguised as goodness. The Friars followed this fiend because he gave them their habits; and at his approach the monks rang their bells and treated him with veneration, while the whole community, apart from a few simple fools, came out to give this tyrant and his henchmen a hearty welcome. But the simple men who stayed within would rather have died than have lived to see Good Faith so rebuked, and Antichrist, that treacherous fiend, reigning over all the people. For these were the mild and holy men who feared nothing that men could do to them, and opposed all deceit and all deceivers. And if any king were to favour such men, or befriend them for a time, the followers of Antichrist would curse him and his fools' council, clerics and laymen alike.

So before long Antichrist had hundreds under his banner, which was carried about boldly by Pride. And by his side was a lord who lived for the lust of his body, who also went to attack Conscience. For Conscience was the leader and defender of all the Christians and the four Cardinal Virtues.

Then Conscience spoke to the holy fools[4] and said: 'You had better come with me into Unity, the fortress of Holy Church. Let us remain there together, and call upon Nature, for love of Piers the Ploughman, to come and defend us "fools" from the limbs of this fiend. And let us call all the common folk into Unity, and tell them to stand fast there, and grapple with the children of Belial.'

Then Nature heard Conscience,[5] and, coming out of the planets,[6] he sent forth his foragers – fevers and fluxes, coughs and seizures, cramps, toothaches, catarrhs and cataracts, scabby skin-diseases, boils, tumours, feverish agues, fits of madness, and countless other foul complaints. And these foragers of Nature so pierced and preyed on the population, that a thousand at least had soon lost their lives. Then on all sides could be heard cries of 'Mercy! Woe! for Nature comes, with dreadful Death, to destroy us all!' And the lord who lived for lust shouted for his knight, Comfort, to come and bear his banner. 'To arms! To arms!' cried this lord. 'Every man for himself!'

And then, before the trumpeters had time to blow, or the herald-of-arms to call out their names, these knights came clashing together in battle.

Hoary Old Age was in the vanguard, bearing before Death the banner that was his by right. Nature followed with a host of cruel diseases, slaughtering thousands with foul contagions, and sweeping all before him with his plagues and poxes. Then Death came dashing after, crushing to powder both kings and knights, emperors and pontiffs. He left none standing, priest or layman, but hit so squarely that they never stirred again. And many a lovely lady, and the mistress of many a knight, sank down and swooned in agony beneath Death's cruel blow.

At last, out of charity, Conscience begged Nature to cease, saying: 'Be still awhile, and then see if they will steal away from the army of Pride and turn true Christians.' So Nature ceased, hoping to see the people amend their lives. And then Fortune began to flatter the survivors,[7] promising them long life; and among all orders of men, married and unmarried, she sent out Lechery, and gathered a great host to oppose Conscience.

This Lechery laid about him with smirking looks, with secret whisperings and affected language, and armed himself in idleness and swaggering airs. He bore a bow in his hand with a sheath of blood-stained arrows, feathered with tender promises and sham betrothals. And he never ceased, with his unseemly talk, from wounding Conscience and the teachers of Holy Church.

Then there came Covetousness plotting and scheming to defeat Conscience and the Cardinal Virtues. He armed himself in Avarice, and lived like a hungry monster. All his weapons were wiles for getting and hoarding, and he imposed on the people with lies and falsification. It was Simony who sent him to attack Conscience, and they preached to the people together, appointing prelates who would side with Antichrist, so that they could keep their temporal possessions. And this Covetousness, in the person of a fierce baron, came to the king's Council and kneeled to Conscience before the eyes of the whole court. And before very long, Honesty fled from court and Falsehood took his place. Meanwhile the Baron, by scattering handfuls of bright gold coins, bore down most of the judgement and wisdom of Westminster Hall. For he need only trot up to a Judge, and tilt at his ear with a few words, like – 'Take this, my good man, and let the matter drop' – to unhorse all his honesty! Then he hurried to the Archbishop's Court and reduced the Law to Simony – not forgetting to bribe the Chancellor of the diocese. He would break up a marriage, which only death should destroy, and fix up a divorce for the price of an ermine cloak.

'Alas!' cried Conscience, 'I would to God this Covetousness were a Christian; he is such a keen fighter, so audacious and persistent, while his purse lasts out!'

But Life only burst out laughing, and went to have his clothes slashed in the new style. And he armed himself quickly in a suit of mockery – for holiness, he thought, was a joke, and courtesy a mere extravagance. He gibed at Loyalty for a slave, and thought Liar a freeman; for Conscience and good advice were nonsense to him.

So with a little good luck, Life recovered his spirits, and he spurred away with Pride, scorning virtue, and ignoring Nature's power to kill; it was nothing to him that she must come in the end to slay all living creatures except Conscience. He leapt aside and grabbed himself a mistress, saying, 'Health and I with our great high spirits will soon rid you of fearing Death or Old Age. While you're with us you can forget about sorrow and stop worrying about sin.'

So Life and his lover Fortune led a gay life together, and at last begot in their glory a lazy urchin called Sloth, who made great mischief. He grew with amazing speed and soon came of age, when he married a drab from the brothels called Despair. She was the daughter of a juryman named Tom Two-tongues, a man who would swear blind that black was white, and was convicted of perjury at every inquest.

This Sloth, being very cautious in battle, made a sling, and threw the dread of despair a dozen miles around him. So Conscience, in alarm, begged Old Age to put up a fight with Despair and frighten him away. Then Old Age seized the sword of Good Hope and prepared himself in all haste. And very soon he drove off Despair, and was grappling with Life himself. Then Life fled in fear to Medicine to beg for his help, and asked for some of his tonic, paying dearly for it in gold, which gladdened the doctor's heart; but all that he got in return was a thin glass helmet![8] Yet he still believed that doctors could stave off Old Age, and drive away Death with drugs and prescriptions. Meanwhile Old Age continued to do battle with him, and at last, by mistake, he struck a doctor in a furred hood. The doctor lost consciousness and died less than three days later.

'Now I see,' said Life, 'that neither Medicine nor Surgery can do anything against Death.' Yet still hoping to recover his health, he took Good Heart, and rode away to the city of Revel, a rich and merry place, sometimes known as Comfort-in-Company.

Whereupon Old Age turned and came after me.[9] He rode straight over the crown of my head and made me bald in front and bare on top. Alas, nothing will ever cover up his tracks – he trampled over my pate so roughly!

'Sir ill-bred Age,' I said, 'clear off with your clumsy manners! Since when was the right of way over men's heads? – You might have been civil enough to ask my permission!'

'You think so, you lazy rascal!' he said, and laid about me more ruthlessly than ever. He struck me under the ear till I was stone-deaf, hit me round the mouth and battered my teeth out, and tied me up with the gout so that I could not budge from home. My wife, seeing my misery, took pity on me, and wished most sincerely that I might be in heaven. For the member that she loved me for and liked to feel (especially at night when we were naked), I could not put to her pleasure, try as I would – Age and she together had crippled it.

Then, as I sat there dejected, I saw Nature pass by; and Death drew near me. Quaking with fear, I cried out to Nature to rescue me from my misery – 'See how hoary Old Age has visited me! Avenge me, Nature, if you will, for I long to escape him.'

'If you want to be avenged,' said Nature, 'go into Unity, and stay there until I send for you. And before you come out again, see that you learn some occupation.'

'What occupation would you advise me to learn?' I said.

'Learn to love,' said Nature, 'and give up everything else.'

'But how shall I clothe and feed myself and make a living?'

'If you love sincerely,' he said, 'you will never lack food and clothing as long as you live.'

So on Nature's advice I set out on my travels, and came to Unity by way of Confession and Contrition. There I found Conscience as warden and protector of all the Christians, and the castle besieged by seven great giants, champions of Antichrist, who were battling hard against Conscience.

Sloth, with his sling, was making a fierce assault, backed by an army of proud priests, at least a thousand strong. They were wearing short jackets and pointed shoes, and carrying long daggers[10] like a band of cut-throats. – These were men who always sided with Covetousness.

'By our blessed Lady,' cried a villainous Irish priest, 'as long as I get good money, I don't give a damn for Conscience! He's not worth the price of a draught of good ale!' And so said scores of others from that country, at the same time letting fly at Conscience with a hail of shot – broad, hooked arrows and sheafs of blasphemous oaths – 'By God's heart' and 'By God's nails,' etc. . . . And they almost razed Unity and Holiness to the ground.

'Help me, Learning,' said Conscience, 'or I shall fall. I am almost overwhelmed by these vicious priests and prelates.'

The Friars heard his cry and came to his help, but as they proved unskilled in their trade, it was not long before he gave them up as useless. Then Need came and said to him: 'These Friars only come out of covetousness, in the hope of getting parishes for themselves. Maybe it is because they

are poor and lack endowments that they flatter the rich for
an easy life. But since they chose cold and wretchedness
and poverty, let them keep it. It would never do to burden
them with church livings! A man who begs for his living
will always be more of a liar than one who sweats for it and
gives it away to beggars. The Friars gave up the pleasures of
this world, so let them live as beggars, or else eat only spiritual
food like the angels!'

But Conscience passed this off with a laugh, and courteously
called in all the Friars and put them at their ease, saying:
'Gentlemen, you are heartily welcome in Holy Church. But
one thing I pray you: that you remain in Unity, live according
to your Rule and envy no one, whether cleric or layman.
Then I will guarantee that you get food and clothing in plenty,
and see that you lack nothing which you need. – But you must
give up studying logic, and learn to love. For Friars Francis
and Dominic gave up their lands and position and education,
so intent were they on holy living.

'And if you long to possess livings, think what Nature
teaches; for she shows how God made all kinds of creatures
in due proportion, fixing a limit to their numbers –

> "He telleth the number of the stars:
>   And calleth them all by their names."[11]

Just so, kings and knights, the protectors of countries,
whenever they appoint officers under them, limit themselves
to a definite number of each kind. And in order that they may
pay their soldiers' wages, they write down the exact figures –
otherwise no paymaster would pay them, however hard they
toiled. Any other folk who turned up on the battlefield would
be treated as plunderers, spoilers of armour come to strip the
dead – men who are detested everywhere.

'Moreover the Rules of all Orders of monks and nuns re-
quire them to have a fixed number. So the same law applies to
Religious as to layfolk – a definite number for a definite
class – for everyone, that is, except the Friars. And by com-
mon sense it follows that it would be sinful to give you Friars
any wages, for heaven knows, your numbers increase beyond

all reckoning! Why, Heaven itself has an even number of souls; only Hell is numberless.[12] So I sincerely wish that you were all down in the Register under the notary's stamp – just so many and no more!'

When Envy heard this, he told the Friars to go to the Universities and acquire logic and law – and also contemplation – and learn to hold forth about Plato, and quote Seneca to prove that all things on this earth should be held in common.

*

Yet I believe that those who preach this doctrine[13] to ignorant people are liars. For God, through Moses, gave men a law, 'Thou shalt not covet that which is thy neighbour's.'[14] And how little is this obeyed in the parishes of England! For it is a parish priest's duty to hear his people's confessions; that is why he is called a 'curate' or keeper – because he must know all his parishioners and heal them and exhort them to do penance and to feel ashamed of their sins when they go to confession. Yet their very shame makes them abandon their curates and run to the Friars, just as some swindlers flee to Westminster – who borrow money, take it there with them,[15] and then beseech their creditors to let them off or extend the loan for a few more years. But while they are in Westminster, they go quickly to work, and make merry[16] on other men's money. It is like that with many of those who confess to the Friars – jurymen and executors for example: they give the Friar a fee to pray for the dead man, and then have a good time with what is left of the money which he had laboured to earn. And so they leave the dead in debt till the Day of Judgement.

*

So Envy hated Conscience, and provided for the Friars to go to College and learn philosophy. Meanwhile Covetousness and Unkindness attacked Conscience, who held fast inside Unity. And Conscience appointed Peace as porter, commanding her to bar the gates to all tattlers and idle gossips. Then Hypocrisy made an assault on the castle, and struggled hard with Conscience at the gates. And he grievously wounded many a wise teacher who fought on the side of Conscience and the Cardinal Virtues.

So Conscience sent for a doctor skilled in hearing confessions. 'Go and heal those that are sick or wounded with sin,' he said. Then this Doctor Shrift concocted a lotion that smarted, and made men do penance for their misdeeds; and he saw to it that Piers' Pardon was properly paid for, with its condition 'Pay back that which thou owest.'

But some disliked this doctor, and sent out letters to ask if there were any surgeon in the town who could apply plasters more gently. For Sir Love-Living-in-Lechery lay there groaning, and whenever he had to fast on a Friday he acted as though he were dying. 'There is a surgeon here,' he said, 'who knows how to handle you gently. He knows far more about Medicine than the parson does, and applies plasters much more pleasantly. They call him Doctor Friar Flatter, Physician and Surgeon.'

'Let him come to Unity,' said Contrition to Conscience, 'for we have so many folk here wounded by Hypocrisy.'

'We don't really need him,' said Conscience; 'I know of no better doctors than the parson, the penitentiary[17] and the Bishop – except for Piers the Ploughman, who has power over them all, for he can grant an indulgence to any who are not in debt. But since you are so anxious, perhaps, after all, I will let Dr Flatter come and treat your patients.'

The Friar very soon heard of this, and hurried off to the Bishop to get a licence to do parish work. He came before him as bold as brass, carrying his letters of recommendation, and very soon got written permission to hear confessions wherever he went. Then he came to the place where Conscience was, and knocked at the gate.

Peace, the porter of Unity, unfastened the gates, and said hurriedly, 'What do you want?'

'I should like to speak with Contrition,' answered the Friar. 'It concerns the health and welfare of you all. That is why I have come.'

'He is ill, and so are many others,' said Peace. 'Hypocrisy

has wounded them so badly that they are not likely to get better.'

'But I am a doctor,' said the Friar, 'and highly skilled in mixing medicines. Conscience knows me well, and has seen what I can do.'

'Well, before you go any further, you had better tell me your name. And please don't try to conceal it.'

Then the Friar's companion answered for him, saying, 'Certainly. This is Father Creep-into-Houses.'[18]

'Oh! Then you can clear off!' said Peace. 'I've heard of your medicine, by heaven! You will have to learn a better trade before you get in here! I knew a man like you, in a Friar's habit, eight years ago. He used to come to the house where I worked, to act as doctor to my master and mistress. And one day, when my master was out, he came and cured our women so well that some turned out to be with child!'

But Courtesy urged Peace to open the gate, saying, 'Let the Friar and his friend in, and give them a good welcome. He may be very shrewd, and for all you know his teaching may persuade Life to leave Avarice and Pride, and begin to fear Death. We may yet see Life embrace Conscience and make his peace with him.'

So, through Courtesy's intervention, the Friar came in, and going in to where Conscience was, he greeted him politely. 'You are welcome,' replied Conscience. 'Can you heal the sick? My cousin Contrition here is wounded. Will you nurse him and look after his sores? The parson's plasters and powders are too strong for him; he is always unwilling to change them, and leaves them on too long. Why, he sometimes lets them go on chafing from one Lent to another.'

'That is far too long,' said the Friar, 'but I think I know how to put things right.'

So he went to examine Contrition, and gave him a fresh dressing called a Private Subscription. 'And I shall pray for you,' he said, 'and for all your loved ones, all my life.' And to another patient he said, 'I shall remember you, my lady, in my Masses and Matins, and you shall share all the spiritual gifts of our Order – for a small charge of course.'

So he went about collecting money, and flattering those who came to him for confession. And Contrition had soon forgotten to weep for his sins, and no longer lay awake at night as he used to do. So, in return for the comfort of an easy confessor, he gave up repentance, the sovereign remedy for all sins.

Sloth and Pride saw this at once, and attacked Conscience more eagerly than ever. And Conscience begged Clergy to help him, and ordered Contrition to guard the gates.

'Contrition is on his back, asleep and dreaming,' said Peace, 'and most of the others are in the same state. The Friar has bewitched them with his cures; his plasters are so mild that they have lost all fear of sin.'

'Then by Christ!' cried Conscience, 'I will become a pilgrim, and walk to the ends of the earth in search of Piers the Ploughman. For he can destroy Pride, and find an honest livelihood for these Friars who live by flattery and set themselves against me. Now may Nature avenge me, and send me His help and healing, until I have found Piers the Ploughman!'

Then he cried aloud for Grace, and I awoke.

AN 'AUTOBIOGRAPHICAL' PASSAGE FROM THE C TEXT

THUS I awoke, and found myself on Cornhill, where I lived with Kit in a cottage, dressed like a beggar – though not, believe me, in high favour with the idle hermits and beggars who hang around London, for I put them into my verses and spoke as Reason taught me.

For I met Reason one hot harvest-time, just as I was passing by Conscience.[1] And though, at the time, I was as fit as a fiddle, and my muscles were in good shape for work, I was fond of an easy life, and had nothing better to do than drink and sleep. And as I roamed along content with the world, and lost in daydreams of times past, I heard a voice, the voice of Reason, rebuking me and saying:

'Why can't you serve at Mass or sing in the choir, or rake the corn for the harvesters, or help them to mow and stack it, or bind up the sheaves? Or why don't you get up early and join the reapers, or find yourself a job as a head-reaper or a hayward, and stand with a horn in your hand, and sleep out at night to guard the corn in my fields from thieves and pilferers? Or why couldn't you cobble shoes, or watch the sheep or the pigs, or get some hedging or harrowing done, or drive the hogs and geese to market? At all events, you ought to do *something* that's useful to the community, and play your part in feeding the old and infirm.'

'Well, to be perfectly honest,' I said, 'I just haven't the strength. I'm no good with a scythe or a sickle, and God knows I'm far too tall to bend down to a labourer's job – honestly, I should never stand the pace!'

'Then have you got an estate of your own to live on?' asked Reason, 'or a wealthy family to provide for you? For you certainly look an idle fellow – one of those spendthrifts, I should think, who can't resist wasting their time and money. Or maybe you beg for your living, and hang around buttery-doors and squat in the churches on Fridays and fast-days, telling some yarn or other. That's not the kind of life that will gain you much credit when you come to where Justice deals out men's deserts – "For God rewards every man according to his work."[2] – But perhaps you're lame in one of your limbs or maimed by some accident, and are excused from working?'

'Many years ago, when I was a boy,' I answered, 'my father and friends found the means to send me to school, so that I came to understand Holy Scripture, and was taught all that's best for my body and safest for my soul – provided, of course, that I persevere in it. And though the friends who helped me then have since died, I have never found any life that suited me, except in these long, clerical robes. If I'm to earn a living, I must earn it by doing the job that I've learned best, for it is written, "Let every man abide in the same calling wherein he was called."[3]

'So I live in London, and also on London,[4] and the tools that I work with are my Paternoster and Prayer Book, and sometimes my Book of Offices for the Dead, and my Psalter and Seven Penitential Psalms.[5] And with these I sing for the souls of those who help me; and I expect the folk who provide me with food, to make me welcome when I visit them once or twice a month. So I go on my rounds, now to his house and now to hers, and that is how I do my begging – with neither bag nor bottle, but only my stomach to carry all my supplies!

'What is more, Sir Reason, I am convinced that you should never force a man in Holy Orders to do manual work. For it says in Leviticus,[6] the Law of God, that men whose natural gifts lead them to take Orders should not toil or sweat, or serve on juries, or fight in the front line or attack an enemy – "Do not render evil for evil,"[7] says the Scripture. For all who wear the tonsure are heirs of Heaven and ministers of Christ, and their job is to serve Him in the churches and choir-stalls. For it is written, "The Lord himself is the portion of mine inheritance,"[8] and again, "The life of meekness does not constrain a man."[9]

'So a cleric's duty is to serve Christ, and leave carting and labouring to ignorant serfs. And no one should take Holy Orders unless he comes from a family of freemen, and his parents are married in church. Serfs and beggar's children and bastards should toil with their hands, while men of noble blood should serve God and their fellowmen as befits their rank – some by singing Masses, and others by book-keeping and advising men how to spend their money.

'But nowadays, bondmen's children are made into Bishops and bastards into Archdeacons; and soap-makers and their sons buy themselves knighthoods, while the sons of true noblemen toil and sweat for them – for they mortgage their estates to ride out against our enemies and to fight for king and country in defence of the people. And the monks and nuns, who should feed the poor, buy up the incomes of knights and make noblemen of their relatives. Even Popes now, and ecclesiastical patrons, are refusing noble blood, and appointing the sons of Simony[10] to keep God's sanctuary. No wonder charity and holy living have disappeared – and will not return till this new fashion wears out, or someone uproots it.

'So pray do not rebuke me, Reason, for my conscience tells me what Christ would have me do. Our Lord loves the prayers of a perfect man and penance done with discretion, more than any other work in the world. "Man shall not live by the fruits of the earth, nor by bread and food alone"[11] – for so the Paternoster bears witness: "Thy will be done" can furnish us with all things.'

'But I don't see how this applies to you,' interrupted Conscience. 'To beg in cities is not the life of perfection – not unless you're appointed to beg by a Prior or Abbot.'

'True enough,' I replied, 'and I confess that I have frittered away my time. But consider: a merchant may lose money again and again, yet if at last he makes some wonderful bargain which sets him up for the rest of his life, what does he care about his previous losses? – Through the grace of God he has acquired a fortune, such as the parables describe: "The Kingdom of Heaven is like unto a treasure hid in a field,"[12] and again, "The woman, when she hath found her piece of silver, calleth her friends and her neighbours, saying, Rejoice with me; for I have found the piece which I had lost."[13] And I too am banking on a treasure – a sudden windfall of God's grace, to begin a new epoch in my life and turn all my past to profit.'

'Then I suggest you get a move on,' said Reason, 'and begin a more reputable life at once, and treat your soul with some respect.'

'Yes, and persevere in it too,' added Conscience – so off I went to church, to worship God.

Then I fell on my knees before the crucifix, beating my breast and sighing for my sins as I said the Paternoster; and as I wept and groaned there, I fell asleep.

Then I dreamt much more than I dreamt before on the Malvern Hills. For again I saw the field, packed with people from end to end, and now Reason, robed like a Pope, with Conscience as his crosier-bearer, standing before the king and preaching . . . (continues as on p. 99).

Appendix B

'THE POOREST FOLK ARE OUR NEIGHBOURS'
C Text, Book x, lines 71–97

THE poorest folk are our neighbours, if we look about us – the prisoners in dungeons and the poor in their hovels, overburdened with children, and rack-rented by landlords. For whatever they save by spinning they spend on rent, or on milk and oatmeal to make gruel and fill the bellies of their children who clamour for food. And they themselves are often famished with hunger, and wretched with the miseries of winter – cold, sleepless nights, when they get up to rock the cradle cramped in a corner, and rise before dawn to card and comb the wool, to wash and scrub and mend, and wind yarn and peel rushes for their rushlights. – The miseries of these women who dwell in hovels are too pitiful to read, or describe in verse.

Yet there are many more who suffer like them – men who go hungry and thirsty all day long, and strive their utmost to hide it – ashamed to beg, or tell their neighbours of their need. I've seen enough of the world to know how they suffer, these men who have many children, and no means but their trade to clothe and feed them. For many hands are waiting to grasp the few pence they earn, and while the Friars feast on roast venison, they have bread and thin ale, with perhaps a scrap of cold meat or stale fish. And on Fridays and fast-days a farthing's worth of cockles or a few mussels would be a feast for such folk. I tell you, it would be a real charity to help men so burdened, and comfort these cottagers along with the blind and the lame.

NOTES AND COMMENTARY

Some of the Notes which follow are taken from the standard
Edition of W. W. Skeat (Early English Text Society, published
by the Oxford University Press), which I have used in preparing
this translation, and I am grateful to the Oxford University Press
for permission to quote from it freely. (All line-numbers men-
tioned in the Notes and the line-numbering of the running head-
lines refer to this edition.) I have also consulted the work of more
recent scholars, and am indebted to the authors and publishers of
all works quoted or mentioned in the Introduction and Notes.

Abbreviation: R. & H. = J. R. Robertson and Bernard F. Huppé,
Piers Plowman and Scriptural Tradition (Princeton University Press,
1951).

INTRODUCTION

1. Cf George Kane, *Piers Plowman. The Evidence for Authorship*
(University of London Press, 1965)

2. Trinity College, Dublin MS D.4.1. 'Memorandum quod
Stacy de Rokayle pater willielmi de Langlond quit stacius fuit
generosus & morabatur in Schiptoun vnder whicwode tenens
domini le Spenser in comitatu Oxoniensi qui predictus willielmus
fecit librum qui vocatur Perys ploughman.'

3. W. A. Pantin, *The English Church in the Fourteenth Century*
(Cambridge University Press, 1955).

4. J. A. W. Bennett, 'The Date of the A-text of P. Pl.' (*P.M.L.A.*
lvii, 3, June 1943) and 'The Date of the B-text of P. Pl.' (*Med. Aev.*,
xii, 1941).

5. Cf George Kane, op. cit.

6. The poem was printed three times in 1550, and reprinted for
the last time by Owen Rogers in 1561.

7. Puttenham, *The Arte of English Poesie* (1586).

8. *Piers Plowman, The A Version* edited by George Kane (Uni-
versity of London Press, 1960); Elizabeth Salter, *Piers Plowman,
An Introduction* (Blackwell, 1963); John Lawlor, *Piers Plowman, An
Essay in Criticism* (Arnold, 1962).

9. Lawlor, op. cit.

10. Lawlor, op. cit.

11. G. R. Owst, *Preaching In Mediaeval England* (Cambridge
University Press, 1925) and *Literature and the Pulpit in Mediaeval
England* (Cambridge University Press, 1933).

Part I. The difference between the themes of the two Parts may be explained by St Paul's distinction between natural and spiritual life in I Cor. xv. 46–9. The Piers of Part I is earth-born, and, as T. P. Dunning has explained ('The Structure of the B-Text of P.Pl.', *R.E.S.*, vii, July 1956), the first Part deals with 'the primary necessity which gives rise to the arts and crafts – the provision of food and clothing and all those major occupations which absorb most of the energies of men in civil society.' Its subject, then, is the reform of society.

Prologue

THE ALLEGORY. *The dreamer is as yet spiritually unsanctified and his judgements are based on temporal standards. The world as he sees it is anarchic: men of every profession are bent on gain, regardless of Tower and Dungeon. The authority of both church and State has become arbitrary, since their Law is no longer tempered by love and mercy. Langland's picture of the setting up of the State dwindles to the comedy of the rats and mice, which parodies the proceedings of the House of Commons in his day and shows politics as a scramble of self-interest. The cat goes unchecked, and though countless lawyers plead at the bar, the world remains lawless.*

1. *In the garb of an easy-living hermit.* i.e. one who did not keep to his cell (see p. 26). Shepherds and hermits were dressed alike.

2. *Looking Eastwards;.* 'The East and the Sun are Biblical symbols of God' – H. W. Wells.

3. *Babblers and vulgar jesters.* Cf. pp. 113–14. On the general significance of these 'false minstrels' throughout the poem, see note 31, Bk xiii.

4. *'He who talks filth.'* There is no such text in St Paul, though L. may have been thinking of Titus i. 10–12, Eph. v. 4, or Col. iii. 8.

5. *Palmers.* Folk who made it their vocation to go on pilgrimages, professing poverty.

6. *Compostella.* The famous shrine of St James the Greater at Santiago de Compostella in Galicia – a favourite resort of pilgrims.

7. *All four Orders of them.* i.e. the Carmelites, Augustines, Dominicans, and Franciscans or Friars Minor.

8. *The worst evil in the world.* The conflict between the Friars and the regular priests is described under the Deadly Sin of Anger, Bk v. Cf. also Pantin, op. cit., 124–6. By 'the worst evil' L. may here mean a permanent Schism. One effect of the Great Schism

was to divide the Friars into two factions, one supporting the Pope, the other the anti-pope Clement; and the latter group elected a rival Minister-General.

9. *Since the Plague*. There were four pestilences during the reign of Edward III, in 1348–9, 1361–2, 1369, and 1375–6. The first of these is generally known as the Black Death, which destroyed at least a third of the population, so that the land was left untilled, and the parish priests could not collect their tithes.

10. *Traffic in Masses*. Literally 'sing for Simony' – i.e. the money received for singing Masses for the Dead in the chantries or side-chapels of St Paul's and elsewhere.

11. *Consistory Court*. An ecclesiastical Court – here a metaphor for the Day of Judgement.

12. *'To bind and unbind.'* Matt. xvi. 19.

13. *Four greatest virtues*. 'Cardinal' is derived from the Latin 'cardo', a hinge. By playing on this derivation, Langland compares the true spiritual 'hinges' of Christendom with those on whom its fate actually turns. Bennett (*Date of the B-text*) points out that Pope Urban VI's denunciation of avaricious cardinals provoked the Cardinal of Amiens to organize a rebel group among the French Cardinals, who in September 1378 elected an anti-pope, Clement VII, of their own nationality. In October of the same year, when the English Parliament met at Gloucester, messengers came begging aid both from the Pope *and* the Apostate Cardinals. This may account for Langland's attack on their presumption over the electing of a Pope. 'If interpreted as referring to the Schism,' Bennett says, 'these lines provide a link between the Papacy and the English scene which corresponds exactly to the sequence of thought in this part of Langland's Prologue.' (For another link between the Cardinals and the English scene, see what the 'ignorant vicar' says about them, p. 242).

14. *Then there came into the field ... etc.'* Langland briefly sets before us the whole political situation, with little direct comment. The fable of the Rats and Mice has some reference to the events of the Good Parliament (1376), though it was probably inserted ironically at the time of the Bad Parliament (1377), which undid all the work of the good one.

J. Jusserand has shown how closely some of Langland's remarks about politics (e.g. about the encroachments of Papal power) resemble certain passages in the Rolls of Parliament: 'In religious, as in secular matters, Langland sides ... heart and soul with the Commons of England.' (See J. Jusserand, *Piers Plowman: A*

Contribution to the History of English Mysticism, London, 1894, especially pp. 71, 112, 128–36.)

15. *A long, lean, crazy fellow*. All the commentators agree in assuming that this must be Langland himself.

16. *An angel of heaven*. In Middle English the word 'angel' was sometimes used of a prophet or a preacher (OED. 2). Owst (*Literature and the Pulpit*) identifies this angel with a popular preacher of the time, Thomas Brunton, Bishop of Rochester, leaning from his pulpit. The sermon he preached – in Latin, since it was a State occasion – on the accession of Richard II is still extant; it voices the complaints of the Commons, and refers to 'the fable of the parliament of rats and mice'.

17. *A horde of rats ... and little mice*. A well-known fable – cf. *Les Contes moralisés* de Nicole Bozon (1320). The rats represent the more influential members of the Commons, the mice those of lesser importance.

18. *A cat*. More likely John of Gaunt than Edward III, as the latter was too old to cause the Commons much trouble.

19. *A mouse who looked very shrewd*. Bennett (*The Date of the B-Text*) says that this mouse, 'whose sentiments the poet seems to approve of', is perhaps Peter de la Mare, who in 1377 put forward the Commons' proposal for a Council to advise the new king Richard. (On the other hand, Owst identifies the 'garrulous fellow' ['goliardeys'] of p. 29 with Peter de la Mare.) This was at the same time as Brunton preached his sermon, in which he showed that the youthfulness of the new king was a matter of general concern.

20. *I heard my father say ... etc*. This part of the mouse's speech, says Bennet (op. cit.) is an allegorical description of the changed situation after Richard's (i.e. the kitten's) accession, when the quarrels between the citizens and John of Gaunt were forgotten for a time.

21. *'Woe to that land ...'* Eccles. x. 16.

22. *While he's off catching rabbits*. This may refer to John of Gaunt's retirement to his duchy at the close of 1377, to enjoy the pleasures of the chase; or to his campaigns against the French in 1378.

Book I

THE ALLEGORY. *The perfect heavenly Church, the daughter of God, who first received the dreamer as a child at the font, now comes to interpret his vision, correct his attitude and explain the proper use of physical things.*

Once he has recognized her, he recalls the baptismal grace he has lost and asks the question from which the rest of the poem's action springs: 'How may I save my soul?' Her answer – a simple statement of the fundamentals of the Christian faith – is that he must seek Truth through the love that is already implanted in his heart, and practise the virtues that all men know by instinct. But he still persists in his inquiry into the ways of the world.

1. *Three things in common.* Cf. Ecclus. xxix. 21, and St John Chrysostom, Twelfth Address on the First Letter to Timothy: 'God gave us every necessary thing as a common possession ... Community of goods is a far more suitable mode of life for us than private property, and it is natural.' The same doctrine was taught by St Cyprian, Pope Gregory the Great, and others. But see Bk xx, ll. 274–6 (p. 253 in present translation).

2. *The story of Lot.* Genesis xix.

3. *Read the Gospel.* Matt. xxii. 21.

4. *Common Sense.* In Langland, this has something of the meaning 'Moral Sense'.

5. *Hanged him on an elder-tree.* The tradition that Judas hanged himself on an elder-tree is often mentioned in Middle English. See also *Love's Labour's Lost*, v. ii. 610. Langland's contemporary Mandeville said that the tree was still standing when he visited the Holy Land!

6. *'God is love.'* See 1 John iv. esp. 6–8 and 11 John 1–2. Truth and Charity (like Falsehood and Wrong) are inseparable, and the rest of the Book develops this theme. Cf. the traditional Scriptural linking of Mercy and Truth, and of Grace and Truth.

7. *Those are St Luke's words.* The reference has not been traced, but as Langland sometimes confuses the different Gospels, he may have been thinking of John xv. 1–6, or of the text quoted by 'Wit' (ix, 62) and Repentance (v, 494), – 1 John iv. 16.

8. *King David in his time.* May refer to 1 Sam. xxii. 2 or 11 Sam. xxiii. 8–39.

9. *Ten Orders of Angels.* Seraphim, Cherubim, Thrones, Dominations, Virtues, Powers, Principalities, Archangels, and Angels. The tenth was the Order of Lucifer, which fell from Heaven.

10. *Understand Truth by the Holy Trinity.* Truth here has partly the sense of Loyalty. Lucifer and the angels were taught truth by the Beatific Vision, that is, by beholding Truth himself. The undivided unity of the three Persons of the Trinity was their perfect example of loyalty or oneness. 1 John iv might again serve as a commentary.

11. *'I will exalt my throne . . .'* Isaiah xiv. 13–14. Cf. also *Paradise Lost*, The Argument to Bk v, and v, 752.

12. *They fell in so strange a way.* This was thought to explain the origin of sylphs (in the air), gnomes (in the earth), and nymphs (in streams and woods), who were less guilty than the rest of the rebellious angels.

13. *My two texts.* 'Render to Caesar' and 'God is love'.

14. *A natural knowledge in your heart.* Cp. v, 615–16, xv, 203–4 and 212, and xvi, 13–16.

15. *By Love, God chose to fashion.* i.e. by Christ. Cf. Eph. iii. 9 and John i. 3.

16. *He taught Moses.* See Deut. vi. 6, x. 12, and elsewhere.

17. *Plant of Peace.* Cf. Isaiah liii. 2 and Rev. xxii. 2.

18. *Taken flesh and blood.* 'And the word was made flesh' (John i. 14).

19. *'With what measure ye mete.'* Matt. vii. 2 and James ii. 13.

20. *'Faith without deeds.'* James ii. 26.

21. *'Give and it shall be given.'* Luke vi. 38. Langland elaborates on the text.

Book II

THE ALLEGORY. *Holy Church shows the dreamer her opposite ('Meed'), the woman who has usurped her place in Church and State. She represents the power of the purse, and 'we begin to see the specific charge in the general indictment against the world of the Prologue is venality – all is for sale, and this is ratified by law, which also, and principally, is for sale' (Lawlor, op. cit.). Her marriage to Fraud, a conspiracy supported by all the public officials, lay and clerical, in the kingdom, signifies the wedding of payment or reward to bribery and corruption. Its chief supporters, Sir Civil-Law and Father Simony, stand for civil and ecclesiastical law respectively, and they control English society. Theology's objection to the marriage introduces the great case of Lady Fee, which is to be heard in the King's Court, and concerns the proper use of payment or reward. All her other followers go into hiding to await the result.*

1. *Lady Fee.* In the original, 'Meed the Maid'. 'Meed' literally meant 'reward', but came to mean bribery. Some scholars say that she represents Alice Perrers, the mistress of Edward III.

2. *Flattery.* Langland's word 'Fauel' also means duplicity and cajolery.

3. *I looked to the left.* 'The left is symbolical of evil' – H. W. Wells.

4. *Her fingers prettily adorned.* Cf. the description of the Whore of Babylon in Rev. xvii 4 ff.

5. *To protect her from poisons.* 'Precious stones were thought to be antidotes to poisons, and remedies for diseases' – Davis.

6. *'Every good tree . . .'* Matt. vii. 17.

7. *I his lover, in heaven.* Cf. the image of the Holy City as a bride, Rev. xxi. 2 and xxii. 17.

8. *'Lord, who shall dwell . . .'* Ps. xiv.

9. *Serpent's-tongue.* Cf. Ps. cxl. 3.

10. *Summoners.* Officers of the ecclesiastical courts, whose duty was to cite and warn offenders to appear in court.

11. *Victuallers.* 'These were the purveyors, who went before a king or great lord in progress, and bought up provisions for himself and his retinue. They often used much oppression, exacting provisions at a cheap rate, and sometimes forgetting to pay for them' – Skeat. The character named Crime ('Wrong') in Bk IV may well represent one of these.

12. *Father Simony and Lord Civil-Law.* For further light on their activities, cf. the paragraph about Covetousness pp. 248–9 (Bk xx, ll. 120–41).

13. *Sciant presentes et futuri.* This is drawn up in the form of a typical medieval charter.

14. *The Pauline Order.* Usually identified with the 'Crutched Friars' who came to England in 1244. They seem to have been especially concerned with the drawing-up of law-suits in the Consistory Courts (see p. 43).

15. *Mund the Miller, and many others.* The witnesses all belong to callings notorious for extortion.

16. *Fee is an honest woman.* See note 1.

17. *'The labourer is worthy . . .'* Luke x. 7.

18. *Westminster.* The Courts of Law at Westminster.

19. *Deans, sub-deans, etc.* All the 'horses' in this paragraph are ecclesiastical Officials of the Diocese, concerned with the ecclesiastical courts.

20. *The Commissary.* 'An officer of the Bishop who exercised spiritual jurisdiction in distant parts of the diocese, where the people could not attend the consistory court' (Davis).

21. *Six months and eleven days.* This, says Dr Bennett (*Date of the A-text*) is 'exactly the period during which the 1359–60 operations (against the French) lasted: Edward III landed at Calais on 28 Oct. 1359, and the Treaty of Bretigny was signed on 8 May in the following year.' In that case, the significance of Liar's

staying among 'minstrels and messengers' for this period may be that these wayfarers spread false rumours about the course of the campaign.

Book III

THE ALLEGORY. *The king is surrounded by courtiers, priests and judges who seek Fee's favours, and in her dealings with them she is shown up as the perverter of justice. The conflict between her and Conscience provides a deeper analysis of the relation between human and divine reward: Conscience sets human standards of payment for service against the millenial ideal of a kingdom governed by divine law – where Law itself will be the servant of Love. 'There begins to rise, above the dead level of this middle-earth, where the* measurable *is the truth to be contended for, the cliff-like outline of perfection'* (Lawlor, op. cit.).

1. *Obtain seats for them.* Literally, 'have their names called over.'

2. *The dulcet undertones.* Langland wrote: 'He mellud this wordes, And seide ful softly in shrifte as it were'; I do not think they had confession-boxes in the fourteenth century.

3. *Beadsman.* A person paid to say regular prayers for another.

4. *Your name engraved in the window.* 'It was usual to introduce portraits or names of the benefactors in stained glass' (Skeat).

5. *A lay-sister.* The Friars could, by means of a 'letter of fraternity', give to a lay person a share in all the spiritual gifts of their Order, so that he became a kind of Tertiary.

6. *Cry out for the notice of men of God.* Cf. Matt. vi. 1. But the phrase 'men of God' might refer to the Friars or priests, and Langland may mean, 'Don't send for the Friars when you want to give alms.'

7. *Have your reward on earth.* Matt. vi. 2.

8. *'Let not thy left hand . . .'* Matt. vi. 3.

9. *'Fire shall consume . . .'* Not from one of the Books of Solomon, but Job xv. 34.

10. *Poisoned Popes.* Cf. the story of the angel heard over Rome, p. 194. But Langland may mean it literally, for 'Pope Benedict XI, who died in 1304, is said to have been poisoned' (Skeat).

11. *Your own father.* An allusion to the dethronement and murder of Edward II.

12. *The king's privy seal.* This remark, and its connexion with what follows, is explained by the following passage from Wyclif (quoted by Skeat): 'Also many worldly peyntid clerkes geten the *kyngis seel*, hym out-wittynge, and senden to Rome for beneficis

moche gold.' (Cf. Langland's remarks about the taking of gold overseas, pp. 58–9.)

13. *The French Wars*. Refers to Edward III's campaign of 1359–60.

14. *Creeping into hovels*, etc. 'Froissart's account of the 1359–60 campaign shows that the English army did suffer real privations of the kind suggested by these lines.' The terrible storm of Black Monday, described by Froissart, 'was merely the crowning misery' (Bennett, *Date of A-text*).

15. *To give it all up*. Alludes to the terms of the Treaty of Bretigny (8 May 1260), by which Edward renounced his claim to the crown of France, and gave up most of his French territories, while the Dauphin agreed to pay for the ransom of his father, King John, the sum of 3,000,000 crowns of gold.

16. *The king receives money* . . . 'The king sometimes accepted a fine from a delinquent who should have been brought to justice, but who thus obtained the "king's peace".' (Skeat). See note 5, Bk IV.

17. '*Lord, who shall dwell* . . . ' Ps. 15. Cf. also Isaiah xxxiii. 14–18.

18. '*In whose hand is wickedness* . . . ' Ps. xxvi. 10.

19. *Unless the Scripture lies*. Cf. Gen. xiv. 21–3.

20. '*They have their reward.*' Matt. vi. 5.

21. *The Book of Samuel*. 1 Sam. xv.

22. *The fate of Agag*. 1 Sam. xv. 32–3.

23. *David shall be crowned*. 1 Sam. xv. 12–14, 16.

24. *Such love shall arise*. This and the following para. is 'largely a paraphrase and commentary on Isaiah ii. 2–5, along lines common to homilists' (Bennett, *Date of the B-text*).

25. *Any man who carries a sword*. 'The frequent enactments against the wearing of weapons by civilians, etc., in the reigns of Edward III and Richard II, show how often the law was disregarded' (Skeat).

26. '*Beat their swords into ploughshares* . . . ' Isaiah 11. 4.

27. *Will be for the souls of the dead*. i.e. they will sing the Office for the Dead, instead of hunting.

28. '*Nation shall not lift up sword* . . . ' Isaiah ii. 4.

29. *Six suns in the sky*. 'The widespread belief in astrology gave rise to all sorts of fanciful predictions' (Davis). 'The present one merely hints at a final time when Jews and Mahometans shall be converted' (Skeat). Skeat also quotes various occasions when the portent of several suns in the sky was supposed to have been seen,

and adds, 'We might ... interpret "ships" and "half a sheaf of arrows" to refer to a portent signifying invasion by an enemy.'

30. '*A good name* ...' Prov. xxii. 1.

31. '*He that giveth gifts* ...' Prov. XXII. 9.

32. '*Prove all things.*' 1 Thess. v. 21.

33. '*But he taketh away the soul* ...' The meaning of the second half of the text is actually obscure, and it is translated differently in the Authorized Version. See Knox rendering and his footnote.

Book IV

THE ALLEGORY. *The petition of Peace against Crime ('Wrong') provides a test case for the rule of Reason and Law, in which Fee exerts all her powers to corrupt the witnesses and the plaintiff himself. Crime (one of the king's purveyors) represents brutal injustice sheltering under the pretence of service to the crown. The sanctity of law is finally upheld, and Fee and all her followers are disgraced. The king is now obliged to accept Reason and Conscience as his counsellors; but to carry out the rule of Law requires the support of the whole realm. So Reason must preach to the people and bring them to confession. The reform of the State depends on the reform of society.*

1. *Cato.* 'Reason probably names his servant after Dionysius Cato, whose Moral Distichs, written in the fourth century, were very popular in the Middle Ages' (Davis). Langland frequently quotes Cato (*Disticha de Moribus*) and treats him as a great authority on ethical questions.

2. '*Destruction and unhappiness* ...' Ps. xiv 7,. quoted in Rom. iii. 16–18. The verse does not appear in the Authorized Version, but only in the Vulgate and Prayer Book.

3. *A petition.* The complaints of Peace are against the evils of purveyance – See note 11, Bk II.

4. *Forestalls my goods.* 'The purveyor seized the produce, so the farmer had nothing to sell at the fairs' (Davis).

5. *Holds your life and lands* ... 'In the royal court, the usual penalty on conviction was placing the culprit "at the king's mercy"; that his goods and chattels were forfeited, unless – which, indeed, often happened – the monarch graciously condescended to accept a fine by way of compromise' (Quoted by Skeat from *Europe in the Middle Ages*).

6. *Pay a ransom.* 'A person arrested for debt or any other personal action might find *mainprise* or bail. ... It is evident that the

finding of mainprise was used for screening rich offenders, and defeating the ends of justice' (Skeat).

7. *Two wrongs don't make a right*. Cunning's words literally mean: 'It is better that compensation should reduce the wrong done, than that the wrong done be punished (beaten) and no reparation be really made.' He plays on the proverbial contrast between 'bote' and 'bale'.

8. *St James is sought*. See note 6, Prologue.

9. *To fill the pockets of the Papal robbers*. See note 12, Bk III. Langland may also be voicing the complaints of the Commons against Papal taxes and impositions, and Italian priests' drawing stipends from English benefices.

10. *Running off to Rome or Avignon*. During most of the fourteenth century the Papal Court was at Avignon, but it was at Rome from 1377–83. Bennett (*Date of the B-text*) quotes a passage from Wycliffe about priests 'who can faste renne to Rome & bere gold out of the lond & paie it for deed leed (bulls?) & a litil wrytinge (indulgences?).' See also the Chapter on 'Anglo-Papal Relations' in Pantin, op. cit. pp. 76–105.

11. *At Dover*. 'Refers to the then existing law – "that no pilgrim should pass out of the realm, to parts beyond the seas, but only *at Dover*, on pain of a year's imprisonment": Ruding's *Annals of the Coinage*, 1840' (Skeat).

12. *Except, of course, for all the merchants* ... This list of exceptions must be intended ironically, since it includes those who were most guilty of the offence.

13. *Nullum malum* ... The point of this riddle is to introduce the Latin words, which come from Pope Innocent III's *De Contemptu Mundi*: 'Ipse est iudex iustus ... qui *nullum malum* praeterit *impunitum, nullum bonum irremuneratum*' – 'He alone is a just judge ... who leaves no evil unpunished and no good unrewarded.'

14. *Estates*. Literally 'escheats' – lands which should have lapsed to the crown when the tenant died without an heir.

Book V

THE ALLEGORY. *Reason's sermon turns attention from human law to the absolute demands of God and their direct application to everyday life. The dreamer himself is now moved to repent and we hear his name, Will (i.e. the human will seeking its proper course), for the first time. The 'follies and knaveries of the world the poet knows' are now 'subsumed under the great traditional heads' (Lawlor, op. cit.). These are the vices that destroy society, and are so firmly rooted in human nature that they lead to a blindness that is almost incurable. Robert the Robber's direct appeal to Christ to pay his debt points to the impossibility of man's making restitution for himself; and Repentance, taking up this theme in his prayer, sketches out the theme of redemption which is to be enacted in Book XVIII. The narrative reaches a joyful climax as the people set out in search of Truth, but they still need a guide. The palmer who has never heard of St Truth represents the outward trappings of a church that has forgotten how to guide its pilgrims. He is contrasted with Piers, the good ploughman who knows Truth by that 'natural knowledge' which Holy Church pointed to in the dreamer. He explains the way of the commandments in precise and simple terms and tries to encourage the people by reminding them of their natural kinship with the heavenly virtues.*

1. *The great gale.* An allusion to the violent tempest which occurred on Saturday, 15 Jan. 1362, and began 'about euensong tyme'. The second great Pestilence was then prevailing.

2. *Rescue Felicity.* She was probably an ale-wife, like Rose the Racketeer (p. 67), and was being punished for selling bad drink. The two sticks were presumably to disperse the crowd.

3. *'The more you love your child . . . '* A common medieval proverb.

4. *'He that spareth his rod . . . '* Prov. xiii. 24.

5. *'I know you not.'* Matt. xxv. 12.

6. *Saint Truth.* Here identified with the Holy Ghost (Cf. Piers' description of His mansion in the human heart, pp. 78–9).

7. *Pride.* In the C-text, the description of Haukyn's pride (pp. 159–61) was added to this, to complete the picture.

8. *Lechery.* In the C-text, the description of Haukyn's lechery (p. 162) is here inserted.

9. *Anger.* In the A-text, this Sin was omitted. Langland here depicts it chiefly through one example of its growth and effects – the bitterness that existed between the Friars and the secular priests.

10. *Grow rich, and ride about on horseback.* 'Wrath here insinuates that the quarrel generally terminates in one of two ways; either the secular clergy turn beggars like the friars, or the friars obtain wealth enough to buy horses like the secular clergy. The quarrel was as to which should hear confessions' (Skeat).

11. *In cherry-time.* The C-text changes this to 'in the henhouse'!

12. *No Prioress . . . hear confessions.* 'It appears that some abbesses did at one time attempt to hear the confessions of their nuns, . . . but this practice was soon stopped by Gregory IX, who has for-

bidden it in the strongest terms. – Decretal l. v. tit. 38. c. x'
(Tyrwhitt, quoted by Skeat).

13. *'Be ye sober.'* 1 Pet. iv. 7, v. 8.

14. *The pound weight she used.* i.e. she cheated the spinners she
employed by using false weights.

15. *The Rood of Bromholm.* 'At the Priory of Bromholm, in
Norfolk, there was a celebrated cross, said to be made of fragments
of the real cross, and much resorted to by pilgrims' (Wright, quoted
by Davis). Avarice could visit it on his journey to or from the
shrine of Our Lady of Walsingham.

16. *Jews and Lombards.* 'The system of money-lending in Eng-
land was established by merchants from Lombardy as early as the
reign of Richard I. They lent money on pawns and on sums due to
the Pope. Both the Lombards and the Jews exacted exorbitant
interest, and were also guilty of clipping coins' (Davis).

17. *For love of the cross.* The word 'cross' frequently refers to
that stamped on the back of coins, and it became a slang word for
coin (as in 2 *Henry IV.* I.ii.253). According to Skeat, sacred
Christian relics were sometimes obtained by Jews as pledges for
money. 'It is clear enough,' he adds, 'what Avarice did: he first
clipped coins and then lent them, taking a pledge which he hoped
would not be redeemed.'

18. *'Showing kindness and lending'.* Ps. cxii. 5.

19. *I have lent ... to lords and ladies,* etc. It was customary to
give part of a loan in the form of goods. When the borrower had
paid back the money with interest, but not the goods, the lender
would then buy back the goods at a very low valuation.

20. *Turned many a knight into a mercer.* 'Avarice, in his dealings
with knights, used to buy silk and cloth from them at a sufficiently
cheap rate; and he now ironically calls his customers mercers and
drapers who never paid anything for their apprenticeship' (Skeat).

21. *'Thou art the slave of another ...'* Source unknown, but
cf. Prov. xxii. 7 and II Thess. iii. 12.

22. *'The sin is not remitted ...'* Augustine Epistles cliii. sect. 20.

23. *'Behold, Thou desirest truth ...'* Ps. li. 6. By the Psalter
Commentary Langland probably means the *Glosa Ordinaria*, which
for this verse quotes St Augustine's comment: 'He giveth indeed
His mercies, yet in such a way that He may satisfy justice; that the
sins of him whom He pardoneth may not go unpunished.'

24. *'With the merciful ...'* Ps. xviii. 25–6.

25. *'God's tender mercies ...'* Ps. cxlv. 9.

26. *'Compared with the mercy of God ...'* A frequently quoted

saying, attributed to St Augustine – Cf. his comment on Ps. cxliii. 2: 'The fire of sin is quenched as if by a wave of mercy.'

27. *Render an account to God.* Cf. Hebr. xiii. 17.

28. *A fish-day.* It was on a Friday and fasting-day that Glutton set out to go to confession.

29. *The hackneyman.* 'A hackney man was one who let out horses on hire' (Skeat).

30. *The Flemish wench.* Skeat quotes Riley's Memorials of London, the Regulation as to street-walkers by night, who were especially 'Flemish women,' that they were forbidden to lodge in the city, by night or by day, but must keep themselves to 'the places thereunto assigned, that is to say, to the stews on the other side of Thames, and *Cokkeslane.*'

31. *A game of handicap.* 'An old game ... played as a sort of trade barter. The difference in value between two articles was estimated by two friends of the sellers, and if these could not agree, an umpire was appointed. In this instance, Bett the butcher acted for Hick, and Robin the umpire decided that Clement should drink at Hick's expense for the extra value of the cloak' (Davis).

32. *Robin Hood and Randolph.* 'No earlier mention than this has been found of the Robin Hood ballads' (Davis). The Earl of Chester may be the one who married Constance, the widow of Geoffrey Plantagenet and mother of Prince Arthur (Earl from 1181 to 1231). Though his exploits are known, no ballads about him have survived.

33. *Auditing Reeves' accounts.* Cf. Chaucer's Prologue, 594 *et seq.*, and *Piers Plowman*, Bk XIX, ll. 456–61.

34. *Vigilate* = Watch! (imperative); a reference to Mark xiii. 37.

35. *The Rood of Chester.* 'The famous cross of Chester at Rood-eye (now spelt Roodee), i.e. Rood Island, was a frequent resort of pilgrims' (Davis).

36. '*Render to all men ...*' Rom. xiii. 7.

37. *Dismas my brother.* According to the apocryphal Gospel of Nicodemus the name of the penitent thief was Dismas.

38. '*Remember me ...*' Luke xxiii. 42.

39. *Has not wherewith to repay.* Cf. Luke vii. 42.

40. *Latro* = robber. The word is used with reference to the expression in Luke xxiii. 39 – '*Unus autem de his qui pendebant latronibus* – And one of the robbers which were hanged.'

41. *O God, who in Your goodness ...* 'The prayer of Repentance is essentially a statement of faith followed by a plea for amendment

and mercy, combining most of the elements of the Apostolic Creed' (R. and H., 74).

42. *O felix culpa.* The full passage, from the Holy Saturday Canticle *Exsultet*, runs: 'O truly necessary sin of Adam, that Christ's death blotted out; O happy fault that merited such a Redeemer!'

43. '*Let us make man.*' Gen. i. 26.

44. '*He that dwelleth ...*' 1 John iv. 16.

45. *At about midday ... the meal-time*, etc. The words 'midday' or 'noon' in Middle English might refer to the period from 12.0 a.m. to 3.0 p.m. (the hour of Nones). But Langland is here speaking symbolically, for midday is traditionally the time when the Devil (or 'Midday fiend') tries a man most severely (cf. Ps. xci. 6 – 'The destruction that wasteth at noonday'), and Christ's death was the time of his greatest struggle with the Devil (see p. 258). Noon is also the time for a midday meal, especially in Religious Houses (cf. C-text, x, 246), and Christ, by His death, fed all his children with His Blood (cf. Song of Sol, i. 7). Moreover, it was at the time of the 'greatest light' that the world was plunged in darkness, and the Light of Christ descended into Hell to 'feed with His fresh blood our forefathers (the patriarchs and prophets) who dwelt in darkness', so that the light of the noonday sun seemed, at the moment of His death, to leave the earth, and light up the darkness of hell.

46. '*The people that walked in darkness ...*' Isaiah ix. 2. Cf. the use of the text on p. 226. In the Apocryphal Gospel of Nicodemus this text is explained as a reference to the Harrowing of Hell.

47. '*I came not to call the righteous ...*' Matt. ix. 13.

48. '*The Word was made flesh.*' John i. 14.

49. '*Yet didst thou turn ...*' Ps. lxxi. 20.

50. '*Blessed is he ...*' Ps. xxxii. 1.

51. '*Thou, Lord, shalt save ...*' Ps. xxxvi. 6 and 7.

52. *Blundered on like beasts.* Cf. Matt. ix. 36 *et seq.* – 'as sheep having no shepherd.' Piers is the labourer whom Christ sends into his harvest.

53. *Dressed like a strange Saracen.* Because of his foreign appearance and the pilgrims' signs that he wore.

54. *Bag and begging-bowl.* 'The bowl and bag were invariably carried, the former to drink out of, the latter to hold scraps of meat and bread' (Skeat). The true pilgrim, Piers, carries his seed-basket ('hopper') instead of a beggar's wallet (p. 83); and Christ commanded his own 'harvesters' to carry none (Luke x. 4).

55. *Souvenirs*. 'Besides the ordinary insignia of pilgrimage, every pilgrimage had its special signs, which the pilgrim on his return wore conspicuously upon his hat or his scrip, or hanging round his neck, in token that he had accomplished that particular pilgrimage' (Quoted by Skeat from Cutts, *Scenes and Characters of the Middle Ages*, p. 167). The phials of holy oil ('ampullae') were the signs of the Canterbury pilgrimage.

56. *Sinai*. 'Pilgrims to Sinai used to visit the convent of St Catharine, with its various relics' (Skeat).

57. *St Veronica handkerchief*. A copy of the handkerchief of St Veronica, which is said to have been miraculously impressed with the features of Christ.

58. *Bethlehem, Babylon*, etc. ... The various sights supposed to be seen at these places are extravagantly described in Mandeville's Travels. 'By going to Armenia, the pilgrim could see Noah's Ark' (Skeat).

59. *By St Peter!* Piers' exclamation, swearing by the saint after whom he is named, suggests at once the first worker in Christ's harvest (Matt. x. 2), and his character as the Rock (Matt. xvi, 18–19). Langland's oaths and asseverations frequently bear a direct, or sometimes an ironical, relation to the allegory, e.g. that of the dreamer on p. 38 (the contrast between Our Lady and Lady Fee), that of the knight on p. 82 (Piers has just given him advice very like that of St James's Epistle), and others.

60. *Riches in St Thomas's shrine*. 'The offerings of numberless pilgrims made the shrine of St Thomas à Becket of Canterbury the wealthiest in England' (Davis).

61. *Love God above all things*. Cf. Matt. xxii. 37–40. As all the commandments depend on these two precepts, 'Piers follows them with a generalized exposition of the commandments' (R. and H., p. 77).

62. *A mansion*. The Castle of Truth is in the human heart – See below, 'You will find Truth dwelling in your heart, etc.'. See also note 14, Bk 1, and cf. Prov. ix. 1 and iv. 23.

63. '*Through Eve the door* ...' A very familiar idea (Cf. the hymn *Ave, maris stella*), though source of this quotation not identified.

64. *When the king is sleeping*. Cf. Ps. xliv. 23, Mark iv. 38.

65. '*As the early dew* ...' Hosea xiii. 3.

66. *Seven Sisters*. The Seven Virtues, opposites to the Seven Deadly Sins.

67. *Mercy*. Here identified with the Blessed Virgin.

Book VI

THE ALLEGORY. *'It was not the principle of spiritual life which came first; natural life came first'* (I Cor. xv. 46). *In Langland's day, the first need was to stave off famine, enforce the Statutes of Labourers and do away with the injustice of waste and idleness that followed the Black Death. The ploughman (provider of society, and symbol of the Christian community) tries to enforce conformity to the law among all classes of society, and is driven to invoke the principle of 'work or want'. But in this he fails: though the knight cooperates, the labourers will not follow suit, and they return to their original anarchy.*

1. *Piers sets the world to work.* Prov. xxiv. 27–34 might serve as a motto for this Book.

2. *Half an acre.* As in modern American speech, this means a small field or strip of land.

3. *A knight.* The knight is introduced here because Langland is following 'the old threefold division of the Church into Oratores (priests), Bellatores (warriors), and Laboratores (commons)' (Skeat). The duty of the second class is to defend God's laws and His Church.

4. *'When thou art bidden . . .'* Luke xiv. 10.

5. *Jack the Juggler*, etc. All these characters are excluded because they gain a false living, without helping Piers to work (in contrast to Piers' wife, below); they therefore cut themselves off from Christian society – ch.II Thess. iii. 10.

6. *'Let them be blotted out . . .'* Ps. lxix. 28.

7. *Before going to bed.* Cf. Deut. xxiv. 12–13.

8. *Holy Rood of Lucca.* 'At Lucca (French *Lucques*) is a crucifix and a famous representation of the face of Christ reputed to be the work of the disciple Nicodemus. William the Conqueror's favourite oath was "By the Face of Lucca"' (Sisam, quoted by Davis).

9. *The wandering preachers.* Possibly an allusion to Wyclif's 'poor priests'.

10. *Blood-brothers.* Cf. p. 133 – 'For on Calvary, etc.'

11. *'Bear ye one another's burdens . . .'* Gal. vi. 2.

12. *'Vengeance is mine . . .'* Rom. xii. 19. and Heb. x. 30.

13. *'Make to yourselves friends . . .'* Luke xvi. 9. Cf. a similar use of this text on p. 103.

14. *'In the sweat of thy brow . . .'* Gen. iii. 19.

15. *'The sluggard will not plow . . .'* Prov. xx. 4.

16. *Whose sign has a man's face.* In medieval art, Mark was

symbolized by a lion, Luke by a bull, John by an eagle, and Matthew by a man. Cf. Rev. iv. 7.

17. *This Parable.* Matt. xxv. 14–30.

18. '*For thou shalt eat the labours* . . .' Ps. cxxviii. 2.

19. *Unless he gets high wages.* 'After the Black Death (1349) labour in England was scarce and the labourers demanded higher wages. The Statute of Labourers (1350) compelled the able-bodied labourers to work for hire at recognized rates of pay, but the provisions of the Statute were not kept' (Davis).

20. *Cato.* Dionysius Cato, op. cit., part of 21st Distich of the First Book.

21. *Saturn has predicted.* The influence of the planet Saturn was malign – cp. Chaucer, Knight's Tale, ll. 1009–11.

22. *When you see the sun awry,* etc. See note 29, Bk III. 'William imitates, not perhaps without ridicule, the mysterious prophecies which were then popular, such as, for instance, the prophecies of John of Bridlington' (Skeat). However, I do not think that, in this context, any ridicule is intended, or that the prophecy is, as Davis suggests, 'intentionally meaningless'. 'The sun awry' presumably refers to an eclipse of the sun, and we know that a total eclipse did occur in 1377. We may assume that the dearth that followed the pestilence of 1376 was also in 1377. 'When a maiden has dominion' may suggest the power of Alice Perrers over the Court, and if, as Bradley suggests, the words 'maistrie' ('magical power') and 'multiply' are used in their alchemical senses – the Maid shall show the magical skill of multiplying gold – this might be a further hint of the corruption brought about by Fee. The 'two monks' heads' might be taken as a portent of the future fall of the monks, as prophesied by Learning in Book x (pp. 121–2).

Book VII

THE ALLEGORY. *Truth's message to Piers means that the pilgrimage may now be abandoned, since men can gain their pardon by honest work and cooperation. This ruling is applied in detail to all the different orders of society. But when the pardon itself is read, it proves not to be an indulgence, but merely the familiar law expressed in the words of the Athanasian creed. Realizing that this cannot save all the people, and that the reform of society has in effect failed, Piers – like Moses on his return from Mt Sinai – destroys the pardon and takes upon himself the burden of a new and higher law: by a life of voluntary poverty and prayer, he will gain for others the pardon which they cannot gain by their own efforts.*

1. *From guilt and punishment.* Normally, a Pardon or Indulgence is only believed to remit the *punishment* due to sins, not to forgive their guilt. This, therefore, is not an ordinary indulgence.

2. *Stay at home.* Literally, this means that the pilgrimage to Truth is to be abandoned. Allegorically, it may imply that the work of building a Christian society on earth, and ploughing the field, is itself the way to Truth, and the best means of gaining a Pardon.

3. *Both the Laws.* i.e. the two divisions of the Ten Commandments – our duty to God, and to our neighbour.

4. 'He who taketh no bribes . . .' Ps. xv. 5.

5. 'Their wages shall be . . .' Unidentified, but cf. Ecclus. xxxviii. 1–2.

6. *Human intelligence*, etc. Cf. p. 238 – 'Your talents are gifts from me.' The C-text says here, 'It is Simony to sell that which is sent by Grace.'

7. 'All things whatsoever . . .' Matt. vii. 12.

8. *Cato.* The 23rd of the *Breves sententiae* prefixed to the Distichs.

9. *Peter Comestor* (d. 1198). Known as 'Master of the Stories', author of *Historia Scholastica*, a paraphrase of the Bible, with many legends added. Langland's quotations are often garbled, and they seem to be made from memory.

10. 'Do not choose whom you pity . . .' Not from Gregory the Great, but Jerome's Commentary (331–420) on Eccl. xi. 6.

11. *Giver is repaying God's gifts.* Cf. Prov. xix. 17.

12. 'Wherefore then gavest thou not . . .' Luke xix 23.

13. 'He is rich enough . . .' St Jerome Epistles, cxxv.

14. 'I have been young . . .' Ps. xxxvii. 25.

15. *Braying like wild beasts.* Cf. Jer. v. 8.

16. 'And they that have done good . . .' These words from the Athanasian Creed are derived from Matt. xxv. 46, the context of which shows the connexion between Piers' Pardon and the long discussion of the works of Charity in the first part of this Book.

17. 'Yea, though I walk . . .' Ps. xxiii. 4. See note 42, Bk XII.

18. 'My tears have been my meat . . .' Ps. xlii. 3.

19. 'Nor be solicitous . . .' Matt. vi. 31.

20. 'The fool hath spoken.' Ps. xiv. 1 and liii. 1.

21. 'Cast out the scorner . . .' Prov. xxii. 10.

22. 'Pay no heed to dreams.' Cato Distich, ii. 31.

23. *Nebuchadnezzar.* Though the reference is to Dan. ii. 39, Langland was really thinking of Daniel's interpreting the writing on the wall at Belshazzar's Feast (Dan. v).

24. *Joseph's dream*. Gen. xxxvii. 9–10.

25. *Biennials, triennials*. Arrangements for the saying of Mass for a departed soul during the period of two, or three, years.

26. *Bishops' Letters*. Cf. pp. 27 and 80. Letters promulgating indulgences.

27. *'Whatsoever thou shalt bind.'* Matt. xvi. 19.

28. *Provincials' Letters*. A Provincial is the monastic superior of a Province, and these are letters of indulgence granted by such superiors.

29. *Fraternity*. See note 5, Bk III.

Part II. The subject of the second Part is the spiritual life, a growth in charity such that the church will at last be equipped to struggle with Antichrist. The dreamer is now alone, and his pilgrimage is set in motion by his bewilderment over the failure of Piers to reform the natural man in Part I. Piers himself has moved at once from the *animale* to the *spirituale*, but the dreamer fails for a long time to find Do-well because he mistakenly looks for it in the world, where it is not to be found. The three lives that he searches for prove in the end not to be three different vocations (layman, priest, bishop), but all one and the same life of patience and charity. 'The good works of the active life are the works of religion and devotion. In other words, the active life is the ascetical life' (Dunning, op. cit.)

Book VIII

THE ALLEGORY. *The friars' plausible allegorizing is not to Will's taste, so he passes on in dreamy detachment till he falls asleep again and meets his double, Thought. 'Thought represents those ideas concerning the way to achieve Truth of which Will is at the moment capable. ... (He) describes Dowel, Dobet and Dobest in terms of externals, with no suggestion of the necessary preparation of the will for good action through faith and grace' (R. & H., op. cit.). So Will turns to Intelligence ('Wit') to see if he can show Do-well in action.*

1. *Two Franciscan Friars*. The friars usually went about in pairs. '"Master of Divinity" was a title much coveted by some of the Order' (Skeat).

2. *He dwells among us*. 'The pharisee of Christ's parable (Luke xviii. 11) had a similar attitude' (R. and H., 102).

3. *'Even a righteous man ...'* Prov. xxiv. 16. Cf. Ps. xxxvii. 24.

4. *A parable.* The parable is hackneyed – Cf. the many parallels referred to by Skeat, and further examples in Owst, *Literature and the Pulpit.* 'His use of a clear example to support false doctrines enforces the dangerousness of the Friar's gifts' (R. and H., p. 103).

5. *Strength to stand.* But cf. 1 Cor. x. 12 – 'Wherefore let him that thinketh he standeth take heed lest he fall.'

6. *With the money of Mammon.* Cf. a similar use of the same text (Luke xvi. 9) by Hunger, p. 87.

7. *Suffer the foolish.* Langland's Thought mistranslates this text (II Cor. xi. 19), taking St Paul's ironical remark as if it were an imperative. Since the *Glossa* makes it clear that he was admonishing the Corinthians *not* to tolerate false prophets, R. and H. (p. 105) may well be right in thinking the mistake deliberate. (On p. 130, Will is admonished to speak out against the Friars, and not to suffer them gladly.) In that case, the weakness of Thought's definitions is apparent – Do-better simply consists in belonging to a Religious Order, a state of life in which one can afford complacently to 'suffer fools', and feel secure in one's own wisdom.

8. *With a hook at one end.* A Bishop's crozier has a hook at the upper end and a spike at the lower.

9. *Wrong Do-best.* i.e. wrong the Church or the Bishops.

Book IX

THE ALLEGORY. *Intelligence is a self-sufficient faculty, who tries to find Do-well in the natural man – a harmonious working together of physical and mental faculties. Man has been given the gift of Sense ('Inwit'), and those who lack this should be protected by the church. Since he sets too high a value on the purely natural powers, Intelligence blames most of the world's misery on the misuse of the flesh and men's failure to obey the laws of marriage – which in turn gives rise to unnatural offspring. But he knows that 'Do-well is a function of the soul, not merely an external compliance with the Law'* (R. & H., op. cit.).

1. *Intelligence* ('Wit'). By means of this faculty, which might be described as man's Mother Wit or primitive natural reason (not, as R. and H. suppose, the 'speculative intellect'), the dreamer begins in earnest to consider man from the cradle to the grave. Intelligence therefore tells him of the creation of the human soul and of the rational nature of man – his 'Good Sense', which is God's greatest gift to him – and this leads on to the subject of marriage.

2. *Earth and air with wind and water*. By 'air' (for which we should expect the element of 'fire,' since the four elements were earth, air, *fire*, and water) Langland means the *upper air* (Latin *aër*, which he confuses with *aether*, and this with *fire*); and by 'wind' the lower air of this world. The heavenly air may be the spiritual element or 'breath of life' which God 'breathed into Adam's nostrils' (Gen. ii. 7 and l. 45 (p. 106) below).

3. *Prince of this world*. Cf. John xii. 31 and elsewhere.

4. '*He spoke and they were created*.' Ps. cxlviii. 5.

5. *Using no intermediary*. He made man directly in the image of the Trinity, invoking the other Persons of the Trinity to assist Him. Langland appears to contradict himself, since he says a little later that God *did* use His word – but not as an intermediary, for all three Persons shared directly in the work, whereas God the Father did *not* share directly in the creation of the beasts.

6. '*Let us make man*.' Gen. i. 26. 'And the father speaks to the Son and the Holy Ghost' – Peter Comestor's comment, quoted by Skeat.

7. *Home is in the heart*. Cf. Prov. iv. 23.

8. '*Whose god is their belly*.' Phil. iii. 19.

9. *All sinners have souls like Satan*. Cf. 1 John iii. 8.

10. '*He that dwelleth in love* ...' 1 John iv. 16.

11. '*I know you not*.' Matt. xxv. 12.

12. '*So I gave them up* ...' Ps. lxxxi. 12.

13. *The Four Doctors*. St Jerome, St Gregory, St Augustine, and St Ambrose – cf. the 'four bullocks', p. 238.

14. *Taught by St Luke*. This might refer to Acts vi. 1–4, but James i. 27 is more relevant.

15. '*The Prelate who does not distribute* ...' Peter Cantor, *Compendium*, cap. xlvii, c. 135. The quotation which follows is from the same chapter, c. 150.

16. '*The fear of the Lord* ...' Prov. i. 7 and ix. 10.

17. '*Whosoever shall keep the whole law* ...' James ii. 10.

18. '*For there is no want* ...' Ps. xxxiv. 10.

19. *He himself was its witness*. i.e. at the Marriage at Cana (John ii. 2) – or he might refer to Gen. i. 28.

20. *Cain*. Cf. 1 John iii. 12 ff. According to medieval legend, Cain was born during the period of penitence and fasting to which Adam and Eve were condemned for their sin. 'Cain, in the Commentaries, is the first in the generation of the wicked' (R. and H., p. 114). The phrase 'Cain's kin' was proverbial in Middle English, like 'Sons of Judas'.

21. *'Behold, he travaileth . . .'* Ps. vii. 14.

22. *God sent an angel to Seth.* Cf. Gen. vi. 1–2. The sons of God who mingled with the daughters of men are, according to some commentators, the sons of Seth mingling with the generation of Cain. The command of God to Seth is not in Scripture, but is probably derived from Peter Comestor.

23. *'It repenteth me . . .'* Gen. vi. 6 ff.

24. *'The son shall not bear . . .'* Ezek. xviii. 20.

25. *'Do men gather grapes . . .'* Matt. vii. 16.

26. *'I am the Truth . . .'* John xiv. 6. The second part of the text, added by Langland, may be a reminiscence of 1 Sam. ii. 6–8.

27. *The Dunmow flitch.* This is 'the earliest known allusion to the singular custom known as that of "the Dunmow flitch of Bacon". The custom was (and still is) – "that if any pair could, after a twelvemonth of matrimony, come forward, and make oath at Dunmow (Essex) that, during the whole time, they had never had a quarrel, never regretted their marriage, and, if again open to an engagement, would make exactly that they had made, they should be rewarded with a flitch of bacon;"' Chambers, *Book of Days'* (Skeat).

28. *Get married.* Cf. 1 Cor. vii. 9.

29. *'While thou art strong . . .'* From some Latin verses by John of Bridlington.

30. *Forbidden times.* i.e. on fasting-days – cf. p. 162.

31. *'To avoid fornication . . .'* 1 Cor. vii. 2.

32. *Those born out of marriage.* R. and H. interpret this, and the whole discussion of marriage, in an allegorical sense – 'those born out of spiritual wedlock' (pp. 79–80). But throughout the Book, Intelligence is speaking of the laws which govern the flesh.

Book X

THE ALLEGORY. *Will's purely intellectual search comes to grief in this Book. Bent chiefly on castigating their enemies, he and his guides are at cross purposes and over-reach themselves. Though she recommends the simple Christian virtues, Study (who assumes that Will is a worldly hypocrite) bitterly attacks the hypocrisy of those who combine gluttonous living with shallow theological speculation. Though Will outwardly submits, he ignores her ascetic teaching and continues pursuing his fine intellectual distinctions. So he hears from Learning a prophetic denunciation of the hypocrisy of learned men in Religious houses, which leads him to suppose that the only corrective*

*lies in the use of force. Scripture's answer drives him to an opposite extreme –
that of recklessly abandoning everything to simple faith, since learning (and
with it, the church and priesthood) has proved useless.*

1. *Scripture*. The word 'Scripture' in Langland means all sacred
writings, the Fathers no less than the Bible.

2. *To teach blockheads*. Cf. Prov. i. 7, xiv. 6, xvii. 16, and xxiii. 9.

3. *'Do not cast your pearls . . .'* Matt. vii. 6.

4. *Grow in paradise*. Cf. Gen. ii. 12. 'Note also the old belief that
stones could *grow*' (Skeat).

5. *Says Job the prophet*. Job xxi. 7 ff.

6. *'Wherefore doth the way . . .'* Not in Job, but Jer. xii. 1.

7. *'Lo, these are the ungodly . . .'* Ps. lxxiii. 12.

8. *'For lo, what thou hast perfected . . .'* Ps. xi. 3 (Authorized
Version here differs from Vulgate).

9. *'We have heard of the same . . .'* Ps. cxxxii. 5–6. This passage
refers to the Ark of the Covenant, but Langland takes it to mean
'We *hear* God spoken of among the wealthy (at Ephrata), but we
only *find* Him among the poor, in country places.'

10. *At St Paul's*. 'The preaching place was in the open air, at
St Paul's Cross' (Skeat).

11. *Isaiah teaches*. Isaiah lviii. 7.

12. *Tobit*. iv. 8.

13. *In a special chamber*. 'With the absence of the lord from the
hall, its festive character and indiscriminate hospitality began to
diminish' (T. Wright, quoted by Skeat).

14. *'The son shall not bear . . .'* Ezek. xviii. 20.

15. *'Every man shall bear . . .'* Gal. vi. 5.

16. *Augustine*. Skeat cites *De Baptismo, contra Donatistas*, lib. 2,
cap. 5. The text is Rom. xii. 2.

17. *The Seven Arts* were contained in the Trivium (Grammar,
Logic, and Rhetoric), and the Quadrivium, or more advanced
studies (Music, Arithmetic, Geometry, and Astronomy). Cf. p. 155.

18. *'If anyone tries to deceive you . . .'* Cato Distichs i. 26.

19. *'Do good unto all men.'* Gal. vi. 10.

20. *'Vengeance is mine.'* Rom xii. 19.

21. *Geomancy*. 'The art of divination by means of lines and
figures, formed orig. by throwing earth on some surface, and later
by jotting down on paper dots at random' (OED). Cf. Chaucer,
Parson's Tale (De Ira) on 'thise false enchantours'.

22. *'I am in the Father.'* John xiv. 9–10.

23. *St Gregory*. xl. Homil. in Evang. lib. ii. homil. xxvi.

24. *'For your teaching is contemptible ...'* A medieval rhymed Latin couplet, unidentified.

25. *'The mote in thy brother's eye.'* Matt. vii. 3.

26. *Buzzard.* A lazy, cowardly kind of hawk, feeding on vermin, and unfit for falconry.

27. *'The blind leading the blind.'* Luke vi. 39.

28. *Hophni and Phineas.* 1 Sam. iv.

29. *'Thou thoughtest that I was ...'* Ps. l. 21.

30. *'His watchmen are blind ...'* Isaiah lvi. 10.

31. *Religion.* i.e. Religious Orders.

32. *A king shall arise.* This famous prophecy 'was merely due to the prevalent views as to the supreme power of the king' (Skeat) – or, rather, the view that he had the power to punish churchmen if necessary; cf. p. 104, where Thought says that Do-well and Do-better (laymen and Religious Orders) agree to crown a king to rule them, etc.

33. *Till you are 'like the chaff'*, etc. I have here paraphrased freely: the original simply says, 'And Barons and Earls shall beat them with the teaching of *Beatus vir* (i.e. the First Psalm).'

34. *'Some trust in chariots ...'* Ps. xx. 7–8.

35. *Constantine's coffers.* This alludes to the belief that the Emperor Constantine originally gave the Pope his territory in Italy, and endowed the Church with vast wealth; cf. p. 194. Langland means that, once the king and the nobles have taken over the management of monastic property (cf. pp. 62, 194), they will then give the friars regular endowments, so that they may cease to beg. The monks of England are called Gregory's children, because St Augustine, who introduced the monastic state into England, was sent here by Pope Gregory the Great (A.D. 592).

36. *The Abbot of Abingdon.* The ancient and famous abbey at Abingdon was said to be 'the house in which the monks ... were first introduced in England, and it is, therefore, very properly introduced as the representative of English monachism' (T. Wright, quoted by Skeat).

37. *'How hath the oppressor ceased ...'* Isaiah xiv. 4–6.

38. *Cain shall awake.* R. and H. explain this, and the whole prophecy, as follows: 'Clergy (Learning) prophesies the destruction of wicked Religious on the day of doom. The king of heaven will come, but before that day, Cain, the Antichrist, will appear, only to be put down by Dowel, the congregation of the loyal faithful' (p. 125). This fits well with the earlier prophecy of

Conscience about the crowning of the New David (p. 52), though other passages (pp. 62 and 194) suggest that Langland anticipated the reformation of the monks by an earthly king. Yet Scripture at once corrects Will when he assumes that Do-well must therefore be 'kingship and knighthood'.

39. *St Paul shows.* Cf. 1 Tim. vi. 9–10.

40. *'There is not a more wicked thing . . .'* Ecclus. x. 10.

41. *Cato.* Dist. iv. 4.

42. *. The Apostles say . . .* Cf. James ii. 5.

43. *Words of St Peter and St Paul.* The dreamer is speaking at random; he may have been thinking of 1 Peter ii. 21, but it is more likely that he had in mind the words of Christ in Mark xvi. 11.

44. *'If ye then be risen . . .'* Col. iii. 1.

45. *'Thou shalt love . . .'* Luke x. 27.

46. *'Vengeance is mine . . .'* Rom. xii. 19. In this passage, Langland elaborates freely on the commandment 'Thou shalt not kill'.

47. *The Book of Life.* Cf. Rev. xx. 12 and 15.

48. *'No man hath ascended . . .'* John iii. 13. (No one knows whether or not his name is written in the Book of Life.)

49. *His judgements were good.* Alluding to the famous judgement of Solomon, 1 Kings iii. 28.

50. *Considers them both damned.* Will is again speaking wildly (in the C-text, this speech is spoken by Recklessness). For a full discussion of medieval doctrine on this question, see T. P. Dunning: 'Langland and the Salvation of the Heathen' (*Medium Aevum* xii, 1943). He points out that Dante *need not* have placed Aristotle and others in hell; and to show that he knew the orthodox teaching, he deliberately placed a heathen, Ripheus (*Aeneid* ii. 426–7) in heaven, because he was, according to Virgil, a very just man. Langland, too, was aware of the true teaching – cf. pp. 149–50.

51. *'The scribes and Pharisees . . .'* Matt. xxiii. 2.

52. *'O Lord, thou preservest . . .'* Ps. xxxvi. 6.

53. *David when he plotted.* II Sam. xi. 14–15.

54. *What Solomon said.* Eccles. ix. 1.

55. *'When necessity is upon us . . .'* A proverbial saying (in a mixture of Latin and Old French), similar to 'What can't be cured, must be endured.'

56. *'There is none that doeth good.'* Ps. xiv. 1 – but he may also have been thinking of Matt. xix. 17.

57. *'When you stand before kings . . .'* Mark xiii. 9, 11.

58. *King David says.* Cf. Ps. cxix. 46.

59. *St Augustine.* Not in a sermon, but in *Confessions*, Lib. viii, c. 8. Cf. Matt. xi. 12 and xxi. 31.

60. '*Go yet into my vineyard.*' Matt. xx. 4.

Book XI

THE ALLEGORY. *In the A-text, the dreamer is here abandoned by his guides and left to learn through experience. In the B version, he now falls into spiritual oblivion, and only returns to the search in old age through a dispute with the friars about the burial rights of his body. In terror for his own salvation, he is now willing to listen to new teachings that pass beyond the level of intellectual debate. His teachers are Scripture, Good Faith ('Lewte', which implies loyalty to the original teaching of Holy Church) and the Emperor Trajan, a living example of one rescued from hell through obedience to the natural law of love. They speak in praise of poverty, kindness of heart and charity, revealing Christ as the friend of sinners. Yet Will still disputes; he turns to the world of Nature to find further confirmation, and reaches the despairing conclusion that God cares for all His creatures except mankind. He is rescued by a new gift, Imagination, the power of recollecting past experience and interpreting the lessons of life.*

1. '*Multi multa sciunt . . .*' From the first words of St Bernard's *Cogitationes Piissimae de cognitione humanae conditionis.*

2. *Pride-of-perfect-life.* Cf. 1 John ii. 15–16. According to a common exposition, these three correspond to the three temptations addressed to Christ by the Devil.

3. '*Man proposes, God disposes.*' This well-known proverb, attributed to Plato, is probably derived from Prov. xvi. 9. The predestinarian views expressed by Will to Learning and Scripture have led him into a slothful fatalism.

4. *Truth himself declares.* He is probably thinking of the words 'Take no thought for the morrow.'

5. *That Intelligence should go to the dogs.* Here, the dreamer's name *Will* seems definitely to stand for the faculty of the human will, and Intelligence seems to be the dreamer's own intelligence. By following Lust, he is doing just what Intelligence warned him against – destroying the image of God in himself.

6. *The friars will love you.* In Bk xx, the friars become the 'many antichrists' of 1 John ii. 18 – thus their connexion here with the Three Temptations mentioned two verses earlier in the Epistle. Throughout the poem, the friars are blamed for conniving at sin and making penance a mockery; they are therefore the servants of

Fee, Fortune, and Antichrist, and are 'not of the Father, but of the world'.

7. '*Sed poena pecunia* . . .' Source unknown.

8. *Would rather bury people*. Owing to their avarice for burial-fees, and for the legacies of their wealthy patrons. This was a common charge against the Friars, repeated by Wycliffe.

9. '*Only contrition* . . .' Unidentified.

10. '*Except a man be born* . . .' John iii. 5.

11. *Good Faith* ('Loyalty') signifies honest living, loyalty to one's moral and social obligations, and the following of Truth as it was first taught to the dreamer by Holy Church. It is possible for a pagan like Trajan to possess this virtue, by his obeying the natural law.

12. *Both those Apostles*. Cf. 1 Tim. v. 20, Tit, i. 13, ii. 15. St Peter said nothing to this effect.

13. '*Thou shalt not hate the brothers* . . .' Levit. xix. 17. The word 'brothers' is applied by Langland to the Friars – see p. 154, '*Among false brethren*', and Note.

14. '*Judge not* . . .' Matt. vii. 1.

15. '*They that sin, rebuke* . . .' 1 Tim. v. 20. Langland, perhaps forgetting the text, actually says, 'The Apostle said something like "Thou shalt not hate the brothers, etc." ' I have inserted, instead, the text he probably had in mind.

16. '*Thou thoughtest that I was* . . .' Ps. l. 21.

17. *Tell tales about people's sins*. i.e. matters recounted to them in confession.

18. *This was her text*. Scripture paraphrases the parable in Matt. xxii. 1–14.

19. '*Ho, everyone that thirsteth* . . .' Isaiah lv. 1.

20. '*He that believeth* . . .' Mark xvi. 16.

21. '*His tender mercies* . . .' Ps. cxlv. 9.

22. *Trajan*. According to a well-known legend, much-discussed in the Middle Ages, St Gregory the Great, remembering the justice of the pagan Emperor Trajan, prayed earnestly for his soul, and was answered by a voice from God, telling him that He had spared Trajan from everlasting damnation in answer to Gregory's prayer. This raised the question whether any man could be released from hell. In most of the versions, Trajan was represented as having been brought back from hell to receive baptism. But Langland derived his rendering from the Golden Legend of Jacobus de Voragine, which does not state that Trajan was restored to life.

23. *See, you great men.* Langland does not make clear who utters this speech – presumably either Good Faith or Scripture. In the C-text, it is put into the mouth of Recklessness.

24. *'He that loveth not . . .'* 1 John iii. 14.

25. *In a poor man's likeness.* Cf. Matt. xxv. 40.

26. *'When thou makest a dinner . . . .'* Luke xiv 12.

27. *Wealthy by His coffers.* Cf. Rom. viii. 16–17.

28. *'As newborn babes.'* 1 Peter ii. 2. This was a familiar phrase ('Quasi modo geniti'), as it was 'used as a name for Low Sunday, or the octave of Easter, because, in the Sarum Missal, the Office for that day begins with this text' (Skeat).

29. *'Whosoever committeth sin . . .'* John viii. 34.

30. *Sons of men.* 'The phrase "children of men" occurs 19 times in the Old Testament, but in the New, not at all; whilst "children of God" occurs ten times in the New Testament, but not once in the Old' (Skeat).

31. *'Bear one another's burdens.'* Gal. vi. 2.

32. *Christ himself said . . .* Luke vii. 48.

33. *'With what measure . . .'* Matt. vii. 1.

34. *When He went to Emmaus.* Luke xxiv. 13–35.

35. *Martha complained aloud.* Luke x. 40–2 – not, as Langland says, in St Matthew.

36. *He put poverty first.* According to traditional interpretation, St Mary Magdalen represents the contemplative life ('the better part'), and St Martha the 'active' life.

37. *'Give me neither poverty . . .'* Prov. xxx. 8.

38. *'If thou wilt be perfect . . .'* Matt. xix 21.

39. *'I have not seen the righteous forsaken . . .'* Ps. xxxvii. 25.

40. *'Nothing is impossible . . .'* Luke i. 37 and Matt. xvii. 20.

41. *'They that seek the Lord . . .'* Ps. xxiv. 10.

42. *'Judge me, O God . . .'* Ps. xliii. 1.

43. *'Put thy trust . . .'* Ps. xxxvii.

44. *By their tonsures alone.* i.e. simply by the fact of being a priest. Cp. Fee's remark about education, p. 46.

45. *'Offend in one point . . .'* James ii. 10.

46. *'Sing praises with understanding.'* Ps. xlvii. 7–8.

47. *Conceived at their beaks.* This curious idea is derived from Aristotle, *Hist. of Animals*, Bk vi. c. ii. Sect. 9. – a mode of conception, he says, that is due to the violence of their sexual desires.

48. *The way that peacocks breed.* 'With respect to the peacock we find the following account in Batman vppon Bartholomè, lib, 12.

c. 31: "And the Pecock is a bird that loueth not his young: for the male searcheth out the female, and seeketh out her egges for to breake them, that he may so occupy him the more in his lecherie." ' (Skeat).

49. *My time is still to come.* Cf. 1 Cor. iv. 5 and the advice of Holy Church to the dreamer to 'hold his tongue', p. 39.

50. *'Be ye subject . . .'* 1 Peter ii. 13.

51. *'Bele vertue . . .'* Cf. Ecclus. xi. 7–9, and Chaucer, 'Frankelyn's Tale', *The Canterbury Tales*, ll. 11085–11092.

52. *'Strive not in matter . . .'* Ecclus. xi. 9.

53. *'And God saw everything . . .'* Gen. i. 31.

54. *Cato.* Distich. i. 5.

55. *'You might be a philosopher . . .'* Boethius *De Cons. Phil.* lib. ii. prosa 7. Cf. also Prov. xvii. 28 and x. 19.

Book XII

THE ALLEGORY. *Imagination is another self, who has known Will throughout the search – 'The dreamer comes face to face with his own experience, long known but not attended to' (Lawlor, op. cit.). Will's captious theologizing is summarily disposed of, and Imagination gives him a balanced view of all those problems that have previously perplexed him – the proper place of Learning and the priesthood in the scheme of salvation, the truth concerning predestination, and the necessity of trusting in God's grace and mercy. The dreamer is now almost cured of intellectual pride, and ready for the great turning-point of Book XIII.*

1. *'And if he shall come . . .'* Luke xii. 38.

2. *'Such as I love . . .'* Rev. iii. 19.

3. *'Thy rod and thy staff . . .'* Ps. xxiii. 4. He takes it to mean that God's corrections turn to consolation.

4. *Cato.* Distich. iii. 7.

5. *'And now abideth faith . . .'* 1 Cor. xiii. 13.

6. *Shrine of Rochemadour.* The Church of Our Lady of Rochemadour (near Cahors) is still a well-known place of pilgrimage.

7. *Do not stray from that path.* Cf. 1 Cor. vii. 8.

8. *Lucifer, Solomon, Samson.* Langland is arguing in praise of loyalty and obedience, so his examples are of those who were disloyal to their own callings, and misused God's gifts.

9. *Hippocrates.* Was said to have murdered his nephew Galen out of jealousy for his knowledge, dying himself from remorse

shortly afterwards. *Virgil* was celebrated as having been a great magician.

10. *Felicia.* Probably the wife of Guy of Warwick, 'to whome in his woinge tyme she made greate straungenes, and caused him, for her sake, to put himselfe in meny greate distresse, dangers and perills; but when they wer wedded and been but a litle season togither, he departed from her to her greate hevynes, and never was conversaunt with her after . . . ' (Quoted by Skeat from Percy Folio MS, ed. Hales and Furnivall, ii, 509, 515).

11. *Rosamund.* 'Higden, monk of Chester, says – "She was the fayre daughter of Walter lord Clifford, concubine of Henry II, and poisoned by Queen Elianor A.D. 1177." Henry made for her a house of wonderful working, so that no man or woman might come to her. This house was named Labyrinthus, and was wrought like unto a knot in a garden called a maze. But the queen came to her by a clue of thredde, and so dealt with her that she lived not long after. She was buried at Godstow, in an house of nunnes, with these verses upon her tomb:

Here Rose the graced, not Rose the chaste, reposes;

The smell that rises is no smell of roses' (Brewer's *Dictionary of Phrase and Fable*). Scott introduced her into *The Talisman* and *Woodstock*.

12. *'Give, and it shall be given . . . '* Luke vi. 38.

13. *'That servant who knew . . . '* Luke xii. 47–8.

14. *'Wisdom puffeth up . . . '* 1 Cor. viii. 1.

15. *'The wind bloweth . . . '* John iii. 8.

16. *'We speak of that which we know . . . '* John iii. 11.

17. *'Thou knowest not . . . '* Continuation of John iii. 8.

18. *Any woman taken.* Cf. Levit. xx. 10.

19. *Saved a woman guilty of adultery.* John viii. 3–11. In the Coventry Mysteries Christ is represented as writing upon the ground the sins of the accusers (Skeat).

20. *'Judge not . . . '* Matt. vii. 1.

21. *The Body of Christ . . . will damn us.* Cf. I Cor. xi. 29.

22. *Levites were the guardians.* Cf. Numbers i. 50–51.

23. *Saul was brought to ruin.* 1 Sam. xiii. 9–14.

24. *Laid hands on it.* Cf. II Sam. vi. 6–7.

25. *'Touch not mine Anointed . . . '* Ps. cv. 15 and 1 Chron. xvi. 22.

26. *'For the wisdom of this world . . . '* 1 Cor. iii. 19.

27. *'And the shepherds said . . . '* Luke ii. 15.

28. *The best burgesses in Bethlehem.* In Matt. ii. 11, the Magi are said to enter a *house* (Vulgate *domum*); whether or not this was

identified with the 'inn' of St Luke, it gave rise to the idea that Christ was born in no mean establishment.

29. *'There was no room for them ...'* Luke ii. 7. The source of the quotation which follows is unknown.

30. *Shepherds and poets.* The traditional association between shepherds and poets was reinforced by the words of St Luke, 'the shepherds returned, *glorifying and praising God.*'

31. *'Blessed is he ...'* Ps. xxxii. 1.

32. *'If the blind lead the blind ...'* Matt. xv. 14.

33. *Saved dozens of mighty robbers.* This alludes to the 'benefit of clergy', the privilege allowed first to clergymen and later to everyone who could read, exempting them from trial by a secular court. A verse from the Latin Psalter was set before one who claimed this privilege, and by reading it correctly he might save his neck. 'Hence the common saying among the people, that if they could not read their neck-verse at sessions, they must sing it at the gallows' (Dr Grey, quoted by Skeat). Though the 51st Psalm was usually selected for this purpose, it is clear from this passage that Ps. 16 was also used.

34. *'Concerning propitiation ...'* Ecclus. v. 5.

35. *'Thou rewardest every man ...'* Ps. lxii. 12 and Matt. xvi. 27.

36. *'Whatsoever the Lord pleased ...'* Ps. cxxxv. 6.

37. *Breed in the foulest manner.* See note 48, Bk XI.

38. *According to the Fables.* Refers to one of the many collections of fables popular in Langland's day. It is not certain where Langland found this interpretation of the peacock, though there is something like it in the fable of the Peacock who complained of his Voice (quoted by Skeat).

39. *In his Logic.* Aristotle describes the lark in his History of Animals; but Langland, who loves to cite important authorities, mentions his *Logic* because Aristotle was looked up to in the later Middle Ages chiefly as 'the teacher of logic, and master of dialectics' (Skeat).

40. *Whether Aristotle is saved.* Cf. p. 124 and Notes.

41. *'The just man shall scarcely ...'* 1 Peter iv. 18.

42. *'Yea, though I walk ...'* Ps. xxiii. 4. Some of the commentators apply this text to the man who walks steadfastly among the heathen, living uprightly though surrounded by unbelief. Cf. the similar use of it by Piers (p. 95), when he is faced with the apparent unbelief of the priest.

Book XIII

THE ALLEGORY. *In this Book Will gives up his striving for intellectual certainty and sets out on the final pilgrimage of the spiritual life. Conscience and Patience, who are able to restrain his impatience when faced with the arch-hypocrite at the High Table, are not self-projections, but God-given graces. For the first time since the search began, Piers is heard of again – as an advocate of the infinite power of love. The crux of the discussion is Patience's riddle, with its hint of a new power (that of perfect charity) symbolized by an* Agnus Dei. *Conscience believes in Patience at once, and leaving Learning behind, all three set out on the same road of patient poverty that Piers took at the beginning. Through their meeting with Haukyn, the Deadly Sins (now subsumed under the category of worldly pride) and the Plain of People are suddenly recalled, the new lessons of humility are applied to the man-of-the-world and the solitary pilgrimage again comes to embrace all mankind.*

1. *What kind of man he was.* The C-text says explicitly, 'A man like a friar.'

2. *'Eating and drinking . . .'* Luke x. 7.

3. *A mortar called Post-mortem.* i.e. The friars eat well now, thanks to the ill-gotten gains of their patrons; but their food is spoilt by a bitter sauce, compounded out of the prospect of torments after death.

4. *'Ye who feast . . .'* Not identified.

5. *'Do penance.'* Matt. ii. 2. All the food eaten by Patience and Will is food of repentance, composed of the Penitential Psalms.

6. *Long-endure.* Cf. Matt. x. 22.

7. *The Miserere.* i.e. Ps. li.

8. *'Blessed is he . . .'* The whole course is extracted from Ps. 32.

9. *'For this shall everyone . . .'* Ps. xxxii. 6.

10. *'A broken and contrite heart . . .'* Ps. li. 17.

11. *'Woe unto them . . .'* Isaiah v. 22.

12. *The sufferings of Paul.* II Cor. xi. 24–7.

13. *'Among false brethren'* ('In falsis *fratribus*') – See note 13, Bk xi. The text (II Cor. xi. 26) is applied to the friars on account of the word 'frater'. The Latin text quoted a little later appears to be a commentary on St Paul's phrase.

14. *The Apocalypse of Gluttons.* By Walter Mapes, a sort of parody upon St John's Apocalypse. It contains this description of monks at supper – 'Each monk becomes demoniac. As pye with pye,

parrot with parrot, the brothers chatter and feed, eat till their jaws swell, and drink till there is a deluge in their stomachs.'

15. *St Aurea*. A solitary at the convent of St Aemilian above the Upper Ebro, Spain (d.c. 1100). She was said to have drunk only such drink as she could distil from cinders.

16. '*Whosoever shall do . . .*' Matt. v. 19.

17. '*The patient conquer.*' Langland constantly repeats this proverb. It is not a Scriptural text (though it expresses the sense of *Matt.* x. 22), but a variation of the proverbial saying '*Vincit qui patitur.*'

18. The inscription ('through the power of the passing-over') must refer to the Passover, the slaying of the paschal lamb and the crossing of the Red Sea, which symbolize a Christian's passing from the Old Law to the new life of grace. Patience is already fortified by this power, but Will is still a neophyte.

19. I interpret the riddle as follows: The Saturday which first set the calendar is Holy Saturday, the day of the Passover, and the middle of the moon is Easter, which gives meaning both to Holy Saturday and Easter Wednesday. On the night of Holy Saturday the neophytes were baptized, passing over into the life of grace. The *sign* of Paschaltide is the Paschal Lamb or *Agnus Dei*. On Holy Saturday the Pope blessed the figures of the *Agnus Dei* that were stamped on discs made from the wax remaining from the Paschal Candles of the previous year. These images were distributed to the faithful and worn as talismans. So the mysterious object which Patience carries is an *Agnus Dei*. The 'wisdom of the following Wednesday' refers to the meaning of that day's Mass and Office, which deals almost entirely with the theme of the *Agni Nevelli* (new-born lambs) or neophytes.

20. '*Perfect love . . .*' 1 John iv. 18.

21. *Earls and Emperors*, etc. Images of the *Agnus Dei* were, in fact, sent by the Pope to kings and important persons as gifts.

22. *Peace between the Pope and his enemies.* See note 27, Book XIX.

23. *Two Christian kings.* i.e. the kings of France and England. As there was a truce with France from 1389 onwards, Langland omitted this remark from the C-text.

24. *To gain more experience* – 'til I have proved more.' Cf. Prov. xix. 11 and Rom. v. 3.

25. *New Year gifts.* 'These were given both *by* the sovereign and *to* him' (Skeat).

26. *A box of ointment.* Cf. Mark xiv. 3.

27. *Zacchaeus*. Cf. Luke xix. 8.

28. *A couple of mites*. Cf. Luke xxi. 2.

29. *Proves you and makes you perfect*. Cf. Jas. i. 3.

30. *Covetousness and Unkindness*. The test of apostolic patience is to endure the unnaturalness of men's greed and hatred without anger, and bring those who live in the 'hungry lands' to repentance. Haukyn, whom the pilgrims now meet, belongs to the 'hungry lands', and they set about the slow task of converting him.

31. *I am a minstrel*. The word 'minstrel' sometimes meant simply a servant having a special function in a household. But the point here is, I think, allegorical. There is a double irony in the dreamer's thinking that Haukyn looked like a minstrel, and Haukyn's humorously calling himself one. Haukyn says this because he thinks he deserves better payment for his service than the minstrels get for theirs; he looks down on them, though he envies their success and popularity. Yet in an allegorical sense, he is really one of them himself. For the false minstrels mentioned in the Prologue and elsewhere throughout the poem may represent all those who use their gifts, not to praise God (like the 'harpers harping with their harps' of Rev. xiv. 2), but for their own glory and temporal reward. 'The false minstrels are not mere jesters or entertainers. They are those who profess the faith but do not work accordingly – who have abandoned Truth for the world' (R. and H., 24). Cf. the 'vain janglers' of I Tim. i. 6.

32. *Robes and fur-lined gowns*. 'Robes and furred gowns were common gifts to minstrels, from the great men before whom they exhibited. . . . Some minstrels were not itinerant, but were retained by rich men as jesters' (Skeat).

33. *Piers and all his helpers*. i.e. for the whole Church Militant.

34. *Wafer-bread*. 'A waferer answers very nearly to what we now call a confectioner . . . They sold ornamental cakes and eucharistic wafers' (Skeat). But Haukyn is also an ordinary baker, and wafer-bread was not merely an elegant confection.

35. *Bread for the Pope*. 'To be taken in a satirical sense. It clearly alludes, I think, to the money contributed to the Pope under the name of Peter's pence' (Skeat). It may also allude to the provisions that had to be supplied to Cardinals visiting England – see p. 242.

36. '*In my name shall they cast out . . .* ' Mark xvi. 17–18.

37. '*Silver and gold have I none . . .* ' Acts iii. 6. It is said that when St Thomas Aquinas visited the Pope, he found him seated by a table covered with piles of indulgence money. 'You see,' said the Pontiff, 'the church is no longer in the days when she could say –

Silver and gold have I none.' 'True, holy father,' said St Thomas, 'and she is as little able to say to the sick of the palsy – Rise up and walk.'

38. *Stratford*. Stratford-at-Bow, Middlesex (Chaucer's Stratford-atte-Bow). 'Here lived numerous bakers, who supplied some parts of London with bread' (Skeat).

39. *The dry April ... Mayor*. There was, in fact, an extraordinary dearth in 1370. John de Chichestre was elected Mayor in 1369 and remained in office till Oct. 1370 (Skeat).

40. '*Do I seek to please men?*' Gal. i. 10 and Matt. vi. 24.

41. '*Whose mouths are full of cursing ...*' Ps. x. 7.

42. '*The children of men that are set on fire ...*' Ps. lvii. 4.

43. *Dame Emma of Shoreditch*. Nothing is known of these particular dealers in sorcery, probably famous in their day. Cf. the song of the idle labourers, p. 31 (though this was more likely to have been about a bawd).

44. '*Where your treasure is ...*' Matt. vi. 21.

45. '*Woe unto you that laugh ...*' Luke vi. 25.

46. '*Those who connive ...*' 'Probably not so much a quotation as a maxim of law' (Skeat).

47. '*Those whose works are proud ...*' Ps. ci. 7.

48. '*He that despiseth you ...*' Luke x. 16.

Book XIV

THE ALLEGORY. *Haukyn, the Active Life of the world, confronts Patience, the first essential stage in the spiritual life and the living proof of the practicability of self-denial. Patience's uncompromising teaching reverses, one by one, all Haukyn's values, dissolving his worldly attitudes and driving home the lessons of contrition and poverty. As Imagination had answered Will's theoretical problems, Patience now gives definitive answers to the practical problems of the spiritual life. The questions raised in Part I concerning food, clothing and wealth are finally answered, and worldliness gives way to a complete trust in God.*

1. '*I have married a wife ...*' Luke xiv. 20.

2. *Contrition of Heart*. Contrition is divided into three parts or acts, viz. contrition of heart, confession of mouth, and satisfaction (see next Note).

3. *Satisfaction*. This is the performing of the Sacramental Penance that constitutes the third part of the sacrament.

4. *'Take no thought for your life ...'* Matt. vi. 25–6.

5. *'Whatsoever ye shall ask ...'* John xiv. 13 and Matt. iv. 4.

6. *'He spake the word.'* Ps. cxlviii. 5. Cf. p. 106.

7. *'Thou openest thine hand ...'* Ps. cxlv. 16. This text is used in saying grace after meals.

8. *Seven Sleepers of Ephesus.* 'The legend of the Seven Sleepers of Ephesus, who were walled up in a cave by the Emperor Decius and awoke alive under Theodosius II, 362 years later, is a Christian version of a well-known folk theme' (Donald Attwater, *A Dictionary of Saints*, Burns Oates, 1938).

9. *'Idleness and abundance ...'* Cf. Ezek. xvi. 49.

10. *Dives* (=rich man) is taken, from the Vulgate, as the name of the rich man of Luke xvi. 19.

11. *'The proud are robbed ...'* Ps. lxxvi. 5. The sense of the Authorized Version here differs from that of the Vulgate.

12. *'Yea, even like a dream ...'* Ps. lxxiii. 20. The Vulgate again differs from the Authorized Version.

13. *'It is difficult to pass ...'* May be a commentary on Matt. xix. 23.

14. *'Come back and keep still ...'* Cf. Isaiah xxx. 15.

15. *Our Reprieve.* The Passion of Christ is the pledge of our Redemption. It is here symbolized by a legal document or Release, giving evidence of man's discharge. Yet a little later Langland says that this document must be drawn up on a parchment made of our own poverty and patience, etc. – in other words, Christ's Passion can only serve as a release, if we fit ourselves for it, and provide the necessary material.

16. *Names engraved in Friary windows.* Cf. pp. 46–7 and note 4, Book III.

17. *Hold their riches in common.* See note 1, Bk I.

18. *'A rich man shall hardly ...'* Intended to refer to Matt. xix. 23.

19. *'And their works do follow them.'* Rev. xiv 13.

20. *'Blessed be ye poor ...'* Luke vi. 20.

21. *If Anger wrestles.* Patience (the speaker) now pictures each of the Seven Deadly Sins wrestling to get the better of a poor man, and shows how they fail to overcome him, because his poverty protects him. The angry oppressor may win the lawsuit against him, but Anger itself does not get the better of him, since it does him no good to be angry.

22. *For He said so himself.* Cf. Phil. ii. 7.

23. *He is like a maiden.* Cf. Matt. xix. 29 and Eph. v. 31.

24. '*Poverty is a hateful blessing . . .*' A paraphrase of a passage in *Speculum Historiale* by Vincent of Beauvais (Lib. x. cap. 71).

25. '*Judge not . . .*' Matt. vii. 1.

26. *The Alton Pass.* 'The wooded pass of Alton, on the borders of Surrey and Hampshire . . . was a favourite resort for outlaws, who there awaited the merchants and their trains of sumpter-horses travelling to and from Winchester' (T. Hudson Turner, quoted by Skeat).

27. *Seneca says.* Precise reference not identified, though Seneca says many things like this in his Epistles.

28. '*A poor traveller sings . . .*' The quotation is actually from Juvenal, Sat. x. 22.

29. *Sweeter than honey.* Cf. the comparison of poverty to the taste of a walnut, pp. 134.

30. *St Augustine.* 'The reference to St Augustine probably means no more than that similar praise of poverty is to be found in his writings (e.g. in *De Civitate Dei*, lib. iv. c. 3.)' (Skeat).

Book XV

THE ALLEGORY. *This, as Lawlor shows, is a book in which true identities ('the reality behind varying names') are revealed. In Anima, the higher spiritual gifts are at last combined with the intellectual faculties. So, in his comprehensive discourse on the theme of universal charity (of which Piers-Christ is now identified as the exemplar), positives and negatives are linked in a single vision, and Will is made to understand that it lies in the nature of the church to bring forth evil fruits as well as good. This discourse is the Prologue to Do-better; therefore, in its survey of the church, it emphasizes the high responsibility of the priesthood, with its apostolic ideal of perfect love linked with poverty – whose end must be the salvation of all men, pagan and Christian alike. Will's personal perplexities, and with them the local problems of England, are now left behind, and the power of love is seen to be all-embracing.*

1. *Paul with his falchion.* 'St Paul is generally represented with a sword, in allusion to his martyrdom' (Skeat).

2. *I am called Life.* In the C-text, his primary name is Free will.

3. *When I complain to God.* Langland seems to have misunderstood the Latin of Isidore (see next Note), '*Dum recolit, memoria est*' – where '*recolit*' means 'remembers, recollects', not 'complains'.

4. *Augustine and Isidore.* The quotation is found in Isidore, *Etymologiarum Liber* xi, cap. 1, and also in *Differentiarum Liber* ii.

cap. 29. As for Augustine, Langland sometimes uses his name as an authority, without any particular passage in mind.

5. '*I will exalt my throne* . . .' Isaiah xiv. 14.

6. '*Not good to eat much honey* . . .' Prov. xxv. 27.

7. *Says St Bernard.* Cf. Epistle cci., vol. i.

8. '*Not to be more wise* . . .' Rom. xii. 3.

9. *Talking abstrusely about the Trinity.* Cp. p. 114.

10. '*Confounded be all they* . . .' Ps. xcvii. 7.

11. '*O ye sons of men, how long* . . .' Ps. iv. 2.

12. *See what the Commentary says.* St Augustine's comment on this verse runs: 'Why then are ye held back by love of temporal things? Why do you follow after the last things, as if they were the first? For ye desire those things to stay with you for ever which all pass away like a shadow.'

13. '*Thou shalt not respect persons* . . .' Langland may have been thinking of James ii. 1.

14. *In the Latin Proverb.* 'The monks had collections of comparisons, similitudes, proverbs, etc., to be introduced in their sermons' (T. Wright, quoted by Skeat).

15. *Whitewashed.* Cf. Matt. xxiii. 27 and Acts xxiii. 3.

16. *St John Chrysostom.* 'The passage here attributed to St John Chrysostom is not to be found in his genuine works. It occurs in the 38th of a set of Homilies on the Gospel of St Matthew, a work of an uncertain author, sometimes called "Opus Imperfectum" from its incomplete state, and printed in some editions of St John Chrysostom's Works as an Appendix to his Homilies on St Matthew. The text commented on is contained in Matt. xxi. 12–20 . . . It is obvious that William's quotation was made from memory. It is clear, too, that the author of the *Opus Imperfectum* was thinking of Isaiah xxiv. 2 – "As with the people, so with the priest."' (Skeat).

17. *Wearing short-swords*, etc. Priests were forbidden to carry weapons, but they frequently ignored this.

18. '*Become as little children.*' Matt. xviii. 3.

19. *Men call me Long Will.* This line can be interpreted as an acrostic (Long-land) by which the author wished to make himself known indirectly.

20. '*Vaunteth not itself.*' 1 Cor. xiii. 4–5.

21. '*For now we see through a glass* . . .' 1 Cor. xiii. 12.

22. '*Trust in the Lord.*' Ps. xlii. 5.

23. *He can paint illustrations*, etc. i.e. He can say the Rosary well (?).

24. *A laundry.* Here a symbol fo self-examination and penance.

25. '*I am weary with my groaning . . .* ' Ps. vi. 6.

26. '*A broken and a contrite heart . . .* ' Ps. li. 17.

27. *Piers sees more deeply.* (See also two paras below.) R. and H. explain this as follows: 'Clerks (i.e. priests) can judge the presence of charity by words and works, but only Piers can see beneath externals into the will. (A footnote here refers us to Matt. ix. 4.) He can penetrate hypocrisy . . . Christ established the power of apostolic discernment into the hearts of men. This function of his divinity he transmitted to Peter (cf. Acts v. 3–4) . . . (and) as part of the apostolic tradition, it is a function of Piers Plowman; in so far as Christ or Piers share this power, they are they same'.

28. '*And God saw their thoughts.*' Matt. ix. 4 and Luke xi. 17.

29. *Recognize charity by appearances.* Cf. Eccles. ix. 1.

30. *Peter, that is Christ.* The text of 1 Cor. x. 4 has here been taken in connexion with Matt. xvi. 18.

31. '*Be not, as the hypocrites . . .* ' Matt. vi. 16.

32. *Edmund.* St Edmund, the martyr, king of East Anglia (d. 870), from whom Bury-St-Edmunds takes its name.

33. *I have never seen him wheedling.* i.e. Though I have seen charity as a priest or monk, I have never seen him as a friar.

34. *He prefers . . . to walk in rich clean robes.* i.e. Charity *prefers,* if possible, to be embodied in the person of an Abbot or Prelate – not that this is often the case; for Langland says below, '*At one time,* charity consorted with great prelates, etc.'

35. *Crimped hair.* The skull-cap of a tonsured monk would show the waved hair on that part of the head which was left unshorn.

36. '*Blessed is the rich man . . .* ' Ecclus. xxxi. 8.

37. *Make and unmake marriages.* Cf. Bk xx, p. 249.

38. '*I will lay me down . . .* ' Ps. iv. 8.

39. *Giles.* 'The legend of St Giles (*Aegidius*), with the incident of the wounded hind, was one of the most popular of the Middle Ages, but it derives chiefly from a tenth-century biography that is utterly untrustworthy. Giles was probably a Provençal and abbot of a monastery on the Rhône, who d. c. 712' (Attwater, op. cit.).

40. *St Paul.* i.e. St Paul the Hermit – 'Venerated as the first hermit. B. c. 230, he went into the Theban desert at the age of 22 and lived alone in a cave for ninety years. Here he was found by St Antony, who on a second visit found Paul dead, c. 342. The account of his life edited by St Jerome is a classic of desert-father literature; numerous stories of varying value are told of St Paul' (Attwater, op. cit.).

41. *Would weave baskets.* He was actually a tent-maker (Acts xviii. 3), but Chaucer (Prol. to Pardoner's Tale) also thought he made baskets.

42. *St Mary Magdalen.* According to a well-known legend now greatly discredited, she and the risen St Lazarus led a solitary life in the South of Gaul.

43. *'Doth the wild ass ...'* Job vi. 5.

44. *'The nature of brute beasts ...'* A commentary (unidentified, but similar to that of St Bruno) on Job vi. 5.

45. *'He hath dispersed abroad ...'* Ps. cxii. 9.

46. *'If you do not give ...'* Partly taken from Peter Cantor, partly from Jerome, Epistle 66, Sect. 8.

47. *The Corpus Christi hymn.* i.e. the *Pange, lingua*, stanza 4 (not that which is sung on Good Friday, but the *Pange, lingua* of Vespers on Corpus Christi).

48. *This is how he did it.* Langland's account of Mohammed is the one which was most current in the Middle Ages. He probably derived the story of the dove from Vincent of Beauvais, *Speculum Historiale* lib xxiii. c. 40.

49. *Put forth leaves.* Cf. Jer xvii. 8 and Ezek. xlvii. 12.

50. *'Ask, and it shall be given ...'* Matt. vii. 7.

51. *'Ye are the salt ...'* Matt. v. 13.

52. *The word 'heathen'.* This derivation is correct – O.E. *haethen* orig. meant 'dweller on the heath', and was a loose rendering of Latin *paganus* (pagus=a village).

53. *The parable in St Matthew.* xxii 1–14.

54. *'My oxen and fatlings ...'* The 'fatlings' ('altilia') of the parable symbolize the newly-baptized, who are innocent and honest, as opposed to the wild beasts or *heathens* whom Langland has just been discussing. These innocent 'fatlings' need example and spiritual nourishment from their priests – so he returns to the main subject of his discourse, the priesthood, and with it, to the central meaning of the parable of the marriage feast.

55. *Calf a symbol of innocence.* Cf. Levit. xi. 3 ff, where it is listed among the clean animals.

56. *'Lo, we heard of the same ...'* See note 9, Bk x.

57. *'Go ye into all the world ...'* Mark xvi. 15.

58. *'Good shepherds,'* John x. 11.

59. *'Go ye into my vineyard"* Matt. xx. 4.

60. *'Ask, and it shall be given ...'* Matt. vii. 7.

61. *'But God forbid ...'* Gal. vi. 14.

62. *The Templars.* An allusion to the suppression of the Order

of Templars (the first military Order of Knights of the Temple, founded 1118) by the Council of Vienna (1312).

63. '*He putteth down the mighty . . .*' Luke i. 52, the *Magnificat*.

64. '*Through your tithes . . .*' Deut. xii. 6.

65. *Constantine*. See note 35, Bk x. The story of the angel was widely current in the Middle Ages.

66. '*Thou shalt not move a sickle . . .*' Cf. Deut. xxiii. 25.

67. '*In my house is neither . . .*' Isaiah iii. 7.

68. '*Bring ye all the tithes . . .*' Not in Hosea, but Malachi iii. 10.

69. '*Lazarus, come forth.*' John xi. 43.

70. '*When the holy of holies . . .*' Cf. Dan. ix. 24, 26.

Book XVI

THE ALLEGORY. *After completing his survey of Charity's work in the world, Anima turns Will's attention to the ultimate source of its growth, both in history and in the human heart. So, in a deeper swoon of mystical vision, the dreamer at last rediscovers his guide, Piers. The complex symbol of the Jesse-tree represents the church bearing its fruit of holy lives, Israel awaiting the birth of Christ, and also the life of grace in the human soul, waiting for the gifts of faith, hope and charity. So the vision of Piers and the tree gives way to one of the birth and manhood of the Saviour-prince who is to do battle with death. Awaking after this foretaste, Will must now gain Faith and Hope before he can share in the mystery of Redemption. The time is Lent, and as the revelation of Passiontide and Easter is close at hand, the allegory moves on with swiftness and surety. Through his meeting with the herald, Abraham ('Father of Faith'), Will gains the first necessary gift, faith in the Trinity. This is explained to him in language that is fraught with images of generation, since it is from the threefold nature of God that the imminent rebirth of mankind must spring.*

1. *A precious tree*. Cf. the image of the tree in Isai. xi. 1, Ps. i. 3, Prov. xi. 30, Jer. xvii. 8, and Rev. xxii. 2. In the C-text, the tree growing in man's heart is called 'The Image of God'.

2. '*Though a good man fall . . .*' Ps. xxxvii. 24.

3. '*Whosoever speaketh against the Holy Ghost . . .*' Matt. xii. 32. Langland's argument is that to sin deliberately, of one's own free will, is to sin against the Holy Ghost; for Free Will can, if it chooses, use the strength of the Holy Ghost to resist sin.

4. *Sprang from the same root*. 'William had in mind the old legend of the Holy Rood, which tells us how the tree of which Christ's cross was made grew up from three stems' (Skeat). Skeat also

refers us to various descriptions of the Tree of Life, and to St Augustine, *De Fide et Symbolo*, ix. 17.

5. *The ground is called Goodness*. Cf. Matt. xiii. 23.

6. *A fruit named Marriage*. The fruits of the tree 'are the just men, those who are directed in the way of spiritual perfection with its three inner states of development; the lowest is matrimony, higher is continence (widowhood), the highest is maidenhood. These are conventional symbols for the three states of spiritual perfection ... The particular symbolic terminology here employed emphasizes the inner quality of the three states, Dowel, Dobet, and Dobest, externally manifest in active, contemplative, and prelatical' (R. and H., pp. 195–6).

7. *The Limbo of Hell*. i.e. the *Limbus Patrum* (Limbo of the Fathers) – the name given to the outermost circle, or outer verge, of hell, where the souls of the patriarchs awaited Christ's descent into hell to release them.

8. '*The fullness of time*.' Gal. iv. 4 – but Langland probably took the phrase from the *Pange, lingua*, stanza 3.

9. '*Ecce ancilla domini*.' Luke i. 28.

10. *Piers the Ploughman*. As Piers represents the ministry of God, it is he who is said to teach Christ how to protect himself against evil. In the C-text, Christ is taught by Free Will.

11. '*For they that be whole* ...' Matt. ix. 12.

12. Literally 'He grew sorrowful' (John xi. 35).

13. '*He hath a devil*.' John xi. 30.

14. '*Satan is your Saviour*.' Cf. Matt. xii. 27.

15. *Knocking over the stalls*. John ii. 15.

16. '*I shall dash this Temple* ...' John ii. 19.

17. '*Tu dicis*.' Matt. xxvi. 25.

18. *The smile and flattering kiss*. Cf. the Responsory in Matins for Maundy Thursday: 'My friend betrayed me by the sign of a kiss ... He who by a kiss committed murder gave this wicked sign.'

19. *Like a mirror*. The mirror is an attribute of vanity (cf. James i. 23–4), holding up to men what they want to see, and so hiding the truth from them. Christ says that Judas will mirror the wishes of many, and so deceive them – he is a beguiler and flatterer (as Satan was to Eve); other people cannot see through him as Christ can. (Cf. Prov. xxix. 5–6.)

20. '*For it must needs be* ...' Matt. xviii. 7.

21. *Leave my apostles alone*. Cf. John xviii. 8.

22. *Battle against Death*. Cf. Hebr. ii. 14 and 1 Cor. xv. 26, 54. Also the sequence *Victimi paschali laudes*.

23. *On mid-Lent Sunday.* The fourth Sunday in Lent. The lessons in The Breviary for this period tell the stories of the patriarchs.

24. *His Father's wisdom.* Cf. 1 Cor. i. 24 – 'Christ . . . the wisdom of God.'

25. *Three things are necessary.* This paragraph is obscure, and I am not sure that my translation brings out its sense correctly. Augustine, in *De Trinitate*, says: 'The mind may be taken as the Father, knowledge as the Son, and Love as the Holy Ghost. Moreover the mind is like a parent and its knowledge like its offspring . . . The third is Love, which proceeds from the mind itself and from its knowledge.'

26. *That which he and his servant suffer.* If the third Person is Love, then these words must refer to God's patience and long-suffering, shown forth by the Holy Ghost.

27. *Types of the Trinity.* Christ, married to Holy Church, begets on earth children (the fruits of the Tree of Charity) who bear the image of the Trinity, and are therefore 'born of God' (*John* i. 13).

28. *And marriage.* Langland now seeks to show how the three types of Christian perfection (Marriage, Continence, Maidenhood) are images of the three Persons of the Trinity.

29. '*My God, my God . . .*' Matt. xxvii. 46 and Mark xv. 34. Christ's exclamation is taken to signify His humanity as distinct from His godhead. His human nature is widowed, because, for a time, it is voluntarily cut off from God – or refuses to exercise the powers of God.

30. *He first had a mother.* Abraham is still speaking of Christ's *human* nature, which shares the nature of widowhood in this respect also. His human nature springs from a human mother, just as His divine nature springs from the power of God the Father, which, as he has already said, is symbolized by wedlock. So, he adds, a human marriage is not complete – it is not a true 'type of the Trinity' – unless it has lawful issue. The birth of children is, therefore, a symbol of the eternal generation of God (the 'procession' of the Holy Ghost from the Father and the Son) in Heaven. But in Heaven there is only one 'source of generation' (since God is one), and God requires no intermediary in His act of begetting, as a man does (cf. p. 106).

31. '*Accursed is the man . . .*' Not in the Bible, but in the apocryphal Gospel of the Nativity of Mary, where the high priest speaks these words to Joachim, afterwards the father of Mary. (The story is told in the *Golden Legend.*)

32. *I saw Him once.* Cf. Gen. xviii. 2.

33. *Circumcised Ishmael.* Gen. xvii. 23.

34. *He promised.* Cf. Gen. xii. 2, xii. 16, Rom. iv. 13, etc.

35. *'As he spake to our fathers . . .'* Luke i. 55, the *Magnificat.*

36. *Do him sacrifice.* Cf. Gen. xiv. 18–19. All these 'tokens'are signs of the Redemption to come, and the story of Melchisedech prefigures the Eucharist. 'As the "foot" ("first stone") of God's faith, Abraham the patriarch is a representative of Christ's priesthood, Piers Plowman, and thus symbolically learns the Sacrifice of the Mass. . . . Abraham's priesthood was confirmed by Melchisedech, not with oil but in the purity of faith, not in the old sacrifice of animals but in the prophetic sacrifice of bread and wine' (R. and H. , p. 202).

37. *Comforted many suffering souls.* Abraham is traditionally the protector of the souls of the just who died before Christ's coming – cf. Luke xvi. 22–23. Langland also calls him God's herald on earth, because he is 'the father of all them that believe' (Rom iv. 11), and in hell too, because 'it was his mission to announce to the rest the promise that in him should all families of the earth be blessed' (Skeat).

38. *Told the souls in hell.* St John the Baptist, the last of the prophets to join those waiting in Limbo, tells the others the news of what is happening on earth – Christ's birth and ministry, etc.

39. *'Ecce agnus dei.'* John i. 29.

Book XVII

THE ALLEGORY. *Hope, coming swiftly on Faith's heels, is carrying the Law of love, since 'What is commanded in the Old Law is promise and hope in the New' (R. & H., op. cit.). Will's natural difficulty in reconciling faith and works – which recalls the earlier problem of Piers' Pardon – is now answered by the appearance of Charity, the Master whom he has so long sought, in the person of the Good Samaritan or Christ. The Samaritan shows, in action and in word, how the Law (which Faith and Hope cannot carry out) is to be fulfilled. His flowing, measured language, with its homely images of hand, light and warmth, applies the doctrine of the Trinity directly to life's problems; love and mercy spring straight from the heart of the godhead, and the only unforgivable sin is the unkindness which quenches this love.*

1. *Hope, a scout.* He represents 'the expectation of the Messiah's coming. Hence he is called a "spy", i.e. a scout' (Skeat).

2. *Sealed with that seal.* 'The Law was to be fulfilled by the death of Christ' (Skeat) – i.e. sealed with His Blood.

3. *'On these two commandments ...'* Matt. xxii. 40.

4. *A Samaritan.* Cf. Luke x 30–7.

5. *Washed the man's wounds.* All these actions symbolize Christ's healing of mankind through the Redemption and the sacraments.

6. *Eaten the whole child.* i.e. eaten the whole Body and drunk the Blood of Christ in the Eucharist.

7. *No one ... has ever passed.* 'The way to Jerusalem was closed through original sin so that no one passed through the world safely except those who lived in Faith or who followed the Law in the will to righteousness [Will, the dreamer, is among these]. But since Christ has assumed man's flesh, the horse of the parable, and has ridden to Jerusalem and in doing so saved the wayfarer, he has made the celestial pilgrimage safe from the attacks of the devil, when his road is followed' (R. and H., pp. 206–7).

8. *'O Death ...'* Hosea xiii. 14 (1st Antiphon for Lauds on Holy Saturday).

9. *Then Faith will be the keeper.* 'After the Redemption, Faith has the power to teach the imitation of Christ, not simply to herald his coming' (R. and H., p. 207).

10. *'I will draw all things ...'* John xii. 32.

11. *'Qui peccat in Spiritum Sanctum ...'* Mark iii. 29.

12. *Murders his grace.* Cf. 1 Thess. v. 19 – 'Quench not the Spirit.'

13. *Quench true love.* 'The point here (i.e. in the whole passage about the torch) is that it is necessary for the individual to have the hot coal of charity in order to ignite the flame of God's mercy' (R. and H., p. 209).

14. *Pay the remainder for him.* Cf. Matt. xviii. 27.

15. *'Verily I say unto you ...'* Matt. xxv. 12.

16. *Pampeluna.* Pamplona, the old capital of the kingdom of Navarre.

17. *'Though I speak . . . '* 1 Cor. xiii. 1.

18. *'Not everyone that saith ...'* Matt. vii. 21.

19. *Dives.* See note 10, Bk xiv.

20. *The flame of man's body.* Since the body is 'a temple of the Holy Ghost' (1 Cor. vi. 19), murder is a sin against the Holy Ghost.

21. *'Avenge the blood ...'* Rev. vi. 10.

22. *'His mercy is over ...'* Ps. cxlv. 9.

23. *Three things.* These are embodied in a commonly quoted

proverb, which is a compilation from Prov. x. 26, xix. 13, xxi. 19, and xxvii. 15.

24. *'My strength is made perfect ...'* II Cor. xii. 9.

Book XVIII

THE ALLEGORY. *The poem reaches its climax in this symbolic drama which reveals to Will the final truth of his search – that the Law, which has proved a stumbling-block, is to be perfectly fulfilled by One who will joust in Piers' arms, that is to say, share man's nature. The vision gives a speaking picture, first, of the liturgy of Good Friday and the Easter Vigil (especially through the imagery of light and darkness, and the* Lumen Christi *standing before hell gates); second, of the doctrine of the Atonement. The dispute between the four Virtues is part of the eternal debate between justice and mercy – irreconcilables that are reconciled by the crucifixion. Christ's passionate speech of self-justification to Lucifer asserts the justice, as well as the triumph, of mercy, and hints that it may ultimately have no limits. In breaking into the prison of hell, Christ also breaks into the darkness of man's soul to rescue it from the bondage of sin. So when Will wakes up on Easter morning, he is prepared at last to receive Holy Communion.*

1. *Palm Sunday.* Langland's phrase for Palm Sunday is *Ramis Palmarum* ('Palm branches'), from the Responsory to the Procession hymn.

2. *About children.* Cf. the Antiphon *Pueri Hebraeorum* ('The Jewish children'), and the words of the *Gloria, Laus,* 'Cui puerile decus prompsit Hosanna pium.' Presumably the children sang the verses and the older people the Responses.

3. *Gloria, laus.* Palm Sunday Procession hymn – the 'Hosanna' forms part of the Antiphons and Responsory.

4. *Receive his golden spurs.* The buckling on of spurs was an essential part of the ceremony of dubbing a knight. 'Cut-away shoes' refers to the fashion of slitting or slashing them by way of ornament.

5. *'Blessed is he ...'* From the Antiphon *Pueri Hebraeorum* – 'and cried out saying, Hosanna to the Son of David; blessed is he, etc.' (Matt. xxi. 9).

6. *'O Death ...'* See note 8, Bk. XVII.

7. *In the judgement seat.* Matt. xxvii. 19.

8. *Longinus.* The name of Longinus first appeared in the Apocryphal Gospel of Nicodemus, and the story is found in the Golden Legend, cap. xlvii.

9. *'When the holy of holies ...'* Cf. Dan. ix. 24.

10. *In accordance with Scripture.* Cf. Ps. lxxxv. 10–11, 13. He refers also to the treatment of this theme in the writings of saints.

11. *From the West.* The conflict between Mercy and Truth, Peace and Righteousness, is symbolized by their coming from opposite poles. Truth and Righteousness, who do not believe in the possibility of the Redemption, come from the colder quarters of the earth. Langland may have derived this idea from Isaiah xliii. 6 – 'Bring my sons from afar, and *my daughters* from the ends of the earth' – the four maidens being frequently referred to as the Four Daughters of God.

12. *The darkness and then the sudden dawn.* i.e the darkness on earth, followed by the light of Christ entering hell.

13. *A tree should win back.* Cf. *Pange, lingua,* verse 2.

14. *'He that goeth down ...'* Job vii. 9.

15. *'Ars artem falleret.' Pange, lingua,* verse 3.

16. *'Weeping may endure ...'* Ps. xxx. 5.

17. *'I will both lay me down ...'* Ps. iv. 8. The First Antiphon of Matins for Holy Saturday.

18. *'Lord, bid me come ...'* Matt. xiv. 28.

19. *The sons of Simeon.* According to the Apocryphal Gospel of Nicodemus, the two sons of Simeon (Luke ii. 25) were raised from the dead at the time of Christ's death.

20. *The giant Jesus.* Samson, carrying off the gates of Gaza, was a type of Christ, breaking the gates of hell.

21. *'Lift up your heads ...'* Ps. xxiv. 9–10. Psalm and Antiphon for Matins on Holy Saturday and on Ascension Day.

22. *Replied Satan.* Satan and Lucifer are two separate persons, as in the Gospel of Nicodemus. Langland makes Lucifer the one who tempted Eve and Christ.

23. *God or God's Son.* Cf. Matt. iv. 3, 6 – 'If thou be the Son of God.'

24. *To Pilate's wife in her sleep.* Cf. Matt. xxvii. 19.

25. *Now shall the prince of this world ...* ' John xii. 31.

26. *'Who is this king?'* Ps. xxiv. 8. The question of the Psalm is asked by Lucifer, and Christ makes the Psalmist's reply.

27. *'The people that sat in darkness ...'* Isaiah ix. 2 and Matt. iv. 16.

28. *'Ecce agnus dei.'* John i. 36.

29. *A reptile with a woman's face.* Langland's word is 'lizard'. 'The words "lizard" and "lady" refer to the fact that the serpent who tempted Eve was sometimes represented with short feet,

like a lizard or crocodile, and the face of a young maiden. Even when the feet do not appear, the face is commonly retained, as in the representation in the chapter-house of Salisbury cathedral' (Skeat).

30. '*An eye for an eye.*' Matt. v. 38.

31. *Sin shall counter sin.* i.e. the sin of crucifying Christ is the counterpart of Satan's sin: it is the poison which will serve as an antidote to poison.

32. *Member for member.* Cf. Exod. xxi. 23–5.

33. *Grace should destroy guile.* Christ's grace towards men should undo what Lucifer's guile had done for them. Since Lucifer used unjust means, Christ can justifiably go beyond mere justice to retrieve mankind from him.

34. '*I came not to destroy . . .*' Matt. v. 17.

35. '*He made a pit . . .*' Ps. vii. 15.

36. *Valley of Jehoshaphat.* Supposed to be the future scene of the Last Judgement. Cf. Joel iii. 2, 12, and 13: from verse 2 Langland may have derived the idea of Christ pleading for the salvation of men at the Day of Judgment, rather than judging them.

37. '*Against thee only . . .*' Ps. li. 4 – since sin is only an offence against himself (Christ argues), He may forgive it if He chooses.

38. *To hang the man again.* Skeat quotes several medieval examples of such resuscitation, one of which occurred at Leicester in 1363: a hanged man revived on his way to the cemetery, and the king, who happened to see the incident, gave him a pardon.

39. '*No evil will go unpunished.*' See note 13, Bk IV.

40. '*I heard secret words . . .*' II Cor. xii. 4.

41. '*Enter not into judgement . . .*' Ps. cxliii. 2.

42. *Ashtoreth.* Orig. the Phoenician moon-goddess (the 'queen of Heaven' of Jer. vii. 18) – in medieval literature, and in Milton, one among the devils.

43. '*Culpat caro . . .*' Hymn *Aeterne rex altissime*, sung at Matins on Ascension Day, verse 2. Cf. also Ps. xlvii. 5, an Ascension Day Antiphon.

44. '*Clarior est solito . . .*' Source unknown, but the ideas are proverbial. Cf. Tobias ii. 22.

45. '*Mercy and Truth . . .*' Ps. lxxxv. 10–11. Cf. also the Kiss of Peace in the Mass.

46. '*Behold, how good and joyful . . .*' Ps. cxxxiii. 1.

47. *Creep to the Cross.* Cf. the Good Friday Service of the Adoration of the Cross (Roman Missal) and its Antiphon: 'We adore Thy Cross, O Lord: and we praise and glorify Thy holy

resurrection: for behold by the wood of the Cross joy came into the whole world.'

Book XIX

THE ALLEGORY. *In a single sweep, this Book takes in the setting up by Christ the Conqueror of his earthly kingdom, its growth, renewal and final corruption and decline – which brings us back to the world as described in the Prologue. Do-best means a return to the world, to take part in the struggle against Antichrist. First, in the contemplative vision that begins in the middle of Mass, Christ's life is retold in terms of kingship and conquest – the language of Paschaltide – and Will sees the application of the fruits of his victory to the world. Then, after the setting up of Christian society under Piers, Christ's vicar on earth, Piers himself and Grace soon disappear, and Pride again attacks the church, bringing intellectual confusion. Her defensive efforts towards renewal are undermined by men's evasion of the one condition attached to the new Law, 'Pay back that which you owe'. Will has now seen in detail the source of the church's, and his own, original corruption.*

1. *All stained with blood.* Cf. Isaiah lxii. 2 and 3.
2. *No name can compare.* Cf. Acts iv. 12 and Phil. ii. 9–12.
3. *A king and a conqueror.* The knight, Jesus, was also the king and conqueror, Christ. The word *Christ* signifies 'The Lord's Anointed', and Langland rightly takes it to refer to the kingship of Jesus – His Messianic power (which the prophets prophesied in terms of conquest). The language of kingship and conquest is found repeatedly in the liturgy of Paschaltide and the Ascension. Especially relevant to Langland's imagery is the hymn *Aurora coelum* (Easter Lauds) –

'While He, the king of glorious might,
Treads down death's strength in death's despite,
And trampling hell by victor's right
Brings forth his sleeping saints to light.' (Verse 2)

4. *'At the name of Jesus ...'* Phil. ii. 10.
5. *Reason, Righteousness, and Pity.* 'The interpretation of the gifts ... is a modification of one of the traditional explanations' (R. and H., p. 219, footnote). The gifts represent the wisdom, justice, and mercy which are the essential virtues of kingship – the gifts by which earthly kings may best honour the heavenly king, Jesus.
6. *Reason like rich gold.* Langland does not contradict himself.

The gifts of Reason, Righteousness, and Loyalty (truth) are all closely connected, and we may suppose that the incense was in a gold receptacle.

7. *Wine a symbol of Law*. i.e. the new wine which Christ made from water represents the new law of charity – 'the transformation of water into wine symbolizes the transformation of the law' (R. and H., p. 219).

8. *A greater name, Do-better*. 'It is when he is celebrated as a triumphant King that Christ appears as Dobet ... Jesus as Dowel is obedient, as Dobet he inspires praise, and as Dobest he brings charity to mankind' (R. and H., p. 220).

9. *'Saul hath slain ...'* 1 Sam. xviii. 7.

10. *'Christus resurgens ...'* Rom vi. 9.

11. *'Thus it behoved Christ ...'* Luke xxiv. 46.

12. *Thomas of India*. The tradition that St Thomas the Apostle preached and was martyred in India is very old.

13. *'Peace be unto you.'* John xx. 19.

14. *'Deus meus ...'* John xx. 28.

15. *'Beati qui non viderunt ...'* John xx. 29.

16. *'Redde quod debes ...'* Matt. xviii. 28, and cf. the essential condition made in v. 35 – 'if you from your hearts forgive not everyone his brother their trespasses.' But Langland makes it clear throughout the poem that the condition attached to the Pardon applies also to debts in the literal sense, and to all ill-gotten gains. 'When any act of injustice ... has been committed, it is not enough to repent in order to obtain pardon; *restitution* is also necessary; that is, we must restore the ill-gotten goods, and, as far as in us lies, repair the injury we have done. Without restitution we cannot hope for pardon from God' (Hart: *A Student's Catholic Doctrine*, p. 224). The traditional teaching also says (as Langland reiterates in his poem) that this obligation rests on all who have taken a guilty part in an act of injustice, including the receivers of goods which have been gained unjustly (op. cit. p. 225). Langland attributes the decay and corruption of the Church in his day to the ignoring of this condition.

17. *Antichrist and his followers*. Cf. 1 John ii. 18 – 'And as ye have heard that antichrist shall come, *even now are there many antichrists*; whereby we know that it is the last time.' Langland's allegory simply follows the hint given in this text: his poem does *not* necessarily imply that he thought that the end of the world was coming shortly, though he may have thought so.

18. *'Diversities of gifts ...'* 1 Cor. xii. 4. Langland's account of

the gifts or graces is 'roughly parallel to that given by St Augustine' (R. and H., 221).

19. *Augustine, Ambrose,* etc. These are the four chief Latin fathers.

20. *The Cardinal Virtues.* As implied in the Prologue, the hinges on which all moral virtues turn.

21. '*Spare me, Lord.*' Langland was probably thinking of Ps. xvi.

22. '*Be strong in mind . . .*' Cato Distich. ii. 14.

23. *Except the prostitutes,* etc. i.e. those 'who deliberately maintain sin against the Holy Spirit and refuse to assist in the task of digging' (R. and H., p. 224).

24. *An ignorant vicar.* 'Unlearned in the sophistry of the Friars' (R. and H.), this vicar is able to reveal to Conscience the real situation in the Church.

25. *Their palfrey's fodder.* Cf. Haukyn's remark about the Pope's palfrey, p. 158–9.

26. *At Avignon.* The Cardinals, especially the French ones, preferred to live at Avignon, and opposed the Papal decisions to move to Rome (1367 and 1377). The six who remained at Avignon in 1377 helped to bring about the Great Schism in 1378. The Jews were popular at Avignon because many were merchants who catered for the ever-increasing needs of the Papal Court. It was a rich Jew who, in 1379, transported to Avignon the Cardinals who sided with the Anti-Pope, Clement; and Clement, especially, protected the Jews (cf. Bennett, *Date of B-text*).

27. *Sends armies to kill.* Langland probably alludes to the war of the rival popes, and is criticizing Urban himself (the true Pope) and his proclamation of a crusade against the schismatics (March 1381). Open warfare broke out in April 1379 (Bennett, op. cit.).

28. '*Sends rain on evil and on good.*' Matt. v. 45. The context of this text is important, for the Pope fails to 'love his enemies', and only 'loves those who love him'. Piers, the true minister of God, follows Christ's counsel of perfection.

29. '*Vengeance belongs to me . . .*' Hebr. x. 30.

30. *Rake in the money.* The Reeve extorts money from the tenants, and the lord gladly accepts it. Cf. Sloth's remark about his auditing Reeves' accounts, p. 73.

31. *Head of the Law.* Cf. the advice of the 'garrulous fellow', p. 29.

32. '*All things are yours . . .*' A legal maxim (?)

NOTES AND COMMENTARY

Book XX

THE ALLEGORY. *Free from all illusions, the dreamer can now describe the battle with Antichrist (i.e. the church versus the world) in terms of a swift and sometimes farcical comedy. Having resisted Lust, Pride and Despair with some success, the Castle is betrayed by timid complacency. Forgetting that the debt of contrition and penance must still be paid, it lets in the unctuous friar and we are back in the world of venality. So Conscience must go out again to search for Piers, so that the church may be rebuilt from its foundations.*

1. *Midday.* Cf. note. 45, Bk v. According to R. and H., midday here signifies the Day of Judgement, 'specifically for Will since he is growing old, and generally for the folk since they live in the Last Age'.

2. *Need, who knows no law.* Langland's teaching on this point is in accord with traditional teaching. The king of the last Book was wrong in claiming to be entirely above the law; but Will, who is in real, physical need, goes to the other extreme – he is over-scrupulous and immoderately self-denying. His discussion with Need represents his own self-questioning about this point. He now has nothing worse to reproach himself with than that he is too meek, and unwilling to beg for his food – a trivial fault compared with the presumption and despair which he gave way to earlier.

3. *'The foxes and birds can creep . . .'* A poetic elaboration of Matt. viii. 20.

4. *'The holy 'fools'.* i.e. the simple men mentioned before – *not* as Skeat supposes, the 'worldly-foolish'. Cf. 1 Cor. i. 23–7.

5. *Nature heard Conscience.* Skeat (note to l. 75) supposes that Conscience, when he calls upon Nature, does not intend him to ravage men with disease. Similarly, in his note to l. 266, he makes the mistake of supposing that Old Age had, up to that moment, been fighting on the side of the Vices. This is to misread the whole description of the Battle. The Diseases, the Plagues, Old Age, and Death himself are all God's ministers, fighting on the side of Conscience and the Virtues.

6. *Out of the planets.* Diseases were supposed to be due to planetary influence.

7. *Fortune began to flatter.* 'The Black Death was followed by a singular recklessness of conduct on the part of the survivors' (Skeat).

8. *Thin glass helmet.* i.e. an imaginary protection or quack remedy.

9. *Came after me.* Ironically, the reckless man of fashion (Life) has escaped Old Age, or managed to forget it; so now, in his indiscriminate onslaught, Old Age attacks Will himself, and forces him to return into Holy Church and prepare for death. So the dreamer is skilfully brought back into the picture, to represent the predicament of every man.

10. *Carrying long daggers.* Cf. p. 182 and note.

11. '*He telleth the number* ...' Ps. cxlvii. 4. In the symbolic language of Scripture, those who are not numbered are sometimes those who lose themselves from God's sight. Cf. Matt. x. 30, Rev. xx. 8.

12. *Hell is numberless.* For the 'even number' in Heaven, see Rev. vii. 4–8. In Job x. 22, Hell is described as a land 'without any order.' Cf. Chaucer, 'Parson's Tale' (*Prima Pars Penitentiae*): 'And eke (also) Job seith, that in helle is non ordre of rule. And al be it so, that God hath create al thing in right ordre, and nothing withouten ordre, but alle thinges ben ordred and numbred, yet natheles they that ben dampned ben nothing in ordre, ne hold no ordre.'

13. *Those who preach this doctrine.* Cf. p. 32, *Three things in common*, and note. Langland is protesting against the scandalous use made of this doctrine by Friars and others, who made it an excuse for extortion, or for rebellion.

14. '*Thou shalt not covet* ...' Exod. xx. 17.

15. *Take it there with them.* i.e. to bribe the judges (Cf. Bks II and IV). The abandonment of creditors and the bribing of judges is here compared to the abandonment of parish priests in favour of the friars, who were also bribed; for they, like the judges, were paid to condone injustice – cf. Fee's 'confession' in Book III.

16. *Make merry* ... i.e. they 'made merry with the officials, whom they treated with the borrowed money' (Skeat).

17. *The penitentiary* (or penitencer) – a priest appointed to hear confessions, assign penance, and give absolution in extraordinary cases, i.e. for very heinous sins.

18. *Creep-into-houses.* II Tim. iii. 6 – 'For of this sort are they which *creep into houses*, and lead captive silly women laden with sins, led away with divers lusts, etc.'

Appendix A

1. *Passing by Conscience.* 'The allusion is to his vision of Conscience in the last Book (IV); still, he is here in a waking dream only, and represents himself as again beholding this creature of his imagination; passing by him indeed, but only to meet another phantom, with whom he converses. The dialogue is really carried on between William's carnal and spiritual natures, between his flesh and his spirit' (Skeat).

2. *'For God rewards . . . '* Ps. lxii. 12.

3. *'Let every man abide . . . '* I Cor. vii. 20.

4. *And also on London.* See p. 9, on the unbeneficed clergy.

5. *Seven Penitential Psalms.* i.e. Psalms vi, xxxii, xxxviii, li, cii, cxxx, and cxliii.

6. *Says in Leviticus.* Deut. iii. 9–12 (?) – though in view of what follows, he is probably referring to Lev. xix. 18.

7. *'Do not render . . . '* I Thess. v. 15.

8. *'The Lord himself . . . '* Ps. xvi. 5.

9. *'The life of meekness . . . '* Not identified.

10. *The Sons of Simony.* i.e. those whose wealth is their only recommendation – who pay good money for their benefices.

11. *'Man shall not live . . . '* Matt. iv. 4 and Deut. viii. 3.

12. *'The kingdom of Heaven . . . '* Matt. xiii. 44.

13. *'The woman, when she had found . . . '* Luke xv. 9.

READ MORE IN PENGUIN

In every corner of the world, on every subject under the sun, Penguin represents quality and variety – the very best in publishing today.

For complete information about books available from Penguin – including Puffins, Penguin Classics and Arkana – and how to order them, write to us at the appropriate address below. Please note that for copyright reasons the selection of books varies from country to country.

In the United Kingdom: Please write to *Dept. EP, Penguin Books Ltd, Bath Road, Harmondsworth, West Drayton, Middlesex UB7 0DA*

In the United States: Please write to *Consumer Sales, Penguin USA, P.O. Box 999, Dept. 17109, Bergenfield, New Jersey 07621-0120.* VISA and MasterCard holders call 1-800-253-6476 to order Penguin titles

In Canada: Please write to *Penguin Books Canada Ltd, 10 Alcorn Avenue, Suite 300, Toronto, Ontario M4V 3B2*

In Australia: Please write to *Penguin Books Australia Ltd, P.O. Box 257, Ringwood, Victoria 3134*

In New Zealand: Please write to *Penguin Books (NZ) Ltd, Private Bag 102902, North Shore Mail Centre, Auckland 10*

In India: Please write to *Penguin Books India Pvt Ltd, 706 Eros Apartments, 56 Nehru Place, New Delhi 110 019*

In the Netherlands: Please write to *Penguin Books Netherlands bv, Postbus 3507, NL-1001 AH Amsterdam*

In Germany: Please write to *Penguin Books Deutschland GmbH, Metzlerstrasse 26, 60594 Frankfurt am Main*

In Spain: Please write to *Penguin Books S. A., Bravo Murillo 19, 1° B, 28015 Madrid*

In Italy: Please write to *Penguin Italia s.r.l., Via Felice Casati 20, I–20124 Milano*

In France: Please write to *Penguin France S. A., 17 rue Lejeune, F–31000 Toulouse*

In Japan: Please write to *Penguin Books Japan, Ishikiribashi Building, 2–5–4, Suido, Bunkyo-ku, Tokyo 112*

In Greece: Please write to *Penguin Hellas Ltd, Dimocritou 3, GR–106 71 Athens*

In South Africa: Please write to *Longman Penguin Southern Africa (Pty) Ltd, Private Bag X08, Bertsham 2013*

READ MORE IN PENGUIN

A CHOICE OF CLASSICS

St Anselm	**The Prayers and Meditations**
St Augustine	**The Confessions**
Bede	**Ecclesiastical History of the English People**
Geoffrey Chaucer	**The Canterbury Tales**
	Love Visions
	Troilus and Criseyde
Marie de France	**The Lais of Marie de France**
Jean Froissart	**The Chronicles**
Geoffrey of Monmouth	**The History of the Kings of Britain**
Gerald of Wales	**History and Topography of Ireland**
	The Journey through Wales and **The Description of Wales**
Gregory of Tours	**The History of the Franks**
Robert Henryson	**The Testament of Cresseid and Other Poems**
Walter Hilton	**The Ladder of Perfection**
Julian of Norwich	**Revelations of Divine Love**
Thomas à Kempis	**The Imitation of Christ**
William Langland	**Piers the Ploughman**
Sir John Mandeville	**The Travels of Sir John Mandeville**
Marguerite de Navarre	**The Heptameron**
Christine de Pisan	**The Treasure of the City of Ladies**
Chrétien de Troyes	**Arthurian Romances**
Marco Polo	**The Travels**
Richard Rolle	**The Fire of Love**
François Villon	**Selected Poems**